The Transnational Condition

Protest, Culture and Society

General editors:

Kathrin Fahlenbrach, University of Halle Wittenberg, Germany.

Martin Klimke, German Historical Institute, Washington, DC / Heidelberg Center for American Studies (HCA), University of Heidelberg.

Joachim Scharloth, Department of German, University of Zurich, Switzerland.

Protest movements have been recognized as significant contributors to processes of political participation and transformations of culture and value systems, as well as to the development of both a national and transnational civil society.

This series brings together the various innovative approaches to phenomena of social change, protest and dissent which have emerged in recent years, from an interdisciplinary perspective. It contextualizes social protest and cultures of dissent in larger political processes and socio-cultural transformations by examining the influence of historical trajectories and the response of various segments of society, political and legal institutions on a national and international level. In doing so, the series offers a more comprehensive and multi-dimensional view of historical and cultural change in the twentieth and twenty-first century.

The Transnational Condition

Protest Dynamics in an Entangled Europe

Edited by

Simon Teune

Berghahn Books
New York • Oxford

First published in 2010 by
Berghahn Books
www.berghahnbooks.com

Cover picture: Dutch cows wear protest signs against the referendum on the
EU constitution in Oosthuizen, 32 km north of Amsterdam, 25 May 2005.
The Dutch word 'Boe' refers to the sound cows make and, like the English
'boo', signals disapproval. © AP.

Library of Congress Cataloging-in-Publication Data

The transnational condition : protest dynamics in an entangled Europe /
edited by Simon Teune.
     p. cm. — (Protest, culture and society ; v. 4)
    Includes bibliographical references and index.
    ISBN 978-1-84545-728-0 (hbk. : alk. paper)
   1. Protest movements—Europe. 2. Social action—Europe.
3. Transnationalism—Europe. I. Teune, Simon.
    HN373.5.T73 2010
    305.80094'09049—dc22

                  2010013212

British Library Cataloguing in Publication Data
A catalogue record for this book is available from the British Library
Printed in the United States on acid-free paper

ISBN 978-1-84545-728-0 hardback

To Dieter

Contents

Methodology and Theory of Transnational Social Movement Research

Abbreviations

AARRG!!	Apprentis Agitateurs pour un Réseau de Résistance Globale
BSF	Belgian Social Forum
CDA	Critical discourse analysis
ESF	European Social Forum
EU	European Union
FTAA	Free Trade Area of the Americas
GJM(s)	Global justice movement(s)
ICT	Information and communication technologies
IMF	International Monetary Fund
INSURA	Individual surveys in rallies
LCR	Ligue Communiste Révolutionnaire
NGO	Nongovernmental organisation
NSM	New Social Movements
PEA	Protest event analysis
RMT	Resource mobilisation theory
SMO	Social movement organisation
SPEB	Socialisme par en bas
SUD	Solidaires, Unitaires, Démocratiques
SWP	Socialist Workers' Party
Vamos	Vive l'Action pour une Mondialisation des Solidarités
WB	World Bank
WEF	World Economic Forum
WSF	World Social Forum
WTO	World Trade Organisation

Tables and Figures

Tables

Figures

Foreword

Sidney Tarrow

'The transnational condition'? What kind of a condition is that, sceptics may ask? Clearly, if it were to be applied to the world in general, 'parochial' would be a word that came sooner to mind than 'transnational' to describe most peoples' condition. Yet, if we shift our focus from individuals to the processes that encompass them, Teune and his collaborators are on to something. 'Transationalisation', Teune defines as 'pluri-local relations of entanglement beyond national borders', deriving the definition from German sociologist Ludger Pries. That definition is useful because it reflects both the scope and the ambiguities of what is happening to the world today: less than outright 'globalisation' – that much-abused term of the 1990s – and more than 'Europeanisation' – a too-Brussels inflected term; less than a 'global civil society', but deeper than traditional inter-state relations. The book does not imply that individuals engaged in transnational relations have been separated from their domestic moorings – on the contrary, the neologism 'rooted cosmopolitanism' makes its appearance more than once. But it does suggest forcefully that these national moorings are neither the prisons imagined by global idealists nor the Shangri-Las wished for by nationalists. Transnationalism is a growing – if ragged-edged and often hard-to-detect – condition of today's world.

Teune and his collaborators are not the first – nor will they be the last – to explore the boundaries and interstices of the transnational condition. Although this book is an expression of a new phase of transnational theorising and research in Europe, it builds on two earlier phases, each of which had much to contribute but left much unsaid: in a first phase, it was the EU that stimulated research on European collective action. Triggered by the growth of European lobbies and public interest groups, this phase was European with a capital letter 'E' and was often motivated by a passionate neo-functionalism that made its practitioners perhaps too optimistic about the prospects for a European civil society developing in short order. Writers in this tradition came close to believing that if a non-state actor was located in Brussels, dealt on friendly terms with European officials and claimed to represent a grassroots constituency, that would qualify it as a 'European social movement'. The fact that many of these groups were facilitated and were often subsidised by the European Commission was recognised, but its implication for representing the *forces vives* of European society was not widely understood. And the fact that one could be 'critical' as well as European would not be driven home until Donatella della Porta and her group's rich contributions to the field. A second phase of research on European collective action reached beyond the boundaries of Brussels into domestic politics and societies, but remained somewhat ambivalent regarding just what European contention might mean. Did it mean being 'Euro-sceptic', a term that implied a negative valence toward the entire European project and was seldom operationalised as anything more than the attitudes found in Euro-surveys? Did it refer to groups that dealt with issues that had been placed on the agenda by the EU, a definition that risked leaving almost nobody out? Did it mean, in Dieter Rucht's telling phrase – 'distant issue groups' – actors concerned with issues outside of their own boundaries, whether or not these issues were European? Or did it mean that actors were framing their claims in European or global terms, whether or not these claims had anything to do with Europe? In the absence of clarity about the meaning of transnational contention, this new and exciting field risked subsiding into a scattering of only rhetorically connected centres of thinking and research.

The third phase of transnational research in Europe proposed an answer to this dilemma. Already glimpsed in the pioneering volume edited by Donatella della Porta, Hanspeter Kriesi and Dieter Rucht, to whom this volume is appropriately dedicated, it focuses on what people do when they engage in activism outside their borders. Do they 'externalise' domestic claims-making? 'Internalise' external issues? Or form transnational coalitions with others like themselves? This book begins to seriously interrogate these questions.

In the new European transnationalism, which has points of light in places as far apart as Aarhus, Antwerp, Berlin, Florence, Geneva, Lausanne and Paris, it is transnational activism that is the focus of theory and research. No longer limited to the NGOs that circulate around the European Commission, its practitioners deal with 'critical' as well as enthusiastic Europeans, focussing on how and where Europeans come together in transnational coalitions, forums and summits. In its empirical rooting and its theoretical sophistication, it has outpaced the study of transnationalism in other parts of the world.

Why this should be the case is in part due to the greater reach of European institutions into the lives of ordinary Europeans than international or regional institutions elsewhere in the world. But it is also the result of a remarkable scholarly and intellectual development: what I dare to summarise as the 'rooted cosmopolitan' of European scholars of contentious politics. I can illustrate this most easily in contrast to scholarship in other regions of the world.

First, compared to the United States, Europeans have overcome the parochialism and the imagined hegemony of US social science, well illustrated by Jackie Smith and Rachel Kutz-Flamenbaum in their devastating, if perhaps unkind, critique of US social movement research in their chapter in this book. Though they may still lack the methodological hard edge of people trained in the United

States, Western Europeans more than make up for it in their sophistication about the meanings and import of transnational contention.

Second, compared to the countries of East-Central Europe, who, for understandable reasons, are still focussed on their own countries' still precocious democratisation, West European scholars have developed a dual focus on European international and domestic politics. (Although younger Eastern Europeans are beginning to pay attention to transnational politics, it is striking that the only Eastern-European contribution to this book was written by a scholar trained outside of the region).

Third, compared to research in much of the global South, European scholars have developed a richer array of methodological tools with which to examine the transnational condition. From the INSURA surveys invented in Paris (Favre, Fillieule and Mayer), but employed by scholars from Antwerp (Walgrave and van Laer) to Lausanne (Fillieule and Blanchard) to Florence (della Porta and her group); to the ethnographic methods used by Ariane Jossin; to the discourse analysis employed by Nicole Doerr; to the 'public sphere' analysis of Christoph Haug; to the media analysis of Thomas Olesen: the scholars whose work is represented in this volume represent an impressive array of methodological approaches. Finally, Europeans have largely avoided the 'paradigm warfare' that shackles much social movement research across the Atlantic. Never tempted by either the rationalist reductionism or the culturalist obsession that have inflected US social science since the 1960s; sceptical of the equally simplistic globalisation paradigms of the 1990s; absorbing, without trying to parrot, imports from US scholarship – as this book reveals, the study of European transnational politics has profited from theoretical and methodological cosmopolitanism. Consider Giugni, Bandler and Eggert's contribution to this volume. Rather than obsess about whether the political process model either is or is not an appropriate tool for looking beyond the nation state, they carry out a careful empirical analysis of how and with what limitations that approach helps them to understand both national constraints on and the shift of scale to the European level of contentious politics. (For truth in advertising, I share their view that 'the national context remains crucial even for transnational forms of contention', but that 'at the same time, the creation of common ways of framing political, social and economic issues makes the gathering of a variety of different groups, organisations and networks possible'.)

Does the locution 'transnational condition' sound messy and indeterminate? Sure it does, because that is the nature of the phenomenon that Teune and his collaborators explore in this suggestive new book. But like all pioneering studies, it asks us to go further, and this in at least three directions.

First, the term 'condition' is disappointingly static. It begs for a better specified account of the mechanisms and processes through which the European condition is becoming more transnational. For example, this appreciative reader of Walgrave and van Laer's chapter would like to know if there has been a growing organisational embedding of the Belgian and other European activists who participate in transnational counter-summits; or whether, returning to Jossin's evocative chapter, there is a growing phenomenon of participation in counter-summits as 'an activist hobby'; or whether, – thinking of Thomas Olesen's chapter, publics are becoming more 'porous' to transnational issues; or whether della Porta's 'critical Europeans' are making inroads on the 'co-opted Europeans of the Brussels-based NGOs' (the recent research of Jennifer Hadden at the Copenhagen Climate Change Summit suggests that they may be). The mechanisms and processes of transnationalisation need to be better specified and examined.

Second, when we use the term 'contentious politics', are we simply employing a different term for European 'social movements', or do Teune and his collaborators intend the term as Charles Tilly intended it, to designate all forms of organised encounters between challengers and their opponents? The inclusion in the volume of Tsveta Petrova's account of East European and Eurasian 'electoral revolutions' suggests a broader compass than 'social movements', as does Christoph Haug's evocation of the 'European public sphere'. But what of Europeans who take their claims to the European Court of Justice or the European Court of Human Rights? Are they within the sphere of 'contentious politics'? This observer would tend to think so, but the authors of this volume do not tell us clearly whether or not they agree.

Finally – and this is the most difficult problem to tackle – how does European contention relate to the broad social changes at work in today's world? In their chapter, Smith and Kutz-Flamenbaum criticise social movement scholars for lacking a connection between the micro-politics of social movements and the macro-social forces in the international system – especially hegemony and neo-liberalism. Building such a link is the next big challenge in social movement research. But I fear we will not make much progress at the level of general theories that derive contention directly from broad sociological trends; it was in reaction to the inadequacies of such models that the advances of the last thirty years were made. What we need is more attention to the actual processes that link broad international social changes to the mechanisms within European contention.

These are serious issues, but they are the kind of issues that are raised because Teune and his collaborators offer us a rich opportunity to raise them. Their book carries forward the 'Berlin tradition' of social movement research begun by Dieter Rucht and his collaborators in the 1990s and promises to take the study of transnational contention 'beyond Berlin' and hopefully beyond the borders of Europe.

Ithaca New York, 6 February 2010

Preface

Long before transnational contention emerged as a major subject issue, research in protest and social movements was shaped by collaboration beyond national boundaries. The analysis of social movements has benefited particularly from the fruitful exchange between US research shaped by organisational and process oriented approaches on the one side, and the Western European tradition drawing on the analysis of new social movements, on the other. Conferences and joint projects helped the understanding of the influence of national trajectories and contexts on the dynamics of protest. Through this collaboration, researchers established a tight-knit community and developed a relatively homogeneous understanding of collective action, including concepts that were acknowledged and used by large parts of the community. In the mid 1990s, the increase in cross-border activism appeared on the screen of social movement researchers. Scholars began to assess the validity of their analytical repertoire – developed to understand movements within national boundaries – for the study of transnational protest.

The intricate genesis of this book is linked to one of the finest scholars of protest and social movements who played a central role in this transnational research network. When I realised that my teacher and Ph.D. supervisor, Dieter Rucht, would celebrate his sixtieth birthday in June 2006, I was determined to continue the academic tradition of a *Festschrift* in his honour. However, I just had to talk to a few experienced colleagues to find out that I was desperately late for such a project. John McCarthy and Doug McAdam encouraged me to think of a colloquium as an alternative to a rash book project. Convinced by the idea of bringing together Dieter with some of his friends and colleagues as well as young scholars of social movements, I organised the colloquium entitled 'Crossing Borders. On the Road towards Transnational Social Movement Analysis'. Most of the chapters in this book go back to papers that were presented during this meeting. Some others were added when the outline for the volume emerged.

I would like to thank the authors of this book for their dedication and patience; John McCarthy and Doug McAdam for their support in the early phase of this project; Konstanza Prinzessin zu Löwenstein, the administrative head of my research unit at the Social Science Research Center Berlin, for making the colloquium possible; Kathrin Fahlenbrach, Martin Klimke, and Joachim Scharloth for the opportunity to make this book part of a series that represents an exciting new wave of research on protest and social movements; Marion Berghahn for her trustfulness and support as a publisher; and Konstanze and Luk for bearing with me during the production of the manuscript.

Berlin, April 2010

Protest in the Transnational Condition

Simon Teune

Inescapable Transnationalism?

It is hard to think about political protest without considering the transnational condition that comes into play in many contentious actions. If it is not the act of protest itself that is organised or conceived of in a transition of national borders, its preconditions and its reception are rarely limited to the framework of the nation state. In a context that is entangled in the sense that political and cultural formations are permeable and interconnected, protest itself is changing just as the social movements that carry many contentious events are changing.

Protest mobilisations teach us about exchange across borders in many ways. They create events of transnational experience to provoke a revision of thought and they change the course of institutional politics. Hence, protests are an indispensable element in the study of transnational politics. For the increasing permeability of national borders and the relevance of protest in that process, the formation of a European community is a case in point. The continent is marked by the European Union (EU) as a supra-national polity with far-reaching competencies and a high degree of integration in the fields of economy and civil society as well as in science and culture. Citizens of a few tens of nations with very different cultural and political histories increasingly conceive of themselves as Europeans. So far, protest mobilisations have played only a marginal role in the master narrative of Europe. Yet, the coordinated protests against the US-led war on Iraq have been prized as marking the 'birth of a European public sphere' (Habermas and Derrida 2003: 291). Such events suggest that Europe emerges not only from above, namely, in EU governance, but also from below as in the organisation of protest (Tarrow 1995; Imig and Tarrow 2001; Mathers 2007: ch. 6). Dissenters offer a grassroots gaze on Europe. They are part of a democratic process to negotiate particular policies and the future of Europe at large (Balme and Chabanet 2008). In Europe and elsewhere, transnational challengers pioneer in the construction of novel communities, in the reframing of problems and in the development of political alternatives. In most cases, joint discussions and mobilisations go back to dense exchanges, despite material and symbolic hurdles, such as travel costs, language barriers and the threat of concerted governmental repression.

The analysis of transnational phenomena shows that the range and density of exchange varies significantly. The global justice movements (GJMs), which are the reference for most of the contributions to this volume, may serve as an example for the concurrence of different degrees of transnational involvement. A large amount of the European global justice activists taking part in local or regional protests are limited in their capacities to go abroad because of time constraints, a lack of money or because travelling for activist purposes is simply beyond their imagination. Their transnational involvement is primarily a cognitive matter. Movement entrepreneurs from across the continent, by contrast, keep in close contact via emails and telephone, and they also meet regularly in places throughout Europe to prepare protest events, campaigns and gatherings.

The objective of this volume is to take protests in Europe as an example for the crosscutting relevance of transnational exchanges. Transnationalism is something that protesters are confronted with, while at the same time they are moulding it. It permeates individual biographies, the configuration of networks and the environments with which protesters interact. The contributions to this volume disclose these different perspectives by probing available concepts in the analysis of collective action.

The terms 'transnational' and 'transnationalisation' are used in this volume not just because the contributions deal with spatially limited phenomena. Compared to 'globalisation' or 'Europeanisation', the concept of transnationalisation – defined as pluri-local relations of entanglement beyond national borders (see Pries 2008) – is less demanding (in terms of scope) and fuzzy (in terms of an agreed upon definition). Adding to this, 'transnational' allows for the continuous relevance of the nation state (Smith 2003: 17). The very term 'transnational' evades the idea of a strict separation between the local or national level on the one side, and a global (or European) level, on the other.

While the focus of this volume is on contemporary protests, it is not insinuated here that the transnational condition is a recent phenomenon. Cross-border exchanges are probably as old as the borders themselves. Several scholars have pointed to transnational protest activities in the past to contextualise what can be observed today (among others Keck and Sikkink 1998: ch. 2). Three waves of transnational protest play a major role in the scholarly literature: (1) the first wave of labour and women's rights protests roughly from the 1850s to the 1920s (see, for instance, Van Holthoon and van der Linden 1988; Rupp 1997); (2) the internationalism inherent to the peace movement, solidarity, and students' movements in the late 1950s to the 1980s (for instance, Rucht 2000; Nehring 2005; Klimke and Scharloth 2008; Klimke 2010); and (3) the mobilisations after the reorganisation of a bipolar world since the 1990s. However, not only transnational protests, but also the contextual processes that have been labelled as globalisation (and should, more adequately, be referred to in the plural form (see Guidry, Kennedy and Zald 2000)) can be traced back over several centuries. The vanishing of borders and the emergence of a global consciousness are much older than the end to World War II (Robertson 2003; Armitage 2004).

The current perception of transnational influences as salient for every day practices may be owed to a cognitive revolution (see Seidman 2000: 339), but it is also based on materially evident developments that have been accelerating within the last two to three decades. The reason for transnationalism to appear on the screen of social scientists is the rise in both the velocity and the density of cross-border exchanges as facilitated by affordable travel and the improved availability of information.[1] It is beyond question that within the last quarter century, these involve and affect more people than ever and that they are pertinent in the domains of the social, the cultural, and the political. As a matter of fact, the transnational condition of protest has also undergone qualitative changes in the same period. The organisation, the environment, and eventually recent protests themselves look different when they are compared to antecedent mobilisations as we will see in the following sections.

The assumed significance of the transnational condition for the development and understanding of protest does not mean that transnational exchange is a natural thing to happen:

> While transnational practices extend beyond two or more national territories, they are built within the confines of specific social, economic, and political relations which are bound together by perceived shared interests and meanings. Without such social closure, without a basic sense of shared meanings and a sense of predictability of results bounding together the actors involved (i.e., social control), it would be unthinkable for any person to try to establish any kind of relations across national territories. (Smith and Guarnizo 1998: 13)

Proximities in the political and cultural tradition make exchanges across certain borders more likely than across others. In Europe, for instance, activists from France would probably establish links with their Italian counterparts rather than with those in Romania, because they assume shared ground with regard to their relation to the state, experiences with forms of protest or conceptions of left and right. Notwithstanding existing hurdles to transnational mobilisation (see also Tarrow 2005: 7), instances of activism beyond borders are manifold and they are on the rise, especially in an entangled continent such as Europe.

The remainder of this chapter aims at sketching some major features of the transnational condition, as it is encountered and generated by social movement activists. Rather than elaborating specific elements of transnational protest, it covers a broad spectre of relevant aspects. The inherent repercussions on protest are then brought forward to social movement theory, which has acknowledged the challenge of transnationalism. The last section introduces the structure of this volume and the individual contributions.

Encountering Transnationalism

Even when political activists try to gain leverage on the national level, they are by no means isolated from the rest of the world. They find themselves in a situation where influences from outside of their political and cultural community impinge on their lives and their political activities in different ways.

The carriers of protest, most prominently social movements, interact with several resonant fields, such as public institutions, economic players, mass media, potential allies, and adversaries, but also a rather indefinite public of citizens who might support a political struggle.[2] These environments are either affected by transnational processes or they are essentially transnational. Thus, protesters act in multi-level contexts that provide complex political, social, and cultural constraints and opportunities for protest.[3] As suggested in the 'boomerang model' by Margaret Keck and Kathryn Sikkink (1998), political opportunities for ambitions to social change might be disadvantageous on the national level, where public claims-making is met with repression, but favourable on a supra-national level, where activists are supported by international networks or political elites (cf. the mechanism of externalisation in della Porta and Tarrow 2005). Protesters are confronted with the same multi-level composition of their environment with reference to factors such as media systems, communities of values or iconic stocks.

It is more than obvious that political opportunities for challengers have changed dramatically since the demise of the Warsaw Pact and the end to a bi-polar world. Supra-national institutions, such as the World Bank (WB), the International Monetary Fund (IMF), the World Trade Organisation (WTO) or the EU have been granted influence on national policies to a varying degree.[4] At the same time, national governments are not shielded against external influences, but they are nested in an international polity that – in the extreme example of the EU – exerts influence on virtually every policy field. This constellation opens up new options for protesters to make their case (Meyer 2003; Tarrow 2005). In many cases, it is neither sufficient nor efficient to address only national institutions, which have been targets of transnational protests since its first wave at the turn of the twentieth century.

Each aspect of political opportunity for challengers that scholars have canonised as institutional access, stability of alignments, elite splits, and repression (see McAdam 1996: 27; Tarrow 1998: ch. 5) has a specific profile in the transnational condition dependent on the policy field. As far as access is concerned, international institutions wordily advocate the integration of 'civil society' in the policy process. In practice, however, the degree of integration is limited by three factors: the issue at stake; the range of organisations that are granted access; and, the role that non-state actors are assigned. Regarding issues such as environmental protection and women's rights, moderate advocacy organisations were granted access to arenas of decision-making in the framework of global governance.[5] At that point, in the mid 1990s, the international trade and financial institutions, by contrast, were not open to dissident voices at all, but at a later stage, they signalled openness in view of harsh criticism. In the EU, attempts to dialogue with the civil society tend to result in an activation of pre-existing contacts privileging resourceful, professional organisations with expert knowledge.[6]

Thematic particularities are also relevant for the stability of alignments and elite splits. On the international level, controversies over issues that split the representatives of national governments open a window of opportunity for challengers. The fact that several political leaders of 'Old Europe' opposed the war in Iraq was one factor that led to an unprecedented mobilisation on a global day of action (Walgrave and Rucht 2010). On the domestic level, elites might disagree about influences from abroad. The compliance with EU directives, for instance, is a constant source of quarrel within the member states and an opportunity for protesters to take influence on legislation.

As far as repression is concerned, governments have reacted to transnational protests with an increased exchange about effective policing. By creating new informational resources and in tactical exchange, repression has undergone a scale shift from the national to the transnational level as well. As a matter of fact, the model of de-escalation in the policing of protest that developed in most liberal democracies has been suspended for transnational protest events, thus raising the costs for participation (della Porta et al. 2006b; on trauma triggered by police violence see chapter 2 in this volume). Despite transnational exchange, national traditions of policing prevail and shape mobilisation in the respective country. However, the degree of repression is to a certain extent also dependent on another transnational factor, namely, the fact that state reactions to protests are observed in neighbouring countries.

While the political regime and its interaction in transnational contention is widely studied, the impact of cultural diversity in cross-border interaction has hardly obtained a systematic status in research, probably because the focus remains on Western Europe and Northern America – two regions with a large overlap in their cultural background.[7] However, it stands to reason that different cultural traditions – patterns of interpretation, collective memories, images, language – reduce the chance that two players have the same in mind when they design a campaign, negotiate claims or experience a transnational protest event. That is to say, the universe of different experiences that is produced by divisions such as class, gender, or race multiplies in the transnational condition (Smith 2002). Protest campaigns that are very successful in one country because they resonate with a prevalent perception of experiences might be restricted to a mobilisation of core activists in another country where the definition of problems does not find fertile ground (Doerr and Mattoni 2007).

A resonant field for social movements beyond political institutions that is relatively well explored is the public sphere. Conceived of as a vital medium for political actors that are poor in resources, the mobilisation of public attention by challengers has been a major field of study. However, most of the research focuses on commercial and public mass media (see for instance Gamson and Wolfsfeld 1993; Koopmans 2004), while face-to-face public spheres such as encounters and meetings, or media such as leaflets or images, hardly play a role (see chapters 3 and 4 in this volume). In the transnational condition, most mass media outlets are restricted to domestic reception, while others are emitted (mostly via satellite and the internet) to a potentially global audience. However, even the primarily national media are 'porous' with reference to events in other countries (see chapter 6 in this volume). In this setting, protest activists try to use the media as a carrier to reach hitherto uninvolved fellow citizens and to communicate their take on society. For global justice issues, they have been relatively successful in entering these public arenas so that coverage on supra-national summits does not happen without reference to criticism and protest (Rauch et al. 2007; Rucht and Teune 2008). However, challengers continue to have poor chances of finding the substance of their criticism in the commercial and public mass media. Moreover, they are evaluated negatively in the vast majority of press articles (Beyeler and Kriesi 2005). In general, commercial and public mass media show an increased propensity to cover political processes in other countries. As protest is more or less acknowledged today as a democratic right, the repression of protests that are framed as democratic and progressive is more likely to be scandalised. Media coverage from a distance helps spread claims and means of protest and at the same time it changes protest interactions in the making. Being aware of the media observation, protesters address an audience beyond national borders. The police employed to contain protests will also adopt moderate tactics once they are in the spotlight.[8]

The permeability of national public spheres is also a basis in understanding discursive opportunities in a transnational context. The dynamics of protest is shaped significantly by public discourse about protest activities (Ferree et al. 2002, ch. 4; Koopmans and Olzak 2004). As soon as they are considered an expression of an urgent problem or even a legitimate reaction to these problems, protests are likely to grow in numbers. In the transnational condition, the ways an issue is discussed in one country can be affected by public discourse in another country, thus shaping protest in that arena. Homosexuality, for instance, is not regarded acceptable by the majority in catholic Poland. The Christopher Street Day, an event to express gay pride publicly, has therefore been inhibited by authorities and attacked by counter-protesters. The participation of activists and politicians from neighbouring countries has made the protests visible beyond Polish borders and has also made discrimination an issue at the EU level. As Felix Kolb (2005) has shown, the public response also impinges on individual social movement organisations. During the press coverage about the anti-G8 protests in Genoa 2001, Attac Germany was constructed as a central player in the GJMs. As a consequence, the organisation grew exponentially and appeared on the screen of domestic decision-makers.

Practising Transnationalism

Social movements and other protagonists making use of political protest[9] are not only confronted with an environment that is shaped by transnationalisation, they are also at the same time part of these processes (Tarrow 2002; Olesen 2005b). Defining themselves beyond borders, they constitute a transnational community and recognise supra-national political structures such as the EU. How exactly do actors of protest deal with the transnational condition and in which ways do they contribute to cross-border processes?

Donatella della Porta and Sidney Tarrow (2005: 3–6) have identified three mechanisms in the mobilisations of social movement activists that have been developed in the transnational condition. Two of them, internalisation and externalisation, are closely linked to the multi-level political opportunity structure (the last one is referred to in the last paragraph of this section). Dependent on the opportunities at hand, social movements use domestic channels to reach change on the transnational level (e.g., farmers address their national government to conserve EU subsidies) or they bypass national governments exerting pressure via other countries or supra-national institutions (e.g., Soviet dissidents use the Helsinki accords of the Conference for Security and Cooperation in Europe to push Western Governments to action).

As soon as cross-border activism aims at sustained protest, stable transnational mobilising structures are needed. In practice, these organisational forms differ significantly in their density and centrality. We can think of a network of groups in a border region collaborating occasionally on a particular issue on the one pole (low density, low centrality), and a transnational organisation with a central leadership that passes orders to national sections on the other pole (high density, high centrality). Protests in the first wave of transnational movements at the turn of the nineteenth century followed a hierarchical and representational model. They were organised by a coalition of institutionalised national associations, such as the Communist International.[10] The 1st of May, for instance, as an international day of action, was initiated by the Second International and realised at the national level by member organisations. Attendants of events in other countries included mostly the leadership of national associations. Today, by contrast, many transnational protests are organised rather horizontally. They are initiated by networks of diverse groups and organisations and tend to include the rank-and-file (see Rucht 2001: 85). Hence, transnational contacts among individual activists are widespread. This does not imply an organisational process based on equality. However, divisions are less visible and rather mediated symbolically (see below). .

Since the 1990s, transnational organisations and networks gained ground complementing the organisational structure of social movements on the national level (Smith, Chatfield, and Pagnucco 1997; Keck and Sikkink 1998).[11] Again, these transnational networks, or coalitions, as Tarrow prefers to call them, differ in duration and intensity of involvement (Tarrow 2005: 166–178). In terms of the action repertoire used in transnational protest, increased mobility and faster communication as well as the routinisation of street protests make joint demonstrations more likely today. While antecedent transnational mobilisations included means such as transnational petitions and congresses, collective travelling to other countries in order to take part in demonstrations is part and parcel of today's repertoire.

As said above, collaboration across borders will not happen as long as there is no perceived commonality between different actors. One way to establish commonality is to frame the issue at stake in a way that bridges existing differences (Smith 2002). For the GJMs, which are diverse not only at the international level, but also at the national level, the multitude of struggles is connected through the master frame of anti-neoliberalism (see della Porta et al. 2006a: ch. 3; chapter 8 in this volume). Defining particular issues and aims as part of this frame allows priests to collaborate with anarchists and trade unionists to be at the same demonstration as ecologists and illegalised migrants.

In the process of finding common ground, activists discover and fortify an identity that connects them as one collective. A transnational collective identity can emerge in direct contacts with people disadvantaged by transnational processes (Cunningham 1999), in protest events, congresses, network meetings (chapter 4 and 5 in this volume) or in a cognitive amplification of domestic struggles that are mentally linked with other localities (Drury, Reicher, and Stott 2003).

Cognitive aspects of social movements, such as frames and collective identity, build on public exchange. Mainstream mass media are one channel to send and receive information, but, as mentioned before, they are biasing messages and they tend to be restricted to national communities. Social movements have thus developed their own publics beyond national borders. These publics emerge through mass media – websites,[12] magazines, radio stations or videos – in online forums and mailing lists, or in direct meetings, physical or virtual. They are arenas in which to exchange information beyond the mainstream and to acknowledge different perspectives. Protesters make use of electronic media that connect them instantly and help to spread their view of events within and beyond their home country. The internet has lowered the threshold of building links with people abroad without mediation. Thus, the diffusion of information and the organisation of protest across national borders are more likely to happen today when compared to the first two waves of transnational activism. Once contentious events are underway, mobile phones and digital cameras are instruments that increase the publicity and spread information from the protesters point of view.[13] Thus, publics are sites of a reaffirmation and redefinition of the self, the we-group, and the environment in which it is situated (see chapter 4 and 5 in this volume). On the transnational level, language is the key hurdle to the establishment of a public sphere and a barrier for being a part of it. While a lingua franca is easy to find in a context of high education and geographical proximity, costly translation is the only remedy to more complex situations of linguistic isolation. Translation is also a way to acknowledge the value of every voice in a meeting and the speaker's specific cultural background.

The panorama of aspects of the transnational condition ends with the third mechanism identified by della Porta and Tarrow (2005: 3–6): diffusion. As transnationalism can be defined as the travelling of social practices, symbolic systems, and artefacts in space (Pries 2008), diffusion is a key element in understanding isomorphism in transnational protests (Soule 2004; Roggeband 2007; chapter 7 in this volume). The mechanism is investigated best for forms of action (e.g., Soule 1999; Chabot and Duyvendak 2002), but it is also relevant for organisational forms, strategies, and cultural expression. Diffusion was conceptualised as a process that rests in personal contacts, which are the carriers for innovations from one country to another (McAdam and Rucht 1993), but it can also take impersonal channels, such as images published in mass media (Biggs 2006). Diffusion is not just a form to spread successful innovations. It is also a prerequisite to connect people in different localities by the way they organise, protest, and conceive of the world. However, as many of the aspects above, diffusion necessitates translation. Concepts that are developed in another context have to be translated and readjusted to the domestic situation (Roggeband 2007).

However transnational the organisation of protest may be, residual differences between different traditions in political culture and political opportunity will remain. Even though the cross-fertilisation of transnational manifestations changes the face of protest, different contexts for its staging contradict a convergence of protest across the globe. Accordingly, national opportunity structures continue to play a role in shaping protest (Josselin 2007), and the forms of interaction that challengers choose are still varied (Wood 2004), depending on national or regional trajectories.

Transnationalisation and Social Movement Research

While the comparison between countries has been a strong domain in the analysis of protests and social movements, the entanglement of phenomena observed in two or more states remained a side issue. For many years, collective action has primarily been conceived of as bound to the borders of the nation state. This is due to both pragmatic reasons in research and a dominant and often times not explicit conceptual focus on the nation state. One reason for the nation state to become the Archimedean point in research is the emergence of modern forms of protest being closely linked to the development of the construction of a centralised national polity (Tilly 1978). As a consequence, the assumption that challengers would conceive of the national polity as their relevant framework was paradigmatic. In order to reach a narrowly defined, short- or medium-term goal, challengers would frame their struggle domestically, mobilise within national borders, and address national decision-makers.[14] A focus on the state and on instrumental practices has been reinforced by the prevalence of approaches highlighting rational choice models (Crossley 2002). In domains of research that focus less on the interplay of protest and political institutions, the nation state is not necessarily reinforced as a central category.

The emergence of an international polity that complements institutions and practices at the national level has made scholars of protest alert of the specifities in transnational contention. A look at the transnational aspects of protest does not necessarily counter a statist or an instrumental bias, but it sensitises scholars to important facets of mobilisation that went unnoticed before. How does cultural difference impinge on the organisation and reception of protest? Who is represented and who is participating in protest events? How do activist publics complement a public sphere that is dominated by commercial and public mass media? Research that aims at getting the full picture of protest will, on the one side, have to abandon the statist and instrumental path. On the other side – and that is the mission of this volume – scholars should allow for the transnational condition as a crosscutting issue. Transnational dynamics impact on many aspects of protest mobilisation, ranging from the activists' identity to their forms of action to the environment that they encounter.

In light of transnational forms of contention, social movement scholars have raised doubts about the suitability of their theories developed in and for a national framework (McCarthy 1997). A decade after this debate gained momentum, researchers – among them the authors of this book – continue the discussion. One fraction of social movement analysts states that the classical agenda of social movement research 'goes quite far in explaining transnational contention' (see, for instance, chapter 8 in this volume), another fraction pleads for a broadening of the perspective (see, for instance, chapter 3 and 4 in this volume), while still others call for a radical change in the theoretical perspective (see, for instance, chapter 10 in this volume).

Several studies have shown that concepts such as political opportunities, framing strategies, or mobilising structures are certainly not obsolete when focussing on transnational protest, but neither is it sufficient just to apply them without further modification. When actors from different geographical arenas come into play, the blind spots of these concepts become all the more significant. Using them unwarily might result in a symbolic reproduction of inequality, for instance, imagining Western activists as the vanguard of transnational change. In these analytical contexts, central features of transnational contention, such as the need for translation and re-contextualisation (Olesen 2005a) or the prevalence of inequalities among activists, are often not addressed properly.

What was true on the national level, that political opportunity structures are not the same for any actor in the field, is obviously valid also on the transnational level. Generalising accounts of political opportunities that focus on structural features of governmental institutions tend to blur the differences in a multi-organisational field where single organisations act according to perceived opportunities (Roose 2003). Having said that access to international structures of governance is open for environmental issues, it is important to take a closer look. Independent from its expertise, an environmental group from the Global South that is poor in resources, radical in its demands, and probably not familiar with official language use will not have the same chances of being heard in a supra-national consultation than its counterpart from the North that is informed about official agendas, is in touch with government officials, and is perceived as an important actor in the field.

Framing strategies have been primarily interpreted as instrumental to reach a certain goal on the basis of a taken for granted rationality. In a transnational setting, framing requires much translation work to unite different standpoints without bending them too much. This translation can be explained with frame alignment processes (Snow et al. 1986). But such an analysis has to account for fundamental differences not only in terms of language, but also in terms of experience and cognitive concepts. In order to evade a paternalist conception of commonality, these processes require a bi-directional exchange about the subject at hand. As Shareen Hertel (2006) shows, for a transnational coalition to improve labour rights in the garment industry, Western organisations that impose their perception of the situation on their target country risk ignoring the ideas and experiences of their counterparts in the Global South.

The last two paragraphs have anticipated what can be said about the analysis of mobilising structures of transnational contention. Mobilising structures are the outcome of processes of negotiation. Thus, transnational networks and coalitions, their formation or failure, can only be understood when the necessary translation work is taken into account. In a similar vein, a look that concentrates on structures in the literal sense tends to obfuscate mechanisms of inclusion and exclusion.

Having mentioned the peril in the use of classical concepts of social movement research, it helps to think outside of the box. What scholars of protest can learn from the transnationalism approach in anthropology, geography, and migration studies is the claim to 'bring back into focus the enduring asymmetries of domination, inequality, racism, sexism, class conflict, and uneven development in which transnational practices are embedded and which they sometimes even perpetuate' (Smith and Guarnizo 1998: 6). Mechanisms of exclusion are also recurrent in the organisation of dissent on the transnational level. Where privileged activists encounter disadvantaged counter-parts, they are at risk to reproduce cognitive and material inequalities. A post-colonial perspective on transnational activism that reflects power relations between activists from the Global North and those from the Global South is therefore a necessary extension to social movement analysis (Thörn 2006). On a meta-level, a post-colonial perspective could also be a remedy to certain parochialism in social movement analysis. In fact, much of the dominant literature in this field tends to generalise results on transnational mobilisations, while the focus remains on activist networks in Western Europe and North America. The perspective of activists in the Global South and analytical accounts from the other hemisphere are necessary to understand these processes as a whole.

This Volume

The limited perspective on transnational mobilisation is also present in this book. Due to the context from which the volume emerged, seven out of the ten chapters that follow this introduction focus on the European GJMs; obviously the empirical findings are bounded, in spatial as well as temporal terms. The contexts in which these national branches of the GJMs emerge are liberal democracies. A look at other historical periods, at thematically different protests, and at different geographical areas would have highlighted other aspects of transnationalisation. Studies that systematically compare the transnational condition for different protests in a diachronic or synchronic perspective are yet to come. Hence, a book that presents evidence from Europe can hardly claim validity for other parts of the world. This is not a book about global social movements or globalisation. Nor does it cover the full range of contemporary mobilisations across borders. However, each contribution to this volume expands the depth of focus with reference to political processes on the European continent.

The following chapters show that transnational contention is more than a scale shift of challengers who organise across borders and address international organisations (as analysed in early studies of transnational protest, e.g., Smith, Chatfield, and Pagnucco 1997; Keck and Sikkink 1998). Transnationalism gives birth to new communities and interpretative frames, it connects distant struggles, it changes the life course of activists, and it bears novel forms of material and symbolic inequalities. While the former of these facets have been addressed extensively in the burgeoning literature in the field, the latter tend to be neglected. After more than a decade of research in transnational contention, some of the contributions to this volume reflect on the state of the art, while others add new concepts and interpretive frames. The conceptual challenge of transnational activism is addressed throughout the contributions.

Assuming that the transnational condition affects all aspects of social movements from the individual protester, to activist communities, to broader sets of societal systems that challengers interact with, this volume addresses three levels at which transnational processes are at work. This way, it is designed to reveal the crosscutting character in which transnationalism impacts on the organisation and the reception of protest. Although the chapters are not limited to any one of these levels, they bring into focus the micro-, meso-, or macro-level of transnational protest. A concluding section is devoted more explicitly to the consequences of transnational activism on social movement analysis.

Drawing on two surveys among participants of the European Social Forum (ESF) and the Belgian Social Forum, Stefaan Walgrave and Jeroen Van Laer open the section that focuses on the micro-level of individual activists. For both events, they compare respondents with a transnational orientation to those who concentrate on domestic politics. Walgrave and Van Laer find out that in the social forum context, transnational activism as opposed to a domestic orientation is associated with the affiliation to a political organisation. Lowering the costs for participation, organisations have an important impact on the composition of transnational social forums.

Ariane Jossin looks in the opposite direction. She shows that the experience of transnational protest also has repercussions on the national constellation of political organisations. Activists dropping off the exhausting peak of mobilisations reinvest their skills and resources in local activism or parties that have approached the GJMs. In a micro-sociological analysis of young global justice activists from France and Germany, she reconstructs the individual experience of counter-summits. Jossin concludes that on the level of individual activists, summit mobilisations are rather multi-national than truly transnational events, with national delegations being separated by the dominance of pre-existing ties and language barriers.

The section devoted to the meso-level of transnational activism combines two chapters that explore the emergence of a transnational public sphere in activists' exchanges. Linking the discussion about a transnational public sphere and research in transnational social movements, Christoph Haug and Nicole Doerr plead for an integration of the concept of assembly publics into both scholarly fields. In a theoretical account, Haug argues for combining the analysis of networks and public arenas to understand the communication flows and deliberations within social movements. Like Doerr, he sees the assemblies of the European GJMs as an important locus for an Europeanisation from below. Doerr complements Haug's chapter by adding empirical evidence about the emergence of a critical Europeanism in the preparatory assemblies of the ESF. The other Europe is, however, framed differently depending on the activists' social and geographical background. Focussing on disadvantaged participants, Doerr shows that inequalities among transnational activists are reproduced in the organisation process of the ESF.

The focus on critical Europeanists is taken up in Donatella della Porta's chapter, which introduces the section highlighting the macro-level of the transnational condition. She reconstructs the emergence of Europe as a frame of reference for criticism and collective identity within social movements. Della Porta argues that contentious episodes are crucial for the emergence of a European public sphere and that they keep the interpretation of Europe open in terms of its core values and geographic extension.

The concept of public sphere is pertinent also in Thomas Olesen's analysis of the Muhammed cartoons conflict. He explains the course of the mobilisations against the publication of these cartoons by referring to the porosity of national public spheres. These are linked with the public spheres in other countries through transnational mass media and 'micro-media', connecting immigrant communities and their home countries. Observing each other, actors in Denmark and many Islamic countries reacted in a transnational dialectic to what was brought to them from abroad.

Tsveta Petrova devotes her chapter to the analysis of a cycle of contention that linked the electoral revolutions in Central Eastern Europe. The demise of authoritarian regimes in many countries in this region can only be understood as an interactive process in which tactical innovations and organising models diffused from one country to another. Petrova underlines that the diffusion process that shaped the development of an entire region rests in the brokerage of protest vanguards, which were supported by external actors. Picking up the concept of waves of protest, she connects the way innovations are taken up with the time of the adaptation.

The concluding section of the volume deals with conceptual challenges to social movement analysis in a more direct way. Marco Giugni, Marko Bandler, and Nina Eggert spell out the classic agenda of social movement research on the GJMs. They contend that the approaches of political opportunity structure, mobilising structures, and framing can explain a great deal of transnational contention. Using this methodological toolkit, Giugni, Bandler, and Eggert arrive at the conclusion that transnational movements such as the GJMs are bound to a great extent to conditions at the national level.

The individual survey, a method that is widely used in the analysis of transnational protest events, comes under scrutiny in the chapter written by Olivier Fillieule and Philippe Blanchard. The authors argue for a careful use of the instrument and warn scholars about conclusions that are tempting to make – inferring organisational networks from activists' multiple affiliations or drawing on surveys in different contexts to make comparative assertions about the GJMs as a whole. Fillieule and Blanchard take surveys at the ESF in Paris 2003 and at the G8 counter-summit in Évian as an example to show the opportunities and limits of the method.

The last chapter, written by Jackie Smith and Rachel Kutz-Flamenbaum, can be read as a conclusion to this volume. The authors contend that scholars of social movements have developed a routine of applying a given set of theories to their object under study without reflecting on the specific situation that is portrayed. They argue for a revival of a macro-structural perspective that takes into account the societal context shaping contentious politics. A focus on national particularities, by contrast, (preferably in liberal democracies) risks neglecting the international power structures that are contested in protest mobilisations. Social movement scholars, Smith and Kutz-Flamenbaum conclude, have to reflect on their role in the construction of contentious politics and position offensively in the struggles that transnational social movements are fighting.

Notes

I thank Thomas Olesen for his helpful comments on an early draft of this chapter.

1. See Rucht (1999: 215–217) for a more detailed account of context factors that spurred the growth of transnational social movement activities.
2. An integration of a complex set of environments has been proposed by several scholars (Rucht 1996, among others) opposed to the political process model that tends to be restricted on political institutions (Armstrong and Bernstein 2008).
3. The environment in which protesters get active is by no means ahistorical. It is the result of continuous contention. Today's activists in Europe can build on the struggles of previous generations, which enforced the right of assembly and the freedom of expression (women in Germany, for instance, were not allowed to engage politically until the early twentieth century).
4. The impact of WB, WTO, and IMF, however, has shrunk after a hegemonic phase in the 1990s. This is due to internal conflict, but also to continuous protest that has put into question the guiding principles of austerity policy and structural adjustment (see, e.g., Smith 2001; Vanden 2003).
5. However, representatives of advocacy organisations in UN conferences on these issues have realised that their influence was only marginal.
6. Expert knowledge is also a key resource in order for transnational social movement organisations to be heard in domestic institutions.
7. But even in the Western-European context, consonance between activists cannot be taken for granted (Doerr and Mattoni 2007; Roggeband 2007).
8. An analysis that confirms this trend on the national level (Wisler and Giugni 1999) is likely to be transferable to the transnational level.
9. In a review of the research literature, Sidney Tarrow (2001: 10–14) discerns transnational social movements, international non-governmental organisations, and transnational advocacy networks as the main actors of transnational contentious politics.
10. According to Susan Zimmermann, the protagonists of the early women's rights movements conceived of the 'international as a multiplication of the national and the national as the basis of the international' (Zimmermann 2002: 288, own translation).
11. Adding to these organisational forms, social forums have become major sites of transnational exchange and a potential space for networking and defining problems (della Porta 2009; Smith et al. 2007).
12. For the GJMs, the city of Seattle is not only connected to successful blockades of the WTO conference site, but also with the foundation of Indymedia, a website that allows a more or less unfiltered publication of reports that was invented to bypass conventional coverage of the WTO protests.

13. By now, content can easily be uploaded to the internet from a mobile phone. This opportunity, plus pager services and hotlines provided during protest events, has changed the development and coverage of protests in the making.
14. This assumption might be obvious for an epistemic community that was socialised in those countries inheriting the ideas of Westphalian sovereignty; it is probably less so for people rooted wherever borders were designed with the ruler or where state power has been more of a pretension than a reality.

References

Armitage, D. 2004. 'Is there a Pre-history of Globalization?' In *Comparison and History: Europe in Cross-national Perspective,* ed. M. O'Connor, 165–176. London: Routledge.

Armstrong, E.A. and M. Bernstein. 2008. 'Culture, Power, and Institutions: A Multi-Institutional Politics Approach to Social Movements'. *Sociological Theory* 26(1): 74–99.

Balme, R. and D. Chabanet. 2008. *European Governance and Democracy: Power and Protest in the EU.* Lanham: Rowman & Littlefield.

Beyeler, M. and H. Kriesi. 2005. 'Transnational Protest and the Public Sphere'. *Mobilisation* 10(1): 95–109.

Biggs, M. 2006. 'The Transnational Diffusion of Protest by Self-Immolation'. *Crossing Borders. On the Road towards Transnational Social Movement Theory, Berlin, 5–7 October 2006,* Social Science Research Center, Berlin. Retrieved 30 August 2008, from http://193.174.6.11/zkd/zcm/pdf/presentation/biggs06_berlin.pdf.

Chabot, S. and J.W. Duyvendak. 2002. 'Globalization and Transnational Diffusion between Social Movements: Reconceptualizing the Dissemination of the Gandhian Repertoire and the "Coming Out" Routine'. *Theory and Society* 31: 697–740.

Crossley, N. 2002. *Making Sense of Social Movements.* Buckingham: Open University Press.

Cunningham, H. 1999. 'The Ethnography of Transnational Social Activism: Understanding the Global as Local Practice'. *American Ethnologist* 26(3): 583–604.

della Porta, D., ed. 2009. *Another Europe: Conceptions and Practices of Democracy in the European Social Forums.* London: Routledge.

della Porta, D., et al. 2006a. *Globalization from below. Transnational Activists and Protest Networks.* Minneapolis: University of Minnesota Press.

———, eds. 2006b. *The Policing of Transnational Protest.* Aldershot: Ashgate.

della Porta, D. and S. Tarrow 2005. 'Transnational Processes and Social Activism: An Introduction'. In *Transnational Protest and Global Activism,* eds. D. della Porta and S. Tarrow, 1–17. Lanham: Rowman & Littlefield.

Doerr, N. and A. Mattoni. 2007. 'The Euromayday Parade Against Precarity: Cross-National Diffusion and Transformation of the European Space "From Below"'. *Campaign Analysis in a Globalizing World, Tutzing, 27–28 April 2007.*

Drury, J., S. Reicher, and C. Stott 2003. 'Transforming the Boundaries of Collective Identity: From the "Local" Anti-road Campaign to "Global" Resistance?' *Social Movement Studies* 2(2): 191–212.

Ferree, M.M., W.A. Gamson, J. Gerhards, and D. Rucht. 2002. *Shaping Abortion Discourse. Democracy and the Public Sphere in Germany and the United States.* Cambridge: Cambridge University Press.

Gamson, W.A. and G. Wolfsfeld. 1993. 'Movemements and Media as Interacting Systems'. *Annals of the American Academy of Political and Social Science* 528: 114–127.

Guidry, J.A., M.D. Kennedy, and M.N. Zald, eds. 2000. *Globalizations and Social Movements: Culture, Power, and the Transnational Public Sphere*. Ann Arbor: University of Michigan Press.

Habermas, J. And J. Derrida. 2003. 'February 15, or What Binds Europeans Together: A Plea for a Common Foreign Policy, Beginning in the Heart of Europe'. *Constellations* 10(3): 291–297.

Hertel, S. 2006. *Unexpected Power. Conflict and Change among Transnational Activists*. Ithaca: Cornell University Press.

Imig, D. and S. Tarrow, eds. 2001. *Contentious Europeans. Protest and Politics in an Emerging Polity*. Lanham: Rowman & Littlefield.

Josselin, D. 2007. 'From Transnational Protest to Domestic Political Opportunities: Insights from the Debt Cancellation Campaign'. *Social Movement Studies* 6(1): 21–38.

Keck, M.E. and K. Sikkink. 1998. *Activists beyond Borders. Advocacy Networks in International Politics*. Ithaca: Cornell University Press.

Klimke, M. 2010. *The 'Other' Alliance: Global Protest and Student Unrest in West Germany and the U.S., 1962–1972*. Princeton: Princeton University Press.

Klimke, M. and J. Scharloth, eds. 2008. *1968 in Europe. A History of Protest and Activism, 1956–1977*. Basingstoke: Palgrave Macmillan.

Kolb, F. 2005. 'The Impact of Transnational Protest on Social Movement Organisations: Mass Media and the Making of ATTAC Germany'. In *Transnational Movements and Global Activism,* eds. D. della Porta and S. Tarrow, 95–120. Lanham: Rowman and Littlefield.

Koopmans, R. 2004. 'Movements and Media: Selection Processes and Evolutionary Dynamics in the Public Sphere'. *Theory and Society* 33(3–4): 367–391.

Koopmans, R. and S. Olzak. 2004. 'Discursive Opportunities and the Evolution of Right-Wing Violence in Germany'. *American Journal of Sociology* 110(1): 198–230.

Mathers, A. 2007. *Struggling for a Social Europe: Neoliberal Globalization and the Birth of a European Social Movement*. Aldershot: Ashgate.

McAdam, D. 1996. 'Conceptual Origins, Current Problems, Future Directions'. In *Comparative Perspectives on Social Movements: Political Opportunities, Mobilising Structures, and Cultural Framings,* eds. D. McAdam, J.D. McCarthy, and M.N. Zald, 23–30. Cambridge: Cambridge University Press.

McAdam, D. and D. Rucht. 1993. 'The Cross-National Diffusion of Movement Ideas'. *Annals of the American Academy of Political and Social Science* 528: 56–74.

McCarthy, J.D. 1997. 'The Globalization of Social Movement Theory'. In *Transnational Social Movements and Global Politics: Solidarity beyond the State,* eds. J. Smith, C. Chatfield, and R. Pagnucco, 243–259. New York: Syracuse University Press.

Meyer, D.S. 2003. 'Political Opportunity and Nested Institutions'. *Social Movement Studies* 2(1): 17–35.

Nehring, H. 2005. 'National Internationalists: British and West German Protests against Nuclear Weapons, the Politics of Transnational Communications and the Social History of the Cold War, 1957–1964'. *Contemporary European History* 14(04): 559–582.

Olesen, T. 2005a. *International Zapatismo: The Construction of Solidarity in the Age of Globalization.* London: Zed Books.

———. 2005b. 'The Uses and Misuses of Globalization in the Study of Social Movements'. *Social Movement Studies* 4(1): 49–63.

Pries, L. 2008. *Die Transnationalisierung der sozialen Welt. Sozialräume jenseits von Nationalgesellschaften.* Frankfurt am Main: Suhrkamp.

Rauch, J., et al. 2007. 'From Seattle 1999 to New York 2004: A Longitudinal Analysis of Journalistic Framing of the Movement for Democratic Globalization'. *Social Movement Studies* 6(2): 131–145.

Robertson, R. 2003. *The Three Waves of Globalization: A History of a Developing Global Consciousness.* London: Zed Books.

Roggeband, C. 2007. 'Translators and Transformers: International Inspiration and Exchange in Social Movements'. *Social Movement Studies* 6(3): 245–259.

Roose, J. 2003. *Die Europäisierung von Umweltorganisationen. Die Umweltbewegung auf dem langen Marsch nach Brüssel.* Wiesbaden: Westdeutscher Verlag.

Rucht, D. 1996. 'The Impact of National Contexts on Social Movement Structures: A Cross-movement and Cross-national Comparison'. In *Comparative Perspectives on Social Movements. Political Opportunities, Mobilising Structures, and Cultural Framings,* eds. D. McAdam, J.D. McCarthy, and M.N. Zald, 185–204. Cambridge: Cambridge University Press.

———. 1999. 'The Transnationalization of Social Movements: Trends, Causes, Problems'. In *Social Movements in a Globalizing World,* eds. H. Kriesi, D. della Porta, and D. Rucht, 206–222. London: Macmillan.

———. 2000. 'Distant Issue Movements in Germany: Empirical Description and Theoretical Reflections'. In *Globalizations and Social Movements: Culture, Power, and the Transnational Public Sphere,* eds. J.A. Guidry, M.D. Kennedy, and M.N. Zald, 67–105. Ann Arbor: University of Michigan Press.

———. 2001. 'Transnationaler politischer Protest im historischen Längsschnitt'. In *Globalisierung, Partizipation, Protest,* eds. A. Klein, R. Koopmans and H. Geiling, 77–96. Opladen: Leske + Budrich.

Rucht, D. and S. Teune. 2008. 'Eine quantitative Analyse der G8-Berichterstattung in den Printmedien'. In *Nur Clowns und Chaoten? Die G8-Proteste in Heiligendamm im Spiegel der Massenmedien,* eds. D. Rucht and S. Teune, 53–75. Frankfurt am Main: Campus.

Rupp, L.J. 1997. *Worlds of Women: The Making of an International Women's Movement.* Princeton: Princeton University Press.

Seidman, G.W. 2000. 'Adjusting the Lens: What Do Globalizations, Transnationalism, and the Anti-Apartheid Movement Mean for Social Movement Theory?' In *Globalizations and Social Movements. Culture, Power, and the Transnational Public Sphere,* eds. J.A. Guidry, M.D. Kennedy, and M.N. Zald, 339–357. Ann Arbor: University of Michigan Press.

Smith, J. 2001. 'Globalizing Resistance: The Battle of Seattle and the Future of Social Movements'. *Mobilisation* 6(1): 1–19.

———. 2002. 'Bridging Global Divides? Strategic Framing and Solidarity in Transnational Social Movement Organisations'. *International Sociology* 17(4): 505–528.

Smith, J., C. Chatfield, and R. Pagnucco, eds. 1997. *Transnational Social Movements and Global Politics: Solidarity beyond the State*. New York: Syracuse University Press.

Smith, J., et al. 2007. *Global Democracy and the World Social Forums*. Boulder: Paradigm Publishers.

Smith, M.P. 2003. 'Transnationalism and Citizenship'. In *Approaching Transnationalisms. Studies on Transnational Societies, Multicultural Contacts, and Imaginings of Home*, eds. B.S.A. Yeoh, M.W. Charney, and T.C. Kiong, 15–38. Boston: Kluwer.

Smith, M.P. and L.E. Guarnizo, eds. 1998. *Transnationalism from below*. New Brunswick: Transaction Publishers.

Snow, D.A., et al. 1986. 'Frame Alignment Processes, Micromobilisation, and Movement Participation'. *American Sociological Review* 51(4): 464–481.

Soule, S.A. 1999. 'The Diffusion of an Unsuccessful Innovation'. *The Annals of the American Academy of Political and Social Science* 566(1): 120–131.

———. 2004. 'Diffusion Processes within and across Movements'. In *Blackwell Companion to Social Movements*, eds. D.A. Snow, H. Kriesi, and S.A. Soule, 294–310. Oxford: Blackwell.

Tarrow, S. 1995. 'The Europeanisation of Conflict: Reflections from a Social Movement Perspective'. *West European Politics* 18(2): 223–251.

———. 1998. *Power in Movement*. Cambridge: Cambridge University Press.

———. 2001. 'Transnational Politics: Contention and Institutions in International Politics'. *Annual Review of Political Science* 4(1): 1–20.

———. 2002. 'From Lumping to Splitting: Specifying Globalization and Resistance'. In *Globalization and Resistance: Transnational Dimensions of Social Movements*, eds. J. Smith and H. Johnston, 229–249. Lanham: Rowman & Littlefield.

———. 2005. *The New Transnational Activism*. Cambridge: Cambridge University Press.

Thörn, H. 2006. 'Solidarity across Borders: The Transnational Anti-Apartheid Movement'. *Voluntas: International Journal of Voluntary and Nonprofit Organisations* 17(4): 285–301.

Tilly, C. 1978. *From Mobilisation to Revolution*. Reading: Addison-Wesley.

Van Holthoon, F. and M. Van der Linden, eds. 1988. *Internationalism in the Labour Movement, 1830–1940*. Leiden: BRILL.

Vanden, H.E. 2003. 'Globalization in a Time of Neoliberalism: Politicized Social Movements and the Latin American Response'. *Journal of Developing Societies* 19(2–3): 308–333.

Walgrave, S. and D. Rucht, eds. 2010. *The World Says No to War: Demonstrations against the War in Iraq*. Minneapolis: University of Minnesota Press.

Wisler, D. and M. Giugni. 1999. 'Under the Spotlight: The Impact of Media Attention on Protest Policing'. *Mobilisation* 4(2): 171–187.

Wood, L.J. 2004. 'Breaking the Bank and Taking to the Streets – How Protesters Target Neoliberalism'. *Journal of World Systems Research* 10(1): 69–89.

Zimmermann, S. 2002. 'Frauenbewegungen, Transfer und Trans-Nationalität. Feministisches Denken und Streben im globalen und zentral-osteuropäischen Kontext des 19. und frühen 20. Jahrhunderts'. In *Transnationale Öffentlichkeiten und Identitäten im 20. Jahrhundert*, eds. H. Kaelble, M. Kirsch, and A. Schmidt-Gernig, 263–302. Frankfurt: Campus.

Transnational Activists
and Organisations

Chapter One

Transnational versus National Activism

A Systematic Comparison of 'Transnationalists' and 'Nationalists' Participating in the 2006 European and Belgian Social Forums

Stefaan Walgrave and Jeroen Van Laer

Introduction

Is activism located at a transnational level any different from activism located at the national or even local level? More concrete: is there any difference in terms of backgrounds, attitudes, or behaviour among activists that are active on a transnational level and activists that restrict their activities to a national level? While the question may seem trivial, the answers to it are important to understand the apparently spreading transnational activism phenomenon and its repercussions for local grassroots activism. Moreover, the question of whether national and transnational activism is different and whether activists active on one of these levels differ from each other remains largely unresolved and heavily debated. Some scholars claim that transnational activism is a distinct type of activism (e.g., Anheier, Glasius and Kaldor 2001), while others maintain that transnational activists are in the first place just common national or local activists rooted in their local settings (Fisher et al. 2005: 105; Tarrow 2005a).

For more than a decade now, social movement scholars have been focussing heavily on the transnationalization of social movements, protest and contentious politics. One of the main issues is whether classic social movement theories are able to explain transnational movement phenomena (McCarthy 1997; see also chapter 8 in this volume). Much of this work focussed on the meso- or macro-level. Scholars examined, among other topics, to what extent political opportunities shifted from the national to the transnational level (Keck and Sikkink 1998; Sikkink 2005). Imig and Tarrow (2001), for example, undertook protest event analysis to investigate whether protest events targeted national or European institutions. Many studies have also focussed on the link and interplay between organisations operating at the local, national and/or transnational level, and how much global issues shape national and local organisations (see especially della Porta and Tarrow 2005). So, to some extent, the contradiction between the national and the transnational level is arbitrary and we are more likely confronted with a continuum. But for the sake of the argument and the analysis a sharp difference will be maintained between national and transnational activism. Recently, studies started to tackle the micro-level aspect of transnational activism as well. At all kinds of meetings or protest events staged by the Global Justice Movement (GJM), students of social movements distributed questionnaires and interviewed participants (della Porta et al. 2006). Especially European Social Forums (ESFs), the periodical meetings of the GJM emulating the World Social Forum (WSF) initially organised in Porto Alegre, appear to have become the home turf of transnational activism scholars (e.g. Andretta et al. 2002; Agrikoliansky and Sommier 2005; della Porta et al. 2006; della Porta 2009). As a consequence, it is well documented who the people are that attend these transnational forums. They tend to be fairly young, highly educated, mostly women and with middle-class backgrounds; they have a left-wing political orientation, they tend to be motivated by diverse values such as democratisation, social justice, solidarity and anti-capitalism, and they distrust the traditional political institutions; many of them are committed activists with active movement memberships and a history of protest participation (della Porta et al. 2006).

Remarkably, very few of these available studies systematically compare transnational activists with national activists. Even the seminal work of Donatella della Porta and colleagues (2006) on the 2002 ESF in Florence, Italy, did not engage in a systematic comparison of national—that is, Italian – and transnational – that is, non-Italian – participants. To be sure, the authors did present some evidence on differences between the nationalities present in Florence, but rather than comparing national with transnational activists, their goal was to demonstrate that people from different countries have different backgrounds that reflect the diverging political cultures and social movement sectors in their respective countries. The point della Porta and colleagues make is that transnational activists differ from each other rather than that transnational activists differ from national activists. However, a systematic national-transnational comparison can be helpful to grasp the drivers of transnational protest and to test whether it really differs from activism that is confined within the national borders.

If transnational activism is something special that is 'produced' by particular prior characteristics, attitudes and behaviour, transnational activists would systematically differ from national activists. If transnational activism, in contrast, is similar to national or local activism, transnational activists would have a lot in common with national activists. Consequently, if both types of participants are fairly similar, chances are high that the same theories can be used to explain both transnational and national/local activism; but if both types of activists differ a lot also different theories are needed to explain their activism or, at least, existing theories should be revised to grasp the particularities of transnational activism.

This chapter, therefore, provides a systematic comparison of 'transnational' and 'national' participants taking part in the same social forums. Surveys among participants in social forums offer an excellent design to test whether transnational activism is different from national/local activism. Consider the World or the European Social Forum. A part of the participants always are locals: they attend an international meeting but they do so in their own region, country or even city. Schönleitner (2003: 136), for instance, has described this 'regional imbalance' for the first WSF in Porto Alegre, Brazil: more than 60 per cent came from South America. Considerable efforts were taken to attract delegates from more countries at the second WSF, also held in Porto Alegre. However, despite these efforts, still more than 55 per cent of the participants came from Brazil alone. The other participants in the same event, people from abroad who travelled to participate in the forum, can be considered as 'pure' transnational activists. The opposite applies to the national social forums that are organised in many countries; almost all of the participants of these forums are nationals. Yet, among these nationals, some have previously attended social forums abroad and thus can be considered transnational activists. It is this double comparison that this chapter builds upon. A few hundred participants were surveyed in the ESF in 2006 in Athens, Greece, and in the Belgian Social Forum (BSF) organised in 2006 in Brussels, Belgium. Within both groups of participants, 'transnational' activists are compared with 'national' activists.

Hypotheses

As mentioned above, few studies have engaged in systematically comparing national with transnational activists or even in theorising on the differences between national and transnational activists. Thus, hypotheses will remain tentative and explorative. The largest effort to systematically chart transnational activism on a micro-level has been undertaken by della Porta and colleagues (2006). They sampled participants at the 2002 ESF in Florence and at the major anti-G8 demonstration in Genoa in 2001. Implicitly, this study, suggestively entitled 'Globalisation from below', claims that people who participate in transnational events share specific common features that may distinguish them from other activists. This becomes clear when the authors state, in the methods section of their study, that they excluded the Tuscans, living close to or even in Florence, from the Italian sample as 'they had a different profile from other participants in terms of sociodemographic dimensions (gender, age, education, social condition): geographically close to the event, Tuscans needed a lower commitment than Italians from other regions to participate in the ESF' (della Porta et al. 2006: 24, emphasis removed). This quote contains the main argument for expecting differences between national and transnational activists: costs to participate in transnational events abroad are much higher and this high barrier can be compensated by, amongst others, a higher commitment. The fact that 'costly' participation in terms of time, money and risk requires a certain structural availability with less conflicting personal engagements is by now a classic postulate of the social movement literature (McAdam 1986).

Sidney Tarrow (2005b: 7) also recognises that 'forming transnational social movements is not easy'. A precondition for the formation of transnational movements, Tarrow ascertains, is the existence of a stratum of what he calls 'rooted cosmopolitans'. Although firmly domestically embedded and drawing on domestic resources and opportunities, these people engage in transnational contacts and transactions. They form a distinct segment in society that was less available before. 'They are a stratum of individuals who travel regularly, read foreign books and journals and become involved in networks of transaction abroad' (Tarrow 2005b: 34). Not all rooted cosmopolitans become transnational activists, to be sure, but they are available to become active in transnational claims-making processes. Tarrow does not make it entirely clear in what precise and measurable respect the transnational activist would differ from the traditional national activist, though. He suggests some differences, but does not advance a testable list of variables: 'they are better *educated* than most of their compatriots, better *connected*, speak more *languages*, and *travel* more often' (Tarrow 2005b: 43, emphasis added). In another publication, Tarrow (2005a) states that transnational and national activists are not separated and isolated, but form a closely knit continuum, which would imply that there are rather few differences between them. Elaborating on the idea of 'rooted.cosmopolitans', Grenier (2004) identifies transnational activists as 'pioneers of global civil society'. They are not detached from local realities, but they have distinct capacities in terms of leadership abilities, education, financial and other resources, and motivation that allow them to connect local and global opportunity structures to pursue their causes. These kind of activists are very often also labelled as 'social entrepreneurs', referring here to business entrepreneurs, who are similar in risk taking propensity and creativity (Grenier 2004: 122).

Fisher and colleagues (2005) surveyed participants in five globalisation protest events and systematically compared local participants, living nearby the protest event, with non-local participants, living elsewhere in the same (or a neighbouring) country. As they had hardly any transnational participants in their samples, they could not focus on comparing transnational with national activists. Their findings about differences between locals and non-locals, though, are inspirational when thinking about national versus transnational activists. They find that non-locals are significantly more informed about the protest by organisations and less informed by the media, that non-locals attended the event more in the company of organisation members, and that non-locals, to a much larger extent than locals, received funding from an organisation to attend the demonstration (Fisher et al. 2005: 114–116). This suggests, similar to the arguments of della Porta and Tarrow, that non-locals and, thus, transnational activists may be more organisationally embedded than their local or national counterparts. Organisations, this evidence suggests, reduce the thresholds and help people overcome the larger barriers (e.g., financially) to participate in protest abroad. If these organisations are then occupied with transnational and global issues, it is even more likely that activists who are members of such an organisation will take part in transnational actions. This is more or less what Diani (2005) found when he studied different social movement organisations in Glasgow and Bristol: those organisations principally more interested in global issues, such as Third World poverty, globalisation, ethnicity and human rights, are also more likely to take part in global actions.

The most elaborate study of national versus transnational activists, to our knowledge, has been undertaken by Isabelle Bédoyan and collaborators (2004). Drawing on a survey of protesters against the EU summit in Brussels, Belgium, in 2001, they test the idea that transnational mobilisation is more difficult than national mobilisation since there are practical, psychological and political barriers that are harder to overcome (see also Marks and McAdam 1999). Drawing on that premise, they find that transnational and national participants in the Brussels' march differed quite extensively. Their results underpin some of the findings mentioned above. The most important differences that they found are related to the demonstrators' *professional situation* (student vs. non-student), to their *organisational embeddedness* (more in company of co-members, more informed by organisations), to their *political interest* and to their more radical *opinions* about politics (more dissatisfied with democracy and representative system, more agree with radical movement strategy) (Bédoyan, Van Aelst and Walgrave 2004). Bédoyan and colleagues conclude that transnational activists 'are young, organized, and radical compared to their Belgian counterparts' (2004: 48).

Wrapping up, the modest available evidence supports the hypothesis that transnational activists differ from national activists in at least three aspects: social-demographics, attitudes and behaviour. First, transnational activists are expected to be younger, higher educated and to be made up more of students. Second, regarding their attitudes, transnational activists are expected to be more radical and critical toward democracy, but, at the same time, more interested in (broad) political issues. Third, and considering behaviour, it is foremost expected that transnationalists are more organisationally embedded (and this, in addition, more likely to be within organisations working on global issues) and have more protest experience than their domestic counterparts. Are these expectations warranted by the facts?

Data and Methods

The above questions will be addressed by means of survey data collected at two different social forum events. Social forums can be considered as the main gathering moments of the GJM. Interestingly for our purpose, the social forum concept, and especially the transnational or global events, have been criticised for being 'champagne activism': 'open only to those who can afford the time and money to fly around the world ... discussing global problems' (Glasius and Timms 2006: 225). Some claim that having sufficient resources or finding proper funding is one of the main issues at transnational forums. Furthermore, social forums are extensively prepared in so-called preparatory meetings, which alternately take place in different countries and these too require time and money (see chapter 4; Van Laer and Verhulst 2007). In the International Council, the organ that sets out the main political guidelines and strategic directions of the WSF, meetings are found to be even more costly and time consuming. Moreover, national level organisations are even being excluded from these preparatory meetings in order to avoid 'the logic of the nation-state' (Schönleitner 2003: 133). In any case, social forums are excellent occasions to scrutinise differences between national and transnational activists. Arguably, though, social forums cover only a part of the current transnational activism. International protest events, for example, may have led to a different dynamic and to different distinctions between national and transnational protesters. The data presented in this chapter only tackle part of the transnational activism puzzle.

One of the surveys presented in this chapter was taken among participants at the fourth ESF in Athens, Greece, 4–7 May 2006; a second survey was taken among participants of the third BSF in Brussels, Belgium, 16 December 2006. Paper versions of both the ESF and the BSF questionnaires were distributed at the forum venues itself: about 600 were distributed in Athens in the first two days and 678 were distributed in Brussels. In Athens, paper questionnaires were distributed in and outside the main hall on the first and second day of the forum. Two interviewers selected each tenth person passing, kindly asked them to fill in the questionnaire and then leave it in a postal box at the main exit or at the stall of the University of Antwerp in the main hall. The initial response rate in Athens was rather disappointing (only 68 questionnaires were completed at the end of the four-day event). In the weeks and months after the forum, participants were therefore contacted via email and invited to participate in an online version of the same survey. Existing email lists (about 700 subscribers) were used and, on top of that, the Greek Organising Committee provided about 1,500 unique email addresses of people who had registered online. A news entry was placed on the official website of the Athens' ESF, inviting attendants to participate in the study. The fact that all communication, practical information, and, more importantly, the ESF registration nearly exclusively went via the internet justifies the use of an online survey, in addition to the paper questionnaires distributed at the venue itself. About 440 ESF participants completed the online survey (see Table 1.1).

In Brussels, 108 paper questionnaires were completed on one day. The interviewers were positioned at the only entrance and exit of the forum venue. Every

Table 1.1. Response Rates of the ESF and BSF Survey, May and December 2006

	BSF Brussels	ESF Athens
Participants	800	35,000
Questionnaires		
Distributed (paper + electronic version)	678	3,000[a]
Response	205	510
Response rate (percent)	30.3	17.0

[a] The number of distributed questionnaires is a rough estimation of the total amount of email recipients and the amount of distributed paper questionnaires at the forum.

participant had to register when entering the building and then immediately received a paper questionnaire together with a postage paid envelope and a little pencil. Along with a very short introduction, each participant was then kindly requested to fill in the survey and leave it by the end of the day in the blue box at the same exit, or to send it via the post once home by using the postage paid envelope. In the weeks immediately afterward, another 87 respondents returned their completed questionnaires. Yet, although the paper version was rather successful (response rate of 29 per cent), the additional online version of the BSF survey was not a great success. For obvious reasons of privacy, the Organising Committee of the BSF did not agree to us sending an email to the BSF participants who had registered online. As a result, only the existing email lists could be used (about 100 subscribers); only 10 of these people participated in the online version. They all indicated also having received a paper version of the questionnaire at the forum. After processing and cleaning the data, a total amount of 510 ESF and 205 unique BSF participants had completed a useful questionnaire.

Since a good indication of the real composition of the entire population at both of these forum events is not available, it is impossible to test whether the returned questionnaires or those filled in online are representative of the BSF and ESF populations. Especially with regard to the Athens' online survey, it is difficult to estimate the bias caused by both the self-selection of respondents as well as the persisting inequalities in terms of internet use among ESF participants who are coming from different countries. With regard to the postal surveys, though, similar research at street demonstrations indicated that the response bias of returned postal questionnaires is minimal (Walgrave and Verhulst 2010). Of course, participating in a social forum is different from participating in a demonstration, but both can be considered as collective action events and the overlap in participants is probably considerable. As indicated by Fillieule and Blanchard (chapter 9 in this volume), differences may exist between people filling in the survey on the day itself or afterward once they are at home. Bivariate analysis comparing the two independent samples (those who filled in the survey at the BSF or ESF itself, and those who filled in the survey at home or online), however, revealed no differences in terms of socio-demographic variables as well as general attitudinal or organisational backgrounds.

Table 1.2 provides some basic socio-demographic descriptives and information on the dependent variable. General socio-demographic features indicate a highly educated (even hyper-educated), slightly male, young to middle-aged constituency. The BSF respondents are, compared to the ESF sample, slightly older, mostly male and relatively less educated.

In terms of the nationality of the attendants of both forums, Table 1.2 clearly documents that the BSF in Brussels was a truly domestic event. Almost 90 per cent of the attendees had Belgian nationality. A few French participants appeared at the BSF, but all of the other nationalities are negligible or entirely absent. This confirms the finding of many other scholars of transnational activism that most GJM events are dominated by local, national activists, and thus are not that

Table 1.2. Sociodemographics, Nationality, and Previous Transnational Participation of ESF and BSF Participants

	BSF Brussels	ESF Athens
Sociodemographics		
Gender (percent male)	55.2	52.7
Age (mean)	44.3	34.6
Educational level None/primary	1.0	0.4
Lower secondary	4.9	2.0
Higher secondary	12.7	8.6
Higher non-university	28.3	8.4
University/doctoral	50.2	77.3
Missing	2.9	3.3
Nationality		
Belgium	89.3	11.8
France	5.4	6.7
Netherlands	1.0	1.6
Spain/Portugal	—	7.5
Italy	1.5	10.0
Germany/Switzerland/Austria	—	7.6
Scandinavia	—	5.9
UK/Ireland	—	9.4
Turkey	—	3.5
Greece/Cyprus	0.5	22.5
Balkan/Eastern Europe/Russia	1.0	9.0
Non-EU	1.5	4.5
(Previous) transnational participation		
No transnational participation	84.4	17.6
Transnational participation	15.6	82.4
N	205	510

global in terms of its participants (see, e.g., Lichbach and de Vries 2004; Fisher et al. 2005). The opposite applies to the ESF participants. Organised in Greece, a fair amount of participants held Greek nationality, but the ESF was a truly transnational event with wide international attendance. The Belgians in the ESF sample seem to be over-represented (approximately 12 per cent). This is probably caused by the fact that the research team was Belgian, reducing the threshold for Belgian participants to take part in the survey. Moreover, some Belgian participants apparently forwarded the email invitation to their own contacts.

Two separate comparisons will be drawn: one among BSF and a second among ESF participants. The BSF participants were asked whether they had participated in the second WSF (January 2002) or in the fourth ESF (May 2006). At the second WSF, a large Belgian delegation was present and it was on that occasion that the BSF was founded. The fourth ESF was the most recent transnational social forum to have taken place at that time. BSF participants who indicated that they attended one or both of these transnational events were defined as transnational activists (16 per cent); the ones who did not attend any of these events were considered as national activists (84 per cent). This straightforward categorisation is rather rough and contains a lot of noise. People may have participated in other transnational events than the two mentioned, but it is the best measure available. Among the ESF participants, a comparable but not identical distinction was made as different questionnaires were used for the BSF and the ESF. Participants from Greece were considered to be national activists, unless they indicated to have participated in one of the following events: the first ESF in Florence (2002), the second ESF in Paris (2003), or the third ESF in London (2004). In that case, these Greek participants were considered to be transnational participants. All other people travelling from abroad to the Athens meeting were also classified as transnational activists. As for the categorisation of the BSF participants, here again some of the Greek ESF participants may have participated in another transnational event than the three mentioned.

As the figures in Table 1.2 show, about 82 per cent of the ESF respondents are classified as transnational activists. There is a striking contrast between the amount of transnational activists at the BSF compared to the amount at the ESF, which suggest a different logic for both events. Since the fundamental idea of a social forum is to provide an 'open space' (Whitaker 2004) where social movement organisations and activists can meet, debate, exchange experience and learn from each other, the level of each event consequently might attract more national (in the case of the BSF) or transnational (in the case of the ESF) oriented organisations or activists. Different levels of the social forum process (local, national, regional and global) are very much related, adopting the same organisational proceedings, drawing on the same democratic and participatory principles and addressing the same topics on neoliberal globalisation (Glasius and Timms 2006). Yet, as Glasius and Timms (2006) describe, each forum has its own specificities. Especially the local and national chapters very often show typical features that merely refer to the 'higher level' social forums as a source of inspiration, but that have still distinct organisational forms or address specialised local topics. This too is an argument that national social forums in general do attract more nationally oriented activists, and that regional social forums attract more transnationally oriented activists, with only a small overlap.

The analyses below consist of a systematic comparison of the national and transnational activists as defined above: to what extent are they different? Note that the BSF analyses draw on a mainly Belgian sample and basically compare Belgians with Belgians, while the ESF analyses compare Greeks with other nationals. Differences between national and transnational activists in the case of the ESF, then, may not only be due to the difference between different types of activists, but also to their different national backgrounds. This caveat must be kept in mind, especially when taking into account variables on which Greeks in general differ from other European populations.

Finally, although differences between national and transnational activists are expected, at the same time, these differences are not anticipated to be very large. After all, all surveyed participants attended the same events and they more or less overcame the same barriers. Also, Greek ESF participants, for example, were confronted with language thresholds when attending the ESF: many ESF sessions, meetings and workshops were organised in another language than Greek, which might have discouraged participation. Moreover, the ESF analyses lump together many nationalities in the broad 'container' category of transnational activists. Bearing the features of their respective countries, there probably are substantial differences within the transnational activist category that may counterbalance and compensate each other. Still, a rough comparison is presented here, as it is the most straightforward way to test the main argument of national versus transnational activism.

Analyses

Table 1.3 contains two logistic regression analyses predicting transnational activism in contrast to national activism. The first column contains the results for the BSF and compares participants with and without previous international social forum experience. The second column documents the comparison between Greek (national) participants without previous experience in social forums abroad, and those ESF participants with previous (Greek) or current (all other nationalities) transnational experience. A binary logistic regression was applied since the dependent variable has only two possible outcomes (national or transnational). As the ratio between the number of cases and the number of variables is rather low, and in order to reduce the number of missing cases, the final models exclude non-significant variables in a backwards procedure. For the specific coding of the different predictors, see Table 1.4 in the appendix. Three

Table 1.3. Logistic Regressions Comparing National with Transnational Activists at BSF and ESF

		BSF Brussels	ESF Athens
Socio-demos	Age (low-high)	n.s.	n.s.
	Gender (male-female)	n.s.	2.387*
	Education (low-high)	n.s.	n.s.
	Student (no-yes)	n.s.	n.s.
Attitudes	Forum identification (low-high)	2.343*	n.s.
	Satisfaction democracy (low-high)	n.s.	n.s.
	Political interest (low-high)	n.s.	n.s.
	Expected outcome forum (low-high)	n.s.	.709***
Behaviour	Organisational involvement (low-high)	1.341*	1.619***
	Member transnational organisation (no-yes)	n.s.	2.211*
	Info-channel social forum (open-closed)	n.s.	2.088*
	Travel organised/reimbursed (no-yes)	—	1.348***
	Protest frequency (none-frequent)	1.947**	—
	N	177	458
	Nagelkerke R2	.229	.250

*, **, *** Coefficients in the table are odds-ratios and their significance: *p<0.05, **p<0.01, ***p<0.001. A backward (likelihood ratio) stepwise procedure was applied.

sets of independent variables can be discerned, each of them referring to the different hypotheses described above: a first set of socio-demographic variables (age, gender, education, and occupational status [student or not]); a second set of attitudinal variables (self-identification with other forum participants, general satisfaction with democracy in one's own country, general political interest and expected outcome of the forum); and a set of behavioural variables (organisational involvement, member of a transnational organisation or not, information channel about the forum, re-imbursement/organisation of travel, past protest frequency). The parameters presented are odds ratios: coefficients larger than 1.0 indicate a positive effect; parameters smaller than 1.0 denote a negative effect.

First of all, both models manage to grasp a considerable part of the differences between national and transnational activists. The Nagelkerke R^2 of the two models is not particularly high, but it is satisfying. Moreover, the explained variance is very similar: local Greek and transnational ESF participants on the one hand, and BSF participants with a transnational participation track record and BSF participants without such a record, on the other hand, are more or less equally different. The ESF model yields more significant predictors. This is most likely due to the much larger number of observations on which the ESF analysis is based (458 compared to 177).

As expected, the main finding is that organisational embeddedness makes a big difference. The more people are part of and embedded in an organisation, the more likely it is that they participate transnationally. Organisations seem to systematically lower the barriers for transnational mobilisation. Organisational involvement (a scale of four distinct organisational variables, see the appendix) is a significant predictor of transnationalism. And more importantly, confirming Diani's (2005) findings, especially those people who are a member of transnational organisations focussing on global justice, Third World issues, or human rights are sparked to take part in transnational activism, at least among ESF participants. Among the BSF participants, transnational organisation membership was not a significant predictor, but the bivariate correlation went in the expected, positive direction. How organisations exactly perform their barrier reducing function can be seen in the two other organisational variables. Organisations, first of all, inform their members in many ways about upcoming international movement events. Technically speaking, transnational activists are more mobilised via closed mobilisation processes, while national activists are informed through open channels such as mass media, friends and posters (Walgrave and Klandermans 2010). Again, this mobilisation variable is not significant for the BSF, but the bivariate correlation goes in the same positive direction. Secondly, organisations take care of the practical worries of their members' transnational participation: they organise the trip, arrange accommodation and they pay for the expenses. In short, in terms of organisations, our data strongly corroborate previous results (Bédoyan, Van Aelst and Walgrave 2004; Fisher et al. 2005). Transnational activism is, much more than national activism, a predominantly organisational embedded activity. This implies that, at transnational movement events, we do not in the first place encounter the movements' grassroots and rank-and-file, but rather the organisational elites. Apart from their organisational distinctiveness, transnational activists, much more than mere national activists, are experienced and veteran protesters. Protest experience was only assessed by means of past protest frequency in the BSF sample, but it is likely that the same would be true for the ESF crowd. Again, this suggests that transnational activism is not the practice of novices, but rather an activity performed by experienced and weathered activists. Only after a certain activist career can people take their activism a step higher to the transnational level. Likewise, on a national or local scale, we are more likely confronted with occasional passers-by who are merely interested in the social forum as an individual, grabbing a taste of it, but who are not a member of or are not representing any organisation. In the BSF sample, for instance, among the national activists, 55 per cent were attending the forum 'as an individual' compared to only 22 per cent among the transnational activists (figures not shown in table).

Regarding both of the other dimensions of activism, socio-demographic background and attitudinal dispositions, we can be brief: they are much less helpful in distinguishing both activist types than the organisational and behavioural variables. Only gender makes a difference in the ESF sample. Transnational activists at the ESF meeting are more likely female than national ESF activists. Structural differences between Greek society and other countries might offer a tentative explanation. First, it might be the case that, in general, female Greeks are less active in social movement organisations compared to other organisations. More likely, the fact that our ESF research design drew mainly on internet surveys probably skewed the Greek sample in terms of gender: of all European countries, Greece is, after Ukraine, the country with the far least internet access. More than three-fourths of the Greeks, in 2005, declared that they had no access to the internet at home or work. In most other European countries, that figure lay below one-third (European Social Survey 2006, round 2). Furthermore, internet access in Greece, the figures show, is very much a privilege of the male population, both in lower as well as in higher social strata. Interestingly, neither age, nor studentship nor education are significant predictors of transnational activism, which goes against the findings of previous studies.

Finally, our attitudinal predictors are not very performant either. Neither general satisfaction with democracy in one's country nor political interest proved to be an important predictor of transnational activism. An interesting result, yet only for ESF activists, is the expectation that the forum would be successful in disseminating the movements' ideas and boost mobilisation.[1] Transnational ESF participants are much less optimistic than their national counterparts. We can only speculate that the Greeks' self-confidence, maybe overwhelmed by the success of having the ESF in Athens, was boosted. One of the organisers of the Greek ESF explained that for many Greeks – often activists rather isolated from other activists in the world – the ESF was indeed an eye-opener, as they 'realised that they were part of a big family engaged in a common fight. Even the organizations most hostile to the EU have found in the ESF the political space they needed to express themselves' (Anastasia Theodorakopoulous, cited in Delmas 2007: 141). Also, the transnational and, as we showed, the more experienced and weathered activists may be more realistic in their expectations about the effect of the ESF than their less experienced and maybe more naive colleagues. Moreover, both the euphoria characteristic of the first ESFs and the media attention are decreasing (Teune forthcoming). This is probably why experienced activists are more sceptical about the ESF's potential impact beyond the GJM. Finally, yet only at the BSF, transnational activists tend to identify more with the forum and other participants than national activists. Despite the clear indications of transnational activists being more of an 'elite' kind of activist, this result can be positively interpreted as a commitment to represent not only one's own organisation, but also the broader movement and movement's grassroots. Either way, firm conclusions regarding the attitudes cannot be drawn; neither can the claim be corroborated that transnational activists are particularly more committed or have consistently different attitudes than national activists.

The models presented here are incomplete. To really test Tarrow's 'rooted cosmopolitans' thesis, for example, information should be included about the private, non-activist related travelling behaviour of the activists and about their command of foreign languages, etc. (see chapter 9 in this volume). That the organisational variables are dominating the models at the expense of the socio-demographic and attitudinal predictors may also be caused by the fact that we did not dispose of the most adequate indicators. However, it makes sense that especially organisational embeddedness matters. As Marco Giugni and colleagues claim in this book, the transnationalisation of collective action and activism probably is a dissymmetric process. Some aspects are more affected by transnationalism than others. The increased role of organisations might be one of these aspects.

Conclusion

In this chapter, transnational and national participants in local and international social forums, the typical meeting place of the GJM, were systematically compared to each other. Participants were surveyed in two social forum events in 2006: the BSF in Brussels and the ESF in Athens. In both samples, transnational activists were distinguished from national activists by drawing on a nationality criterion and on the self-reported participation in previous transnational social forums. Furthermore, transnational activism is considered as physically moving across borders, which does not include those activists who might report that they are pursuing global causes and issues without actually travelling abroad. The extent, to which activists in fact conceive their engagement as being transnational activism, is a question that Ariane Jossin more adequately tackles in the next chapter. Here, we explicitly focussed on activists being geographically active on a transnational level or a national level. We recognised the shortcomings and limitations of this operationalisation, but consider it to be a first step to further study the relation between national and transnational activism.

The relevance of our exercise is empirical as it is theoretical. Empirically, very few studies directly assessed whether the geographic level of activism really makes a difference. Some asserted that transnational activism is just an extension of national activism; others claimed it to be something entirely different. Theoretically, the geographic level of activism is relevant as large differences between the two types of activists might challenge mainstream activism theory, which has been devised for activism within the confines of the national state.

So, is transnational activism then any different from national activism? Substantial differences were found between the people who were merely active in their own country and the people who travelled abroad to participate in movement events. Particularly important was the organisational embeddedness of the transnational activists. Much more than national activists, transnationalists tend to be formally backed by and engaged in organisations; they tend to officially represent these organisations in the forum; they often belong to the decision-making circle in their organisation; their travel and accommodation have likely been arranged for them and their expenses are frequently paid by their organisation. This is not to say that personal motivations for being active on a transnational level are not important, on the contrary, they are. For instance, we also find transnational activists (although only at the BSF) identify more strongly with the social forum process. But, as Jossin also concludes in the following chapter, the backbone for transnational activists is largely an organisational one: (national) groups and networks function like an anchorage for those activists who want to stay active on a transnational level. Thus, while our data only offer a snapshot of an activist career, Jossin already offers some hints that the same (organisational) factors are important in sustaining transnational activism.

Social movement and protest theory has recently witnessed an increase in attention for informal networks, micro-mobilisation contexts, etc. (see e.g., McAdam 1988). Also, in thinking about transnational activism and especially about the GJM, it is a common practice to emphasise the informality, networked, non-hierarchical and direct character of participation practices and action repertoires (della Porta 2005). The evidence presented here suggests, in contrast, that, much more than in national activism, organisations play a key role in producing transnational activism. The explanation is simple: transnational activism entails more costs than national activism. Organisations, probably more than informal arrangements, can help potential participants in overcoming these problems and taking the thresholds. The barrier-lowering capacity of organisations has been known for a long time (Klandermans and Oegema 1987). Yet, these qualities of organisations become again more relevant in a new context. As the cost of participating in national events has probably gone down over the years – protest participation is up and protest has become normalised – organisations have probably lost some of their indispensability regarding national activism. Examples of mobilisation without formal backbones abound in the recent protest literature. The scale shift of activism to the transnational level, however, brings organisations back in. In the end, we do not need a separate theory to tackle transnational activism, but we can simply rely on the existing mobilisation and participation theories with a renewed respect for the strength of organisations. Transnational activism is simply national activism with more restrictions.

Note

1. The question was formulated as follows: 'How big are the chances that the BSF/ESF will boost mobilisation or give visibility to the common targets of the movements participating in the BSF/ESF?'

References

Agrikoliansky, E. and I. Sommier, eds. 2005. *Radiographie du mouvement altermondialiste*. Paris: La Dispute.

Andretta, M., et al. 2002. *Global, noglobal, new global. La protesta contro il G8 a Genova.* Rome: Laterza.

Anheier, H., M. Glasius and M. Kaldor, eds. 2001. *Global Civil Society 2001.* Oxford: Oxford University Press.

Bédoyan, I., P. Van Aelst and S. Walgrave. 2004. 'Limitations and Possibilities of Transnational Mobilization: The Case of EU Summit Protesters in Brussels, 2001'. *Mobilization* 9(1): 39–54.

della Porta, D. 2005. 'Multiple Belongings, Tolerant Identities and the Construction of "Another Politics": Between the European Social Forum and the Local Social Fora'. In *Transnational Protest and Global Activism,* eds. D. della Porta and S. Tarrow, 175–202. Lanham: Rowman & Littlefield.

———, ed. 2009. *Democracy in the European Social Forums. Conceptions and Practices.* London: Routledge.

della Porta, D., et al. 2006. *Globalization from below: Transnational Activists and Protest Networks.* Minneapolis: University of Minnesota Press.

della Porta, D and S. Tarrow, eds. 2005. *Transnational Protest and Global Activism.* Lanham: Rowman & Littlefield.

Delmas, C. 2007. 'European Social Forums (ESF)'. *transform!* (1): 140–142.

Diani, M. 2005. 'Cities in the World: Local Civil Society and Global Issues in Britain'. In *Transnational Protest and Global Activism,* eds. D. della Porta and S. Tarrow, 45–67. Lanham: Rowman & Littlefield.

Fisher, D.R., et al. 2005. 'How Do Organizations Matter? Mobilization and Support for Participants at Five Globalization Protests'. *Social Problems* 52(1): 102–121.

Glasius, M. and J. Timms. 2006. 'Social Forums: Radical Beacon or Strategic Infrastructure?' In *Global Civil Society 2005/6,* eds. H. Anheier, M. Glasius and M. Kaldor, 190–238. London: Sage Publications.

Grenier, P. 2004. 'The New Pioneers: The People behind Global Civil Society'. In *Global Civil Society 2004/5,* eds. H. Anheier, M. Glasius and M. Kaldor, 122–157. London: Sage.

Imig, D. and S. Tarrow, eds. 2001. *Contentious Europeans.* Lanham: Rowman & Littlefield.

Keck, M.E. and K. Sikkink. 1998. *Activists beyond Borders: Advocacy Networks in International Politics.* Ithaca: Cornell University Press.

Klandermans, B. and D. Oegema. 1987. 'Potentials, Networks, Motivations and Barriers: Steps towards Participation in Social Movements'. *American Sociological Review* 52(4): 519–531.

Lichbach, M.I. and H.G.E. de Vries. 2004. *Global Justice and Antiwar Movements: From Local Resistance to Globalized Protests.* N.p., Department of Government and Politics, University of Maryland.

Marks, G. and D. McAdam. 1999. 'On the Relationship of Political Opportunities to the Form of Collective Action: the Case of the European Union'. In *Social Movements in a Globalizing World,* eds. D. della Porta, H. Kriesi and D. Rucht, 97–111. London: Macmillian Press.

McAdam, D. 1986. 'Recruitment to High-Risk Activism: The Case of Freedom Summer'. *American Journal of Sociology* 92(1): 64–90.

————. 1988. 'Micromobilization Contexts and the Recruitment to Activism'. In *From Structure to Action. Comparing Social Movement Research across Cultures,* eds. B. Klandermans, H. Kriesi and S. Tarrow, 125–154. Greenwich: JAI-Press.

McCarthy, J.D. 1997. 'The Globalization of Social Movement Theory'. In *Transnational Social Movements and Global Politics: Solidarity beyond the State,* eds. J. Smith, C. Chatfield and R. Pagnucco, 243–259. Syracuse: Syracuse University Press.

Schönleitner, G. 2003. 'World Social Forum: Making Another World Possible?' In *Globalizing Civic Engagement. Civil Society and Transnational Action,* ed. J.D Clark, 127–149. London: Earthscan Publications.

Sikkink, K. 2005. 'Patterns of Dynamic Multilevel Governance and the Insider-Outsider Coalition'. In *Transnational Protest and Global Activism,* eds. D. della Porta and S. Tarrow. Lanham: Rowman and Littlefield.

Tarrow, S. 2005a. 'The Dualities of Transnational Contention: "Two Activist Solitudes" or a New World altogether?' *Mobilization* 10(1): 53–72.

Tarrow, S. 2005b. *The New Transnational Activism.* Cambridge: Cambridge University Press.

Teune, S. forthcoming. 'The Limits of Transnational Attention. Rise and fall in the European Forums' Media Resonance'. In *The Revolution Will Not Be Televised? Media and Protest Movements.* Oxford and New York: Berghahn Books.

Van Laer, J. and J. Verhulst. 2007. 'Social Forums and the Celebration of Diversity: Internet Technology between Radical Democracy and Factual Technocracy'. *ECPR 35th Joint Sessions of Workshops,* Helsinki, 7–11 May 2007.

Walgrave, S. and B. Klandermans. 2010. 'Patterns of Mobilisation'. In *The World Says No to War: Demonstrations against the War in Iraq,* eds. S. Walgrave and Dieter Rucht. Minneapolis: University of Minnesota Press.

Walgrave, S. and J. Verhulst. 2010. 'Selection and Response Bias in Protest Surveys'. *Mobilization* (forthcoming).

Whitaker, C. 2004. 'The WSF as Open Space'. In *The World Social Forum: Challenging Empires,* eds. J. Sen et al, 111–121. New Delhi: The Viveka Foundation.

Appendix

Table 1.4. Independent Variables and Their Operationalisation

	Range	Operationalization
Attitudes		
Forum identification	1 'low' – 5 'high'	Rescaled summation of three 5-point scale questions: 'I have a lot in common with the other people present at the BSF/ESF', 'I identify strongly with the others present at the BSF/ESF', and 'I feel committed to the other people present at the BSF/ESF'
Satisfaction democracy	1 'low' – 4 'high'	4-point scale question: 'In general, are you satisfied or dissatisfied with the functioning of democracy in your country?' with 1 'completely dissatisfied', 2 'dissatisfied', 3 'satisfied', and 4 'completely satisfied'.
Political interest	1 'not at all' – 5 'very much'	5-point scale question: 'How interested are you in politics?'
Expected outcome	1 'little chance' – 7 'high chance'	7-point scale question: 'How big are the chances that the BSF/ESF will boost mobilisation or give visibility to the common targets of the movements participating in the BSF/ESF?'
Behaviour		
Organisational involvement	1 'low' – 5 'high'	Participants were first asked whether they represented an organisation at the forum or just participated as an individual. If they were a delegate, respondents were further asked to indicate what position they had in this organisation and whether they got paid for the work they did for this organisation. These three questions resulted in a new scale ranging from 1 'non-delegate', 2 'unpaid, active member' 3 'paid, active member' 4 'unpaid staff', to 5 'paid staff'.
Member transnational organisation	0 'no' – 1 'yes'	Respondents were asked whether they were an active, passive or board member of the following organisations: church or religious organisation, student organisation, union or professional organisation, political party, women's right organisation, sport-recreational organisation, environmental organisation, art/music/educational organisation, community organisation, charity organi-

sation, global justice organisation, third world organisation, human rights organisation, peace organisation and anti-racist or migrants' rights organisation. If respondents were an active or board member of a global justice, third world or human rights organization this variable was coded as one. All others were coded as zero.

Info-channel social forum	0 'open' – 1 'closed'	If a respondent was informed about the forum via radio or television, newspapers, posters, flyers, family, friends, people at school or work, or via personal email, this variable was coded zero. Those who got informed via member magazines, websites or email lists of an organisation, or via people within an organisation, were coded as one.
Travel organised/ reimbursed	1 'not at all' – 6 'completely by an organization'	Participants were asked whether they had organised their trip to the ESF by themselves or whether it was an organisation that arranged travel and accommodation. Also we asked them whether the costs for their ESF participation were reimbursed 'completely', 'partially' or 'not at all' by an organisation. Both questions were simply multiplied to indicate the extent to which an organisation was responsible for travel and expenses.
Protest frequency	1 'low' – 6 'high'	6-point scale indicating protest frequency during the last 5 years: 1 'never' 2 'only once' 3 'between 2 and 5 times', 4 'between 6 and 10', 5 'between 11 and 20', 6 'more than 20'

Chapter Two

How Do Activists Experience Transnational Protest Events?
The Case of Young Global Justice Activists
from Germany and France

Ariane Jossin

Introduction

For many observers, the rise of the global justice movements (GJMs)[1] in the late 1990s represented the advent of a transnational civil society. These movements rapidly spread their influence to all five continents. One of the most influential organisations, Attac, was established in thirty-nine countries.[2] And, the World Social Forum – traditionally hosted by the city of Porto Alegre in Brazil – was held in Asia and Africa in 2004, 2006 and 2007.

Some time after the initial positive reactions to the GJMs, various sociological studies called into question the actual level of its transnationalism. Studies focussing on the GJMs in western countries reminded us of their strong national roots (della Porta 2007; Sommier, Fillieule and Agrikoliansky 2008). Furthermore, one of the rare comparative studies of the spearhead organisation Attac has shown that the demands made by GJMs are, to this day, primarily motivated by national daily politics (Uggla 2006), a point which had also been made by other monographs and articles (e.g., Tarrow 2005a; della Porta 2005). These observations lead to quite loose definitions of what is a transnational social movement. The definition offered by Sidney Tarrow requires socially mobilised groups, whose members are present in at least two countries, that interact contentiously with authorities from at least one foreign country, or with an international institution or a multi-national economic actor (Tarrow 2000).

Chapter one showed the different characteristics of national and transnational global justice activists, but could not address relations between individuals across borders. This aspect will be tackled in the comparative study presented in this chapter. It shows the weak relations between the GJMs in France and Germany, thus challenging – mostly North American – studies insisting on the emergence of a transnational civil society (Wapner 1996; Smith, Chatfield and

Pagnucco 1997; Florini 2000; Guidry, Kennedy and Zald 2000; O'Brien et al. 2000). As Daniel Mouchard wrote, different assumptions about the transnational dimension of social movements mostly go back to different methodological approaches (Mouchard 2005: 130): on the one side, an approach from below, on the other, a rather aerial approach of the movement.

Opting for an empirical and micro-sociological approach, one can just come to the conclusion that the transnationalism of the movement is essentially situated at the level of the targets of the GJMs, i.e., the supra-national institutions. It is also situated at a cognitive level among the activists, as they often refer to foreign personalities to define their activism. However, transnationalism is hardly visible during counter-summits at the level of networks, nor in the everyday activities of global justice activism. This confirms that international dynamics cannot be analysed separately from the local and/or the national scale (Braudel 1985; Bayart 2004: 13–132; Gobille 2005: 144).

Among all of the studies on the GJMs, few have focussed on transnational activism from a micro-sociological perspective. This is what this chapter has set out to do. It is based on findings from a qualitative longitudinal research (conducted from 2002 to 2007) that focuses on the biographies of eighteen young global justice activists in France and Germany. The particular interest of young people for the GJMs contradicts the reputation of indifference to politics that is usually associated to this part of the population (Percheron 1991: 30). This particularity motivates the focus of this chapter on a sample of young activists.

The GJMs are often introduced as being a movement of young people. However, when we observe the sociodemography of certain events or certain organisations of the GJMs, such as the flagship organisation Attac, this assertion seems questionable. Why then is there this reputation of a movement of young people? Obviously, this is due to the nature of events that are mainly covered by mass media: the counter-summits, which are the most obvious showcase of a transnational 'movement of movements'. In fact, the majority of those who feel attracted to these events are young activists.[3] More particularly, they can be found in the 'alternative villages' especially constructed for the occasion: 77.5 per cent of activists in the alternative villages in Évian were younger than 29 years, and the percentage is the same for those who took part in the street blockades.[4] The organisation of the Intergalactic Village of Annemasse (5,000 participants) was run by about thirty activists between the ages of twenty and thirty years old. The journey of 900 German activists to the same counter-summit was organised by three young Attac activists of the same age.

The study of eighteen individual cases is complemented by an ethnographic study of the counter-summits held in Évian (2003) and Heiligendamm (2007) on the occasion of meetings of the Group of Eight (G8). To focus on these transnational protest events of the GJMs means that the deliberative moments of the movement (social forums, alternative forums) and the activities of the GJMs organisations in their domestic societies are excluded from the analysis. This text will instead concentrate on those special moments of the GJMs during which activists stage primarily symbolic events to mark their critique of neoliberal globalisation. It will not focus on the political motivations and claims of the young activists, but rather analyse the effects of transnational activism on the political involvement of these young people.

The analysis of activist biographies over a period of five years aims at understanding the appeal of global justice issues and transnational protest for these young people. It turns out that the activists' expanding activities beyond the borders of their homeland have important repercussions on their situation at home. It will be shown that, in practice, transnational activist experiences are oftentimes restricted to travelling from one country to another: their demands and the networks that are forged during these protests are far more 'multi-national' than 'transnational'. As the example of the G8 counter-summits shows, almost exclusively national activist networks persist also at transnational events. Having observed the transnational dimension within the sample of activists and the field of study, it will be possible to identify those elements that are truly transnational and distinguish them from those only appearing to be transnational.

The first section of this chapter focuses on the sociodemography of the sample, in order to observe the relation between the activists' social profile and the transnational dimension. The second part blends the young activists' experiences with observations at the G8 counter-summits in Évian and Heiligendamm, resulting in a challenge of the taken for granted transnational exchange within the GJMs. The third section discusses the 'burn-out' experienced by activists after several years of commitment to the GJMs. In the end, the return of most activists to the national political realm will be considered.

The Sample: 'Rooted Cosmopolitans', Young and Well-off

The eighteen activists in the sample represent different ideological standpoints: some are Trotskyites involved in the organisations *Socialisme par en bas* (SPEB, – Socialism from below) and Linksruck (both sister organisations of the British Socialist Workers' Party, SWP); others are part of the German autonomist *linksradikale* scene; another fraction has joined Attac in France and Germany and comes from diverse backgrounds (Trotskyites, ecologists, greens, etc.), and finally some are activists of *Apprentis Agitateurs pour un Réseau de Résistance Globale* (AARRG!!, – Trainee Agitators for a Global Resistance Network) who were involved in the Pink and Silver Block, a carnivalesque protest form that questions gender ascriptions and has been present in many of the global justice demonstration marches.

Most of the activists are among the informal 'leaders' of their respective global justice groups. At the same time, they are connected to other organisations, such as immigrant defence associations, ecologist groups, or NGOs. For a number of reasons, the particular sample is not representative of global justice activists in France and Germany. The activists that have been followed for several years are more or less homogeneous with reference to age, social status and the movement sector in which they are active. Activists who are primarily attached to NGOs or trade unions are not part of the sample; none of the interviewees belongs to the black block or is simply older than thirty-four years of age.

In 2003, the first year of the study, the average age of the sample is twenty-five years. The young age heavily influences the manner in which the activists participate. Because family, marital and professional constraints do not affect them, they are able to devote much of their personal resources to political activism. All except one of them have recently graduated (five or eight years of post-A-Level education) or they are students with a long university career. Except for some Trotskyite activists who were not raised as a member of the middle class, their social profile is particularly reminiscent of the constituency of the New Social Movements (NSMs) in the 1970s (Brand 1987).[5] The constellation that they are for the most part from the wealthier social classes, have reached a high level of education and have time at their disposal reinforces the tendency toward involvement (Bourdieu 1984; McAdam 1988).

The privileged position in their domestic society is combined with a strong link with other countries. More than half of the eighteen activists of the sample have spent a prolonged period (other than on holiday) in a foreign country (in Europe, Africa, North or South America), typically in the context of a university exchange, scientific research or work for a NGO. This recalls the concept of the 'rooted Cosmopolitan': the young people remain in contact with local or national networks and resources even when they are moving, both physically and cognitively, outside the borders of their home country (Tarrow 2005b: 29–56). These rooted Cosmopolitans are in no way the 'losers of globalisation'. On the contrary, they profit from an increased permeability of borders. A large-scale study of global justice activists during the European Social Forum in Paris in 2003 similarly showed strong links with foreign countries (Gobille and Uysal 2005: 112–115). The fight of these activists for global justice is therefore rather a 'moral demand' than a struggle for their own rights and benefits.

Getting Involved in Global Justice

All of the eighteen young people in the sample started their activist trajectories at the local or national level, half of them in left wing, radical left or green political parties. Having had disappointing experiences in these parties, they joined the GJMs between 1998 and 2001. In making this decision, the form in which the GJMs are organised played a central role. Their entry into the GJMs should therefore not only be seen as being motivated by convictions or adherence to an ideology. It must also be seen as an emotional process, and as the adoption of an anti-authoritarian, radical position. When the young activists are asked about the characteristics of the GJMs that attracted them, they mention its flexible nature; its function as a network and the new links made between political issues; the power of diversity rather than the pursuit of power; the 'invisibles' (average citizens or activists) coming to the fore and the rejection of the culture of prescribed speakers; the coexistence of disparate political directions; the extensible temporal and spatial scales (short- and long-term; local and international activity); the feeling of a 'new movement'; and, finally, its transnational dimension.

The characteristics that attracted the young activists are not present within the GJMs on a continuous basis, but they emerge in specific events or situations. The movement takes shape primarily in moments of contestation at supra-national summits (protest) and at continental and World Social Forums (debates), during which the different organisations, the networks and the disparate activists come together. The activists in the sample have rather attended counter-summits than social forums, which essentially offer debates, meetings and conferences. However, social forums are also more popular with the French than with the Germans. All of the French activists apart from one had been to several of these forums, while only half of the Germans attended social forums, and if so, it had never been outside of Europe. This difference between French and German activists is essentially due to two factors. Firstly, the French activists have greater financial resources – most of them are paid for their studies. Secondly, the more grassroots oriented German activists conceive the organisation of the forums as too hierarchical.

Between the transnational events, the activities and the demands of global justice organisations focus on national problems, such as the defence of public services or campaigning at the moment of national elections, etc. This is more evident in France, as the comparison of press communications by Attac organisations in France, Germany and Sweden has shown (Uggla 2006). One factor that accounts for this strong national anchorage in France is the predominance of 'traditional' political organisations, such as parties and trade unions, within the national branch of the GJMs. The German movements, by contrast, inherit more of the NSMs (Rucht, Teune and Yang 2008; Sommier 2008).

At times of international mobilisation, in the context of social forums and counter-summits, demands are made on an international scale, questioning, for example, the legitimacy of supra-national decision-making bodies. Nevertheless, this repertoire of demands remains relatively unclear and blurred when compared to claims on the national level. In fact, when we ask the activists what it means to them to be a global justice activist, half of them claim to be anti-capitalist or anti-(neo)-liberal, the other half claim to 'fight for a better world', 'fight against injustice', 'cast a spell on the world', 'be part of a joint global front'. Others mention, in passing, that the term global justice is, above all, a generic term that allows for the renewal of activist terminology, or a *portmanteau* word that smartly conceals old ideologies. Thus, the movement appears as something new without discouraging young activists with concepts that are historically or ideologically loaded, such as 'Trotskyism', 'communism', or 'anti-capitalism'.

This generic term also allows them to mobilise widely over political breaches and bring together or construct, at one specific moment, very broad coalitions, from NGOs to anarchist activists, from ecologists to religious activists.

Compensation for Lacking Social and Cultural Capital, or Affirmation thereof?

The young activists consider transnational activism as an important experience and a progress in their individual lives. When asked about the symbolic rewards they draw from their involvement, they mention, in no specific order, sociability, the acquisition of knowledge, recognition and higher prestige related to their knowledge. Activism and, more particularly, transnational activism are perceived as an opening and an opportunity for activists to enhance their social skills. Improved status and recognition, obtained in the course of their involvement, are considered as a means of compensating for insufficiencies in parental upbringing. This is the case for one of the German Trotskyite activists, who perceives his involvement as a real advancement:

> I come from a fairly poor family background. Education was not considered important. We almost never went on holiday because we couldn't afford to. … That's to say that my view of the rest of the world was extremely limited and not only with regards to politics. In every aspect, my involvement has been a liberation. It's as if someone were living in a musty house and suddenly someone opens the window and fresh air pours in … and you can finally look outside and see that there's a world beyond these four walls. It's been a liberating experience. I've met completely different people. It was like going on holiday. I've learnt lots of things about the world, which I wasn't able to do before. It's been like – this term has religious connotations – like a revelation! For the first time I feel important. It was freedom!

In the midst of this revelation, this activist decided to aspire to higher education, which he gave up, however, shortly afterward. Although he feels that his field of vision has opened up and he senses new possibilities thanks to his involvement as an activist, it does not change the fact that the reality is something completely different. He is the only activist who does not have the time or the financial means to go to international or transnational events. If he actively contributes to their preparation, he does so from the headquarters of his organisation in Berlin. His activism is limited to German soil. A monthly salary of 500 Euros and work scheduled for the weekends – so that he can work voluntarily as an activist during the week – make trips abroad impossible. This social inequality has until now mostly been shown for Southern countries,[6] but is also a factor of exclusion in the European GJMs.

However, the person cited here is an exception amongst the ranks of the young global justice activists who, as seen before, are mostly from well-off backgrounds, have a lot of free time at their disposal and for whom travelling abroad is part of the cultural capital inherited from their parents. Thus, these activists perceive transnational experiences more as an affirmation of a pre-established social and cultural capital.

Differences of cultural capital and in the socialisation of activists do also play a role within the GJMs. The specific characteristics of transnational organisation tend to favour the younger generation of activists. Firstly, commitment beyond the national context is made easier for young people due to a continental or global conscience that would be more extensive for this generation than for senior activists (Jung 2005; Tarrow 2005b: 56). The newcomers' experiences with politics are made in a different context than that of their parents' generation. The ideological bipolarity of the world, the left-right polarity of the national political debate and boundaries within Europe are just some points of reference that have lost some of their clarity, if they have not literally been shattered completely. Through this, the sphere of political activity has widened beyond national boundaries, calling back into question the relevance of a strictly national collective movement (Muxel 2001: 38).

Secondly, the qualities required to take part in counter-summits characterise most of the young people and students committed to these movements: a certain flexibility, linguistic knowledge, free time and a desire to spend a few days in uncertain conditions in alternative villages. With the exception of those who are paid for their involvement, it is difficult for older activists, who are integrated into family and professional life, and are socialised within the context of traditional and national activism, to fulfil these conditions. These qualities are particularly useful for counter-summits, less so for the social forums that attract a much more varied age range.[7] The social forums offer translation services (the Babels network of voluntary translators), permanent accommodation and a centralised organisation.

The question of organisation leads to the consideration of a third point: the advantage that skills in Information and Communication Technologies (ICT) may bring during the preparation and organisation of counter-summits. This preparation, being relatively de-centralised, is mainly done via the internet. A study conducted in France comparing the internet use of Attac activists shows that the younger group can be distinguished by an increased use of the internet to organise their activities. While 89 per cent of activists between 20 and 30 years of age make use of the internet, the percentage declines strongly with the age of the activists (Trautmann 2001: 85). Adding to this, individuals who are more socially advantaged – according to cultural and economic capital – than the average also use the internet more readily for communication purposes. The internet allows the organisation of transnational events by limiting international trips prior to counter-summits. As a potential for non-centralised communication between many people, the internet also allows for the opening up of decisions to a wider audience. Underlining these advantages of the internet does not mean to be naïve about the reality of horizontal organisation via the internet or the solidity of relationships formed via this medium (Tarrow 2005b: 138). However, its use makes the circulation of information possible at an international level. It particularly brings issues to the attention of individuals who are not part of an organisation – this group of activists makes up the majority of the people involved in counter-summits. The intensity of electronic communication and the feeling of being in constant contact with other global justice activists prior to counter-summits also promote a feeling of community and awareness of being a concrete unit, an essential feeling within these vague networks (Mann 1991: 38–39).

The combination of these characteristics (flexibility, linguistic knowledge, free time, a command of ICT) partly explains the greater participation of young people in these transnational showcases otherwise known as counter-summits. Similarly, on a meso-level, certain recent global justice organisations are being pushed to the front of the protest scene due to the predominance of young activists. The French network of young global justice activists *Vive l'Action pour une Mondialisation des Solidarités* (Vamos, Long live the action for the globalisation of solidarities),[8] for example, which represents only a handful of individuals, occupies a key place in the French global justice scene. Vamos has achieved this position by taking charge of the mobilisation for the counter-summits in France and abroad, notably in the organisation of coaches for Parisian Attac activists and then in the organisation of the Évian counter-summit in 2003.

The Importance of Transnational Experiences in the Motivation of Young Activists

The G8 counter-summits can be taken as an example of how young activists experience the transnational dimension. The following section argues that: a) The actors perceive these events as a form of political pastime or 'civil leisure'; b) The propensity of the activists to go from one counter-summit to another without building transnational networks prior to or following them leads us to question the transnational substance of these convergences; c) Finally, we will ask if transnational experiences influence the biographic trajectories and political activities of these young people and if this transnational access is only made possible by the qualities held by young people rather than senior activists.

The Revival of Protest – Counter-summits as an Activist Hobby?

The rise of the GJMs led to a revival of protest, which had mainly taken place on a national level until then. As seen before, the transnational character of the

GJMs is essentially realised at times of international protest: in counter-summits and social forums. The young activists in the sample seized upon this increase in opportunities for activism and embraced the global justice frame shortly after its emergence, most of them during a counter-summit. Almost all activists have attended a great number of these counter-summits, French activists more so than their German counterparts. One of them had been to eight counter-summits, seven of which were abroad (Europe, Central and North America); the others had attended between three and seven of these events. Only one French activist had never been able to partake in counter-summits at all. The German activists had participated in two, three or four counter-summits, respectively. One of them had never been able to travel, due to professional constraints and financial difficulties.

Why do young activists go abroad so often for these counter-summits? Their reasons for preferring counter-summits as a form of protest are not purely political. Many activists also see this part of their political activity abroad as a way of giving their travels meaning. Some even combine them with tourist trips. In a study of activists at the Quebec protests against the Free Trades Area of the Americas (FTAA), Heather Mair (2003) has developed the concept 'civil leisure' to name this phenomenon. Leisure is not perceived as a self-serving and consuming behaviour, but as a public and collective engagement. These activities then in turn have repercussions on the lives of the activists, who find themselves more open to all that is foreign and who develop a transnational identity, as one of the activists from Germany reports:

> Being an activist has changed my way of life, meaning that I'm on the road or abroad more often, that I speak English more often than before as well, and that I'm learning other languages. It's become very important to me to have an international presence.

Some young supporters of the GJMs, including those in the sample, alternate local or national activism with transnational gatherings. Others focus their involvement on counter-summits and become 'global justice globetrotters', as one of the organisers of the Évian counter-summit (2003) observes:

> Whether for [the counter-summits of] Genoa, Brussels or Seville, it was noticeable that a large majority of the people who filled up our coaches did not belong to an activist organization, but were people who move around for these kinds of events, and who very often do not protest locally at all. This is really why anarchist and libertarian critics of the GJMs call it a consumerist activism, a travelling activism for globe-trotters, who go to large summits and then do nothing on the local level.[9]

The phenomenon of activists going from one counter-summit to another without taking part in any form of activism in between has also been called 'event hopping' (Rucht 2002) or 'summit hopping'. The notion of selective engagement has been supported by a survey conducted during the Évian counter-summit: 72 per cent of those interviewed did not go as members of an organisation and 62 per cent had come with friends (Bandler and Sommier 2003; Durand 2005).

As we can see in the case of the Évian and Heiligendamm counter-summits, activists' involvement abroad is also a recreational experience, which combines political commitment and enjoyment. The global justice activists stay in the region for several days – generally between two and five days in total. From 2003 onward, alternative villages close to the official venue hosted challengers of the G8 summits: in Annemasse, Lausanne and Geneva in 2003 during the Évian summit and at Rostock, Reddelich and Wichmansdorf 2007 on occasion of the Heiligendamm summit. These gatherings are appreciated as alternative places to put utopias into practice and to build on the desire for the social change of global justice. The villages are divided into 'barrios'. These small areas are named according to the geographical and political kinship of the groups present there (North/South Barrio, queer barrio, anarchist barrio, etc.). Discussions focussing on political content are rare in the alternative villages. Although they were still present to some extent in the form of debates at Annemasse in 2003, they have declined in the following counter-summits, which were almost exclusively focussed on sociability and the preparation of protest, e.g., role playing exercises to prepare for road blockades. Political debates and the presentation of political demands are institutionalised outside of the alternative villages, in the 'alternative forums', mostly visited by members of NGOs, Attac members, political parties and trade unions.[10]

In the alternatives villages, apart from protest preparation, activists participate in a cultural programme that includes film screenings and concerts. They also benefit from facilities provided by the organisers such as bars, a children's playground, spaces to relax, showers, etc.

However, alternative villages do not only have a relaxed festival-like atmosphere, they are also the site where the fight for global justice is played out on stage. Geographical proximity to places where heads of state meet allows activists from these villages to actively show their opposition to supra-national organisations, which are rather abstract entities between the counter-summits. The huge number of police officers[11] at these counter-summits intensifies the feeling of being at the centre of the action. Most activists see these counter-summits as an opportunity to stage political opposition and to show their resistance to what a lot of them call 'the system'. For some, one of the motivations to become an activist is the myth of revolutionary heroes. A German Trotskyite says:

> I used to read a lot of children's books published then in the GDR. …
> They worshiped the Russian and German Revolution. The characters
> were real heroes and I found it fascinating, it was great you know! I
> always wanted to make a radio transmitter all by myself. I was a kid

from the GDR and I was pissed off that I lived in a socialist country where people had already done it all and where nothing was left for me to win through fighting, through activism … That's why I wanted to be a revolutionary pretty early on.

At a time when 'routine' street demonstrations are no longer seen as subversive (Offerlé 1990), counter-summits offer a perfect occasion and context to live this revolutionary myth. The distance from home for foreign activists, the range of opportunities given by the rural environment in the vicinity of the summit, the exhilarating effect of the number of activists and the feeling of being part of an international dynamic all make the activities an adventure. Use of military jargon to describe blocking actions reinforces this feeling.[12]

Counter-summits: Transnational or Multi-national Events?

National Affinities within Alternative Villages

One tends to believe that these counter-summits linking activism and pleasure are also taken as an opportunity to meet global justice activists from neighbouring countries. It is important to note that the crossing of borders does not go without saying. Counter-summits could have an international effect without the activists leaving their home countries. This would be the case if the counter-summits took place offsite: for example, French activists could have organised a demonstration in Paris to protest against the G8 summit in Heiligendamm in June 2007.[13] The motivation to cross borders in order to protest has developed only progressively during global justice activities in Cologne against the meeting of the European heads of state and the G8 summit (1999), in Seattle against the WTO (1999) and in Prague against the IMF and the World Bank (2000).

So what exactly motivates activists to travel? Firstly, it comes down to an isomorphism between the ways of protesting and the targets (Gobille 2005: 144). This means that the transnationalisation of political decisions goes hand in hand with transnational protest. Not only the insurgent frames and their demands transcend the national level, but also the protest activities transcend it. Secondly, the activists' travelling is justified by the desire to appear in large numbers. On the one hand, they seek to evaluate their mobilising potential and to attract media attention through the power of numbers. On the other hand, activists hope to disrupt the official event by the sheer number of demonstrators. This aim was set by many activists who organised the blockades and the symbolic marches during the summits of Évian and Heiligendamm.

It is an empirical question, however, if these protest events are also used to build transnational coalitions, coordinations or networks, to confront their experiences and to build a community against neoliberal globalisation. During the counter-summits in Évian and Heiligendamm, the transnational character was primarily expressed in the shared methods of the European GJMs rather than in the form of coalitions or networks. This is the case for the counter-summit model that is passed on from one host country to another. The G8 counter activities were based on the following model: 1) two or three alternative villages; 2) blockades surrounding the summit; 3) an alternative summit organised by Attac and NGOs; 4) a unitary mass demonstration.

How did the European activists collaborate during the counter-summits of Évian and Heiligendamm? The French counter-summit of Évian in 2003 included an exceptional participation by German activists, who all arrived on the same train. These 900 activists, who were mainly close to or members of Attac, arrived at the alternative villages in Annemasse, which had been installed and organised by French networks. In the camps, the social exchange of the Germans with other activists was to a large extent limited to their compatriots. The assemblies they attended were almost exclusively filled with German activists. Likewise, the events around the alternative villages organised by Attac Germany only mobilised their constituency. For instance, 150 German Attac activists went swimming in Lake Geneva, eight of them disguised as the G8 heads of state and floating on tyres, while other German Attac activists hung a banner on a motorway bridge. This lack of cooperation between activists from Attac Germany and Attac France is surprising within the framework of an organisation and a movement that claim to be transnational. Joint activities were limited to the main demonstration and blockades.

In 2007, at the Heiligendamm summit, the same phenomenon was experienced by French activists. They arrived at the venue in small numbers (50–60 of them arrived in smaller groups of friends or alone, others came together with trade unions or political groups); in the alternative villages, they stayed mostly among themselves. A relatively trivial reason for this national seclusion was linguistic problems. The languages spoken in the assemblies at Évian and Heiligendamm were French and German, respectively. English was used as a lingua franca but only to a small extent. Simultaneous interpreting systems resolved this obstacle only partly. Moreover, the language barrier made it difficult for foreign activists to participate in decision-making, thus becoming an obstacle to the villages' non-hierarchical organisation. Decisions previously made in the national preparatory process in Évian and later in Heiligendamm stressed the foreign activists' feeling of exclusion.

National Consequences of Transnational Events

What are the consequences of these transnational initiatives? Oddly enough, they are formed less at an international level than at a national level. These counter-summits bring together political groups that hardly collaborate in domestic politics. In the context of counter-summits, national groups tend to be able to transcend political dissent. One example of this was Block G8, created for the Heiligendamm summit. Block G8 brought together 125 mostly German political organisations. Despite a range of different ideologies – from religious groups to radical left groups – they agreed on one common platform in order to organise road blockades. In Évian, the blockades were also an opportunity to bring together people from various political backgrounds. Upon their return, the German Attac activists gave an overview of these unexpected coalitions:

> There were many different activists taking part in the blockades, which reminded us of the beginning of the movement in Seattle. While some kept the police away by throwing stones at them and others were trying to extinguish tear grenades just a few steps from the French riot police, Attac Campus [German and French Attac Youth Branches, A.J.] provided wooden barricades to protect us against tear gas. At the back, the activist groups discussed the events, and just behind them, their delegates held a plenary session to discuss which tactics to adopt. Behind them, from within a large bus, the Amsterdam Independent Media Centre broadcasted the events. Young IG-Metall [German metal workers union, A.J.] members supplied the blockade with water, starting from the Intergalactic Village campsite, using a coach from Cologne. Just behind that, inside a French bus, you could eat a hot meal for two Euros. In the middle of all this, a big Pink and Silver group, danced and sang, unfazed, on carnival rhythms. We had dreamed of this kind of unity for years![14]

The French counter-summit groups worked alongside the Germans and the Dutch, but they hardly ever mixed. This is partly due to the principle of affinity groups, which is based on mutual confidence, acquaintance of the group members and sharing of goals and values, thus encouraging people to stay with activists they already know. The affinity groups bring together five to fifteen activists in very homogenous entities. This homogeneity in language and in desire for action is necessary to build a feeling of trust within the groups and to react quickly in case of police repression (Durand 2005). The language barrier between affinity groups, which had already posed an obstacle at the alternative village campsites, became all the more obvious during the protest actions. German activists regretted that language posed an obstacle to direct democracy during the creation of road blockades.

In the case of France, it was in the preparation of this very summit that the consequences of transnational activities on the national arena were most evident. The establishment of three alternative villages in Annemasse led to unexpected coalitions. Initially, the idea of sharing one sole village between the anarchists, libertarians, Trotskyites and reformists allowed these activists to get together around one table in Paris and Lyon before the Évian counter-summit. Not only were activists of differing ideologies brought together, but also were activists from different cities of the country (Lyon and Paris mainly). This coalition with a very unique character came, however, to a halt due to political differences a few weeks after the work on the multi-group project began.[15] One coalition in particular was born after this experience and deserves to be mentioned. The network connecting No Vox, which defends the so called *sans* – 'withouts' (without papers, without lodging, without employment, etc.) – with Vamos, a network of well-educated, affluent young activists, was a consequence of the blurred lines that separate groups in global justice. It lasted well beyond the counter-summit in Évian. Both groups were able to profit from their new coalition: while the movement of the 'withouts' was said to have had problems entering the GJMs (*Le Monde*, 16 November 2003), No Vox was able to get a foot in the door with the help of Vamos, which, in turn, was able to join the network for disadvantaged activists.

The Unitary Demonstrations of G8 Counter-summits

As mentioned earlier, common actions by activists of different nationalities are essentially limited to the unitary demonstration and the road blockades. However, here it would again be more correct to call these actions multi-national rather than transnational, as activists stay within groups of the same nationality during these common initiatives. The unitary demonstration at counter-summits brings together activists of all kinds, from NGOs to anarchists, from trade unionists to reformist parties and immigrant defence associations. Most of the demands made during the demonstrations remain uncertain and challenge the legitimacy of the G8 in general: 'Shut down G8', 'Fight war, fight racism, fight capitalism, fight G8', 'The world is not for sale', 'G8: Highway to Hell – We go for Heaven on Earth for everyone', 'No G8', 'Smash capitalism, fight the G8-summit', 'Another world is possible', etc. Other demands simply stem from the local or national origins of the activists. Flags and banners presented during the mass demonstration in Rostock included symbols of the German anti-nuclear movement, Turkish communist flags, a banner in German reading 'Yes to the welfare state, no to privatisation', the SED[16] flag, etc.

Apart from those NGOs, whose repertoire of demands is traditionally international, many groups rarely try to shift their demands to the transnational level during the unitary demonstration. One initiative that was an exception to this rule during the events in Évian came from feminist activists from different countries. They united in a single-sex camp and created a banner for the purpose of the unitary demonstration reading: '3 billion clits against the G8'. However, this initiative did not have as much success as the camp, as only a handful of women joined the camp's block during the demonstration. The majority of the other feminists in fact rejoined the blocks of their respective local or national organisations (Jossin and Mathieu 2006). Among the blocks in the demonstration, only the black block and Attac branches from different countries showed a certain unity transcending their national origins. For most of the participating activists, these coalitions are nevertheless limited to the period of the counter-summit. They are set up several months before the counter-summit via internet forums and electronic communication, and do not last once the unitary demonstration is over.

There are other international networks that get together during these big global justice gatherings, for instance, two networks that prioritise light-hearted approaches toward activism. One of these is the Pink and Silver Block, which came into being during the Prague counter-summit in 2000. It incorporates young activists dressed in pink and silver and accompanied by a *batucada* (a samba percussion ensemble). The other network is the Clandestine Insurgent Rebel Clown Army, which also adopts frivolity as a method of disrupting supranational summits. These activists wear costumes combining clown outfits and military uniforms. They ridicule the police by mocking the officers' behaviour. Even if the Pink and Silver Block and the Clowns' Army show a visual unity due to their disguises and a tactical unity, the groups still tend to be divided along national or even local lines. The preparations that are demanded by these theatrical or musical activist actions beforehand (notably, the numerous rehearsals) make it difficult to find common ground across borders. Yet they manage to rehearse all together in the alternative villages shortly before the actions. However, the transnational nature of these networks is mostly reduced to a visual identity and to shared values such as light-heartedness, non-violence and anti-authoritarianism.

Disillusionment with Transnational Events and a Return to the National Realm

Having learned about the nature of the transnational events that the young activists were part of, the remainder of the chapter will review the consequences that these experiences have. In 2005, three years after the first series of interviews, the spirit of global justice activism that was very much alive before, had declined in the lives of the interviewees. At the time of our second series of interviews, only three of the eighteen activists monitored were still active in global justice groups, but not in a direct way. It should be noted that the first cycle of interviews with these eighteen activists took place during the ascendant phase of the European GJMs, the second in its rather stagnant or descendant phase.

Apart from the general crisis of the GJMs, we must consider personal reasons when we try to understand the interviewees' retreat from global justice activism. As young people progress into the 'social career of the adult' and acquire the characteristics of 'maturity' – a job, accommodation, a partner and/or children – (Juhem 2000) – they place less importance on their commitment to political activism. Modifications to protest and the global justice scene (disbanding of groups, conflicts of representation within Attac, etc.) have also played a role in this distancing from the GJMs. However, above all, it is burn out, a mixture of fatigue and disillusionment with initial expectations (Fillieule 2005: 30 and 64), that can be observed among the activists. Moreover, the characteristics of the movement that had initially attracted the young activists (time and geographical scope, intensity of the protest-schedule, fluidity of commitment, variety of demands, etc.) had also lost their appeal.

Political mobilisations abroad, which filled these young people with enthusiasm, have since come under criticism. Several interviewees criticise the lack of demands within counter-summits. They highlight these as mere representations of the masses. Referring to the counter-summits, one French activist speaks of the 'Cannes Festival of Activism'. Another one says: 'everyone wants to say they went to the counter-summits. But the networks that are supposed to be created between organizations … I don't have the impression that it really works'. Subsequently, the 'activist tourism', which inspired a certain exoticism in left wing activism, has proven to be costly in time and money. At the time of the second wave of interviews, the majority of activists had finished their engagement in the counter-summits. Only two out of eighteen went to the G8 summit in Gleneagles in 2005. One activist, commenting on his non-participation, said 'Gleneagles wasn't my idea of a holiday destination'.

As seen before, counter-summits are the concretisation of the fights against supra-national decision-making bodies and they are an occasion for clashes with the police. Some activists consider them as a chance to gain prestige, by demonstrating strength, bravery and virility. Summit activism has, however, a downside, namely, repressive violence and the trauma of being hit by a truncheon (Memmi 1998). This is what some of the protesters have experienced – not only those who are prone to confrontation with the police. One interviewee from the German autonomist scene, for example, was present at the Diaz-School in Genoa when it was attacked by the police after the G8 summit in 2001. As a result, he did not attend any further protests either at the national nor the international level. Similarly, AARRG!!, a small Parisian activist network, came to the forefront of the global justice scene during the protests in Genoa. This was thanks to their experiences of civil disobedience, happenings and their knowledge of ICT and graphics. However, the familiarity with the codes and language of the GJMs were not supported sufficiently by a solid structure. The small size of the group and its horizontal structure resulted in an overburdening of AARRG!! activists. Several of them have been injured, imprisoned or deeply shocked as a result of an incorrect strategy and heavy police repression at the counter-summit. Consequently, nearly all of the AARRG!! activists decided not to attend any further counter-summits. One of them notes:

> When we arrived in Genoa, we were *the* anti-globalization movement or French global justice movement. Ultimately, in terms of numbers, we were ridiculous. There were twenty of us and even though we had ideas, we were in a country we didn't know particularly well. … And

when they told us, we had to pull down gates or a well-guarded wall. ...
[laughs] It wasn't easy at all! Usually we used to compensate for our low
turnout by looking for ideas and concepts. But there came a point when
we couldn't do it anymore because we were out of our depth.

By the time of the second wave of interviews, the social forums were also rejected
by the young activists who were part of the research. They criticised primarily the
centralised and often rigid forms of debate that bored young activists and turned
them away. The move by these forums toward a less radical stance and the stronger presence of non-governmental organisations remain strong criticisms from
the point of view of young activists. As a French activist from Attac puts it:

> It's as if these events were a trade fair or a market place. Propositions
> we had made once are now lost in the background noise of discussions,
> where everyone – even those on the political right – adopt them. There
> are people who just come to see what it's all about and those who come
> to the odd concert and whilst they're there, they come to the debates.
> I get the impression that these social forums are dwindling too. I was
> shocked to see lots of suits going to see the Manu Chao gig or some-
> thing on fair trade and thinking 'Yeah, that's interesting. I'd really like
> to buy fair trade products.' And it is interesting because they wouldn't
> have thought about it before. But that also implies that the movement
> might be taking too much of a softly-softly approach.

Four to seven years since their involvement in the GJMs, the activists have dis-
tanced themselves from the movement and from political mobilisations abroad.
The question remains as to how these young activists incorporate their transnational experiences in their countries of origin.

Transnational Experience: an Added Bonus for Young Activists

Advantages gained at the transnational level have repercussions at the national
level, where these activists reap the benefits of their actions. The 'activist capital'[17]
or experience gained in the GJMs allows the young people to situate themselves
in the competitive market of activism. Thus, some of the young activists consider
their transnational experiences as an added bonus to put on their political CVs.
Half of the interviewees view the GJMs as a step toward integration in a national
organisation or a political party.

The combined experience made with the organisation of counter-summits
or finely interwoven networks at the international level – 'event coalitions', as
Sidney Tarrow calls them (2005b: 171) – allow these young people to integrate

in traditional organisations without going through their hierarchical structure. The parties young people turn to, either simply by voting in elections, or by becoming a member, are those that have themselves invested in the GJMs: the French Ligue Communiste Révolutionnaire (LCR, Revolutionary Communist League) and the German Die Linke (The Left). A meso-sociological study of the French GJMs has indeed shown how investing in this transnational movement can be part of a strategic positioning for outsider organisations (Sommier 2008: 104–105). Thanks to this investment, the LCR has been able to reinvent itself and attract young recruits. The German PDS has been able to redefine itself by joining with other leftist groups and individuals to form Die Linke, thereby ridding itself of the label it inherited from the German Democratic Republic (GDR).

Nearly all of the French activists observed in our investigation joined the LCR. This is partly because activists have a tendency to get involved in political organisations that are present in their own field of political activity and partly because activists have more of an opportunity to invest their 'capital' or experience gained in the GJMs within these parties or organisations.

Several of the activists who did not join a party after having left the GJMs have turned to defending the rights of immigrants without legal documentation and, to this end, remain in a sector that often cognitively crosses national boundaries. In Germany, the exercise of institutional power by Die Linke does not encourage the activists to adhere to such a structure, since their mistrust of certain institutions remains rife. Most German activists have returned to activism on a local level in ecological groups, or in supporting immigrants and those living in precarious conditions. Only one of the activists returned to the German Green Party. Finally, the activists from the Trotskyite party, Linksruck, have rejoined the German Die Linke following the advice of their international organisation.[18]

Conclusion

Transnationalism seems to be a rather abstract category for many global justice activists – even for those who travel abroad. They consider themselves to be part of a global movement, but most of their activities are restricted to national activist communities. As a consequence, the young activists' transnational experiences impact above all on the national level. As seen before, almost all of the interviewees broke away from the GJMs to fall back on local or national commitments. The activist and personal capital collected at the international level was thus reinvested. In the same way, on the meso- and macro-level, the GJMs had repercussions on the national partisan landscape. This impact particularly affected the revival of the LCR in France and the creation of Die Linke in Germany. Another repercussion is the growth of new alliances between activist groups at the national level. Even if few of them last beyond the counter-summits, due to the high cost of the task of coalition, it is true that certain unforeseen links are forged far from the political dissensions on national soil.

The transnational level also brings about the formation of groups on a local scale. Indeed, mobilisation for a transnational event requires the building of local networks. To fill coaches and trains, certain activists have created local groups of reduced size, radically fluctuating according to the transnational agenda. This is the case for Vamos, for example, created in Paris at the time of the counter-summit of Genoa. These small groups constitute a local anchorage for those activists who want to continue their political work between counter-summits. However, it is a struggle for their activities to root on a local level, since the topic of global justice remains abstract beyond supra-national meetings.

There are not many examples of networks that succeed in outlasting counter-summits and social forums, Peoples' Global Action, which was founded in 1998 and is still active today is one of them (Maiba 2005). These coalitions – though they bring together actors of different nationalities or political leanings – require a coalition work, expensive in time and money (Staggenborg 1986). However, the setting up of transnational networks such as Euromayday, which focussed on those living on the margins and united players of global justice, suggest that certain international bonds have actually remained.

The activists that have been followed over the years keep a transnational conscience in terms of political references and figures they use to describe their commitment. And, except for the SPEB and Linksruck activists, all of them still feel attached to the GJMs, even if they are not active anymore. Even if the activists we have studied have progressively turned their backs on this kind of transnational activism, the counter-activities at Heiligendamm have shown that the turnover of activists and the arrival of new global justice recruits continue to sustain the counter-summits. Given the homogeneity of the group studied, we should, however, stay cautious in our conclusions. They cannot be generalised for the GJMs as a whole.

Notes

I would like to acknowledge the support of students and teachers of Leeds University's MA in Applied Translation, who volunteered to translate this chapter. The final version is the work of Laura Chamberlain, Alison Clark, Melanie Cole, Carolyn Collier, Steve Deegan, Caroline Eden, Jessica Hartstein, Melissa Michaux, Kate Tench, Rebecca Tuckley, Rebecca Watts and Paul Wilmot.

1. The plural term 'movements' is adopted here to draw attention to the diversity that characterises this 'movement of movements'.
2. The membership figures of Attac, however, vary greatly from one country to another.
3. Except for the street demonstrations traditionally organised at the time of the counter-summits, which succeed in bringing together many activist generations.

4. Results are from a quantitative study among 2,300 activists at the counter-G8 in Évian lead by the CRPS (La Sorbonne, Paris 1) and the Universities of Lausanne and Genève. If all activists are taken as a basis, 42 per cent were younger than 25 years, 66 per cent younger than 31 years (Fillieule et al. 2004).

5. The inclusion of anarchist or black block activists in our sample would most certainly have made it less homogenous in terms of social and educational status.

6. Recent studies have analysed these inequalities at the World Social Forum in Bamako (2006) and in Nairobi (2007); the participation of African delegates was largely subsidised by countries in the North (Sulmont 2004; Pommerolle and Siméant 2007). Without it, the activists probably would not have been able to go to these global justice forums due to a lack of financial means.

7. At the European Social Forum in Paris-Saint-Denis, half of the activists were over 35 years of age (Gobille and Uysal 2005).

8. Vamos is a Parisian network of individuals and organisations that was created for the counter-summit in Genoa (2001).

9. Interview carried out in 2005 by Lilian Mathieu (CNRS, Sorbonne University, Paris 1). On the same subject, see the unpublished manuscript on the Évian counter-summit by Lilian Mathieu and the author (2006).

10. The 'Sommet pour un autre monde' and the 'Alternativgipfel' took place in Annemasse and in Rostock, respectively. None of the activists in the sample visited them.

11. For the Évian counter-summit, 16,000 police were recruited as well as a hundred pieces of army equipment were gathered (e.g., planes and 60 helicopters) (*Le Monde*, 29 May 2003). The same number of police was sent to the Heiligendamm counter-summit (which represents the biggest security operation since the immediate post-war period in Germany), and 1,100 soldiers joined them. In addition, a twelve kilometre fence was put up around the area of the summit (*Le Monde*, 25 June 2007).

12. Cf. the report written by activists from Attac Germany, which condemns the use of military language because 'violence starts with language'. Évian-Auswertung, written by Alex Arteaga, Olivier Powalla, Cosima Santoro, Birgit Schneider and Sascha Wolff. Internal document from Attac Germany.

13. For example, this was the case with the international day of action against the war in Iraq on 15 February 2003 (Tarrow 2005b: 15).

14. Critical Review of the Évian Summit by Lukas Engelmann, Oliver Pye and Pedram Shahyar. Internal document from Attac Germany.

15. Disputes surrounding the term 'anti-capitalist' split the initial village in two: VIG (Village Intergalactique) and VAAAG (Village Alternatif Anticapitaliste Anti-Guerre), to which a single-sex female village was added, the Point G (G-Spot).

16. SED: Sozialistische Einheitspartei Deutschlands, the Socialist Unity Party of Germany and former governing party of the GDR.

17. 'Activist capital' are skills activism allows to develop, as, for example, working with media, networking with other groups, debating skills, developing public speaking, gaining insight into political structures, etc. (Mair 2003).

18. The Trotskyite SPEB and Linksruck left Attac within months after having (re)joined the LCR and Die Linke, respectively.

References

Bandler, M. and I. Sommier. 2003. 'Le contre-sommet du G8 d'Evian: éléments pour une sociographie des militants altermondialistes'. *GERMM Colloquium 'Les Mobilisations Altermondialistes'*, Paris, 3–5 December 2003.

Bayart, J.-F. 2004. *Le gouvernement du monde: Une critique politique de la globalisation.* Paris: Fayard.

Bourdieu, P. 1984. *Questions de sociologie.* Paris: Les Editions de Minuit.

Brand, K-W. 1987. 'Kontinuität und Diskontinuität in den neuen sozialen Bewegungen'. In *Neue soziale Bewegungen in der Bundesrepublik,* eds. D. Rucht and R. Roth, 30–44. Frankfurt: Campus.

Braudel, F. 1985. *La dynamique du capitalisme.* Paris: Arthaud.

della Porta, D. 2005. 'Multiple Belongings, Flexible Identities and the Construction of Another Politics: Between the European Social Forum and the Local Social Fora'. In *Transnational Movements and Global Activism,* eds. D. della Porta and S. Tarrow, 175–202. Lanham: Rowman and Littlefield.

———, ed. 2007. *The Global Justice Movement: Cross-national and Transnational Perspectives.* Boulder: Paradigm Publishers.

Durand, C. 2005. 'Le mouvement altermondialiste: de nouvelles pratiques organisationnelles pour l'émancipation'. *Mouvements* 42: 103–114.

Fillieule, O. 2005. *Le désengagement militant.* Paris: Belin.

Fillieule, O., et al. 2004. 'L'Altermondialisme en réseaux: Trajectoires militantes, multi-positionnalité et formes de l'engagement: les participants du contre-sommet du G8 d'Evian (2003)'. *Politix* 17(68): 13–48.

Florini, A-M. 2000. *The Rise of Transnational Civil Society.* Washington: Carnegie Endowment for International Peace.

Gobille, B. 2005. 'Les altermondialistes: des activistes transnationaux?' *Critique internationale* 27: 131–146.

Gobille, B. and A. Uysal. 2005. 'Cosmopolites et enracinés'. In *Radiographie du mouvement altermondialiste. Le second Forum social européen,* eds. E. Agrikoliansky and I. Sommier, 105–126. Paris: La Dispute.

Guidry, J., M. Kennedy and M. Zald. 2000. *Globalization and Social Movements. Culture Power and the Transnational Public Sphere.* Ann Arbor: The University of Michigan Press.

Jossin, A. and L. Mathieu. 2006. 'Le Village Intergalactique et le point G'. Unpublished manuscript.

Juhem, P. 2000. '"Civiliser" la banlieue. Logiques et conditions d'efficacité des dispositifs étatiques de régulation de la violence dans les quartiers populaire'. *Revue française de science politique* 50(1): 53–72.

Jung Jai, K. 2005. 'Globalization and Global Identities: Over-time and Cross-National Comparison from the World Values Surveys in 1981–2001', *Annual meeting of the Midwest Political Science Association,* Chicago, 7 April 2005.

Maiba, H. 2005. 'Grassroots Transnational Social Movement Activism: The Case of People's Global Action'. *Sociological Focus* 38(1): 41–63.

Mair, H. 2003. 'Civil Leisure? Investigating the Relationship between Activism, Free Time and Social Change'. *Leisure/Loisir* 27(3/4): 213–238.

Mann, P. 1991. *L'action collective. Mobilisation et organisation des minorités actives*. Paris: Armand Colin.

Memmi, D. 1998. 'Le corps protestataire aujourd'hui: une économie de la menace et de la présence'. *Sociétés Contemporaines* 31: 87–106.

McAdam, D. 1988. *Freedom Summer*. Oxford: Oxford University Press.

Mouchard, D. 2005. 'Les altermondialismes'. *Critique internationale* 27: 129–130.

Muxel, A. 2001. *L'expérience politique des jeunes*. Paris: Presses de Sciences Po.

O'Brien, R., et al. 2000. *Contesting Global Governance*. Cambridge: Cambridge University Press.

Offerlé, M. 1990. 'Descendre dans la rue : de la 'journée' à la 'manif''. In *La manifestation*, ed. P. Favre, 90–122. Paris: Presses de la Fondation Nationale des Sciences politiques.

Percheron, A. 1991. 'Au miroir grossissant de la jeunesse'. *Autrement* 122: 30–42.

Pommerolle, M.-E. and J. Siméant. 2007. 'African Voices and Activists at the WSF in Nairobi. The uncertain Ways of Transnational African Activism'. *European Conference of African Studies*, Leiden, 11–14 July 2007.

Rucht, D. 2002. 'Von Seattle nach Genua – Event-hopping oder neue soziale Bewegung?' In *Eine andere Welt ist möglich*, ed. Attac Deutschland, 50–56. Hamburg: VSA-Verlag.

Rucht, D., S. Teune and M. Yang. 2008. 'La genèse des mouvements altermondialistes en Allemagne'. In *La généalogie des mouvements antiglobalisation en Europe. Une perspective comparée*, eds. I. Sommier, O. Fillieule and E. Agrikoliansky, 115–142. Paris: Karthala.

Smith J., C. Chatfield and R. Pagnucco. 1997. *Transnational Social Movements and Global Politics. Solidarity beyond the State*. New York: Syracuse University Press.

Sommier, I. 2008. 'Sur la généalogie de l'altermondialisme en France'. In *La généalogie des mouvements antiglobalisation en Europe. Une perspective comparée*, eds. I. Sommier, O. Fillieule and E. Agrikoliansky, 87–114. Paris: Karthala.

Sommier, I., O. Fillieule and E. Agrikoliansky. 2008. *La généalogie des mouvements antiglobalisation en Europe. Une perspective comparée*. Paris: Karthala.

Staggenborg, S. 1986. 'Coalition Work in the Pro-Choice-Movement: Organizational and Environmental Opportunities and Obstacles'. *Social Problems* 33(5): 374–390.

Sulmont, R., 2004. 'Forum social africain: émergence d'une mobilisation transnationale africaine'. DEA dissertation. Paris: Sciences Po.

Tarrow, S. 2000. 'La contestation transnationale'. *Cultures & Conflits* 38–39: 187–223.

———. 2005a. 'The Dualities Of Transnational Contention: "Two Activist Solitudes" or a New World altogether?' *Mobilization* 10(1): 53–72.

———. 2005b. *The New Transnational Activism*. Cambridge: Cambridge University Press.

Trautmann, F. 2001. 'Internet au service de la démocratie ? Le cas d'Attac'. *Les Cahiers du CEVIPOF* 30: 3–56.

Uggla, F. 2006. 'Between Globalism and Pragmatism: Attac in France, Germany, and Sweden'. *Mobilization* 11(1): 51–66.

Wapner, P. 1996. *Environmental Activism and World Civic Politics*. Albany: SUNY Press.

Meso-Level

Transnational Networks, Transnational Public Spheres

Chapter Three

Public Spheres within Movements:
Challenging the (Re)search for a European Public Sphere

Christoph Haug

Introduction

The transnationalisation of social movements goes hand in hand with the transnationalisation of public spheres. In fact, social movements have often contributed to the diffusion of vital information across borders, creating awareness of social problems both at home and abroad. Because of this capacity to mobilise public opinion across borders, transnational social movements are generally seen as actors who are engaged in contentious debates. These debates and struggles over meaning take place within the given frameworks of communication, especially national media systems. Social movements – like other actors – feed these with claims in a coordinated way in different countries, e.g., in transnational campaigns, by staging protest events in various countries at the same time, or by addressing the international media at events where journalists from different countries are present anyway (e.g., summits).

More recently, however, increasing attention is being paid to the creation of transnational public spaces created *within* the movements themselves, displaying the diversity present in these movements and the processes of communication taking place in transnational arenas, such as the social forums or the like.

To explore such communicative spaces and the specific conditions that they provide for transnational communication and the transnationalisation of social movements, case study approaches – with their tendency to create context sensitive knowledge – seem adequate. However, research should not let slip the possibilities to discover more general patterns. A conceptual framework to facilitate such generalisations remains a desideratum. This chapter suggests that theories of the public sphere are perhaps best equipped to analyse the communicative spaces within social movements. But incorporating 'public spheres within movements' into existing theories of the public sphere also challenges common notions of the public sphere that focus on the arena of the mass media.

Such an approach of theoretical cross-fertilisation – or as today's activists say: mutual 'contamination' (della Porta and Mosca: 2007) – can be instructive for both social movement research and the currently flourishing field of empirical research on the European public sphere (henceforth: EPS research). The next section starts with a critical assessment of some of the common assumptions prevalent in this research field. It is argued that integrating the public spheres within movements into this field of research could address significant shortcomings and challenge dominant elitist conceptions of the European public sphere.

Drawing on the established notion in EPS research that the European public sphere is a set of interlinked arenas, an arena model of the public sphere is proposed as a common reference point for both social movement and EPS research.

The EU and Media-content Centred Approach to the European Public Sphere

In the early 1990s, EU institutions became increasingly concerned about the lack of support by citizens (Brüggemann 2005: 65), which has further declined throughout the 1990s (Sifft et al. 2007: 128). This triggered not only an (internal) political debate about changing the 'arcane policy' of the EU (Brüggemann 2005: 65) toward a more transparent information policy, but also an academic debate about the 'public sphere deficit' (or the communication deficit) in Europe. This debate revolves around the question of whether and under what conditions a public sphere might possibly emerge at the European level as a democratic counterweight to institutional policy-making in the EU and hence could strengthen the 'legitimacy of European governance' by 'narrowing "the widening gap between the EU and the people"' (Sifft et al. 2007: 128).[1]

Besides this monitoring function vis-à-vis European institutions, a second commonly mentioned function of a (would-be) European public sphere is to create a sense of a European identity amongst the citizens of the EU, or – more generally – to form a common European public opinion (cf., e.g., Risse and van de Steeg 2007: 2; Sifft et al. 2007: 130–132).

A process of Europeanisation of the mass media is perceived as the key dimension for the emergence of a European public sphere. And since a system of European-wide mass media is not in view (Gerhards 1993), research has focussed on the processes of Europeanisation within the national media in Europe (or rather: in the EU). As Neidhardt (2006: 52) summarises, the diagnosis of the extent to which a European public sphere already exists varies in a wide range depending on different theoretical assumptions and operationalisations of the public sphere. The purpose of this section is, however, not to discuss the various operationalisations, but to assess more broadly the stance that EPS research has taken: its preoccupation with mass media content and with the EU polity.

There seems to be an agreement that the aim of EPS research is to identify and analyse a possibly emerging space of transnational communication in Europe with regard to its democratic functions in relation to powerful institutions. However, in the realisation of this goal, EPS research has – if with best intentions – often adopted the top down perspective on the European public sphere that still persists in EU institutions (Brüggemann 2005). This perspective reflects a specific normative model of the public sphere related to representative liberal theories of democracy. According to this model, the public sphere is the domain of elites who divide the public space amongst themselves according to their relative strength, though allowing some space for experts as their advisors (Ferree et al. 2002a: 291–292).

From this normative point of view, it seems sufficient to limit the analysis of the public sphere to mass media content, determining the relative space occupied by various actors and perhaps evaluating whether the space occupied by the actors is in line with their 'real' importance in the policy-making process. In this perspective, it does not matter whether or not the actors engage in public dialogue or if certain groups are empowered or disempowered through public discourse (Ferree et al. 2002a). Accordingly, EPS research treats mass media arenas as the given basis of a transnational public sphere. A European public sphere is thought to (potentially) emerge within this given framework through cross-references between nationally bounded arenas or by the increased salience of EU-related issues in these separated arenas. The internal democratic (or non-democratic) forms of organisation of these arenas or the question of ownership seem to be beyond the horizon of EPS research, despite the fact that it is highly contested in EU policy research whether mass media should be considered as commercial goods (subject to deregulation and marketisation) or as cultural goods (subject to democratic control) (Brüggemann 2005: 62).

Perhaps the creation of new transnational arenas of communication and their interrelation with existing arenas has been considered of little importance simply because the mass media provide few examples for such arenas (e.g., Euronews). But the main obstacle seems to be the notion of the public sphere as a medium for policy-makers to inform citizens about relevant policy decisions made by the EU. However, while it is correct that information about policies is a prerequisite for citizens to evaluate them critically, there are two reasons that this should not lead to seeing citizens only as passive recipients of information.

The first reason is that a review of democratic theory reveals at least four different democratic models of the public sphere: representative liberal, participatory liberal, discursive and constructionist (Ferree et al. 2002a). All but the representative model put strong emphasis on the inclusion of active citizens in public debate. Participatory liberal theories of democracy, for example, emphasise the empowerment of citizens in and through debate (ibid.: 297), discursive theories of democracy promote the notion of dialogue amongst citizens (ibid.: 303), which became quite fashionable in the discourse of the political elites as well.

When the EU commission uses 'dialogue' as a 'prominent catch-word' (Brüg-gemann 2005: 68) rather than engaging in serious dialogue with citizens or fa-cilitating dialogue amongst citizens, this should not lead scholars in interpreting dialogue mainly as a dialogue amongst elites within the media, in front of the (passive) citizens of Europe. Neglecting other normative models of a democratic public sphere beyond the representative liberal one, EPS research has burdened itself with an elite bias that prevents the serious reconsideration of the demo-cratic role of the public sphere at a transnational level (cf. Fraser 2005). It has so far failed to provide knowledge about 'transnational "spaces" where citizens from different countries can discuss what they perceive as being the important challenges for the Union' (Commission of the European Community 2001: 12), let alone any advice on how the proliferation of such spaces could be advanced in order to democratise the EU.

The second reason not to conceive of citizens as mere recipients of elite communication is a functional one. In order to grasp processes of the Europe-anisation of the public sphere in their full capacity, and to assess their potential role within a 'multilevel structure of sovereignty' (Fraser 2005: 6) in 'the current postnational constellation' (ibid.: 7), EPS research needs to approach the 'public sphere deficit' from the perspective of the governed. It is important to note that 'the governed' are not only affected by decisions made by governments or EU in-stitutions. Also, multi-national corporations and global institutions such as the G8 or the WTO have an increasing influence on citizens' lives. Obviously, the question of democratic legitimacy today arises not only with regard to national and transnational polities, but more than ever also with regard to transnational private powers such as multi-national corporations.

As Fraser (2005: 6) points out, the problem of conceptualising the public sphere at the transnational level is the mismatch between 'at least four kinds of community, which do not map onto one another today: 1) the imagined commu-nity, or nation; 2) the political (or civic) community, or citizenry; 3) the communi-cations community, or public; 4) the community of fate, or the set of stakeholders affected by various developments (included here is "community of risk")'.

EPS research seems to be concerned with the realignment of the first three of these communities only: the imagined community of Europe, a European cit-izenry and a European public sphere. From the perspective of the people affected by political decisions, though, the most urgent problems are the misalignment of the community of fate (one could also say 'the community of all those affected') with: 1) the citizenry (= democratic deficit) and 2) the public (= communica-tion deficit, in the sense of lacking space to discuss common concerns). In other words, communicative spaces are needed, where all of those affected can discuss and identify common problems arising from such transnational decisions.[2]

For this task, neither a pan-European media system nor the Europeanisation of national mass media (alone) seems to be of much help. Within the framework of the nation state (with an established liberal representative systems of government), an approach that sees the mass media as the 'master forum' (Ferree et al. 2002b: 10) may be adequate. However, in the context of the transnational polity of the EU, with its lack of legitimacy becoming increasingly evident, the study of the public sphere cannot be limited to media content analysis. This approach risks – politically – reproducing established power structures[3] and – scientifically – losing out on processes of Europeanisation 'from below' that are taking place in civil society across Europe. With numerous interconnected 'deliberative arenas' (e.g., Bobbio 2003) being created at the transnational level in Europe on one side, and the persistence of nationally structured media systems, on the other, there is no reason to assume *a priori* that the mass media actually do constitute the master forum of a public sphere at the European level (and should thus be studied with special regard).

Studying the European public sphere from a perspective that seeks to critically address power relations and their legitimation will hence need to include the study of public arenas at different levels. Gerhards and Neidhardt (1990) – in their widely recognised (but never translated) article – have distinguished three levels of the public sphere: Simple *encounters* amongst people in their daily life; organised *assembly publics*; and the professionalised *mass media*.

The different characteristics of encounters, assembly publics and the mass media (see Table 3.1) can reveal different aspects of the transnationalisation of the public sphere because they constitute different types of public situations, each with their specific 'contribution' to an emerging European space of shared communication.

Table 3.1. Characteristics of the Three Levels of the Public Sphere
(Inspired by Gerhards and Neidhardt (1990) with Additions and Slight Modifications by the Author)

	Examples	Audience	Permeability of audience and speaker roles	Degree of organisation	Continuity of the framework	Rationality of communication	Legal protection
Mass media	TV, radio, newspapers, magazines	*recipients*	*very low*	*high (technical)*	*stable*	*lay-orientation*	*freedom of press*
Assembly publics	conferences, mailinglists, group-meetings	*participants*	*medium–high*	*medium (thematic)*	*temporary / recurring*	*thematic / expert orientation*	*freedom of assembly*
Encounters	at the hotelbar, supermarket, street, etc.	*bystanders*	*high*	*low (spontaneous)*	*episodic*	*situational*	*freedom of speech*

Public Encounters

Public encounters happen rather randomly when people meet in public places: in the street, at the hairdresser, in a waiting queue, at the scene of an accident, etc. They are not organised in any way regarding themes of communication, speaker roles, etc. The focus of communication in encounters evolves in the situation itself. But this does not mean that public communication in encounters is not pre-structured at all: in encounter situations where specific agendas, rules of talk and normative assumptions are not available, speakers have to relate to a more general 'default situation' with a commonly recognised code of conduct of how to behave and what to (not) talk about. For Goffman (1963), who analysed the ordinary US middle-class milieu in the 1950s and 1960s, the default situation was generally given and quite clear to all (middle-class citizens) involved in a public encounter: 'In any given society, different situations will be the scene of many of the same normative assumptions regarding conduct and of the same situational rulings' (ibid.: 216). Unlike assembly publics – which often exhibit their own (sub-cultural) rules of conduct – encounters have to rely on shared cultural habits established outside of the situation of a specific encounter. Often, the mass media provide a reference point. But also other communities of shared experience can be a source of common reference, e.g., gender, class, race or generation-related experiences.

What is interesting about encounters in the context of the Europeanisation of the public sphere is to observe what happens in transnational encounters with different cultural traditions and with no common media as reference available, i.e., when Goffman's assumption of a given society does not apply anymore: which frame of reference is nevertheless established in such a situation, and how? And if communication fails, why?

At first glance, it might seem impossible to study such transnational encounter-publics because they occur rather randomly. But in times of high mobility, cheap travel and open borders within Europe, transnational encounters in border-region shops or bars, in airports, at the camping site, or in the context of international protest events are common. Observing (and possibly recording) such encounters between people of different cultures can provide insight into the specificities of transnational and intercultural public communication in everyday life and their contribution to the transnationalisation of the public sphere.

Assembly Publics

Assembly publics are organised around specific topics and thus provide a shared frame of reference that can be taken for granted when communicating in this specific arena. The program of a conference or the agenda of a meeting empowers the communication in this arena by giving it a certain direction or structure. At the same time, it also constrains it by excluding off-topic contributions.

Though Gerhards and Neidhardt (1990) tend to limit assembly publics to face-to-face meetings, it can be argued that the crucial characteristic of assembly publics is that – in principle – they allow for active participation of any member of the audience (though usually not everyone actually does speak up), i.e., audience and speaker roles are readily exchangeable. This means, that email lists, online forums, chat rooms or telephone conferences can also be considered as assembly publics. Apart from such formal structures, also informal 'group styles' (Eliasoph and Lichterman 2003: 737) may be relevant in these arenas.

Very often, in such publics we find a specific public opinion[4] that is different to that of the mass media or 'mainstream' public opinion in general. Besides, they are usually not oriented toward a lay audience like the mass media, but rather toward experts or special interest groups. Eder and Trenz (2003) have already shown that such specialised public arenas may not only be strongly Europeanised, but also relevant for policy building at the European level. If we consider theories of democracy beyond the representative model, we can see that non-established public actors involved in the creation and maintenance of deliberative arenas within civil society are generally regarded as crucial for the democratic process (Habermas 1989: 474; Neidhardt 1994: 10; Commission of the European Community 2001: 14f.; Fung and Wright 2001; Ferree et al. 2002a: 301).

Indeed, the recent popular politicisation of European politics through protests related to the referendums on the Constitutional Treaty and the 'no' votes in France and the Netherlands reveal that the long observed 'public silence' of these actors can no longer be interpreted as a sign of agreement (cf. Fossum and Trenz 2006: 73). In fact, this 'silence' turns out to be no silence at all, but rather a silence observed by those limiting their view to the mass media.

Including all Levels of the Public Sphere in the Analysis

Although the diffusion of ideas from the level of assembly publics to the mass media is highly selective and biased in many ways (Gitlin 1980), there have been significant instances where transnationally coordinated social movements have managed to mobilise 'global' public opinion to major problems of injustice by lifting their concerns into the mass media in various countries (Olesen 2006; Thörn 2007). In Europe, social movements are increasingly adapting to the high relevance of the EU institutions (della Porta 2005, and chapter 5 in this volume) and creating their own public spaces through interlinked assembly publics, most prominently in the ESF process (Doerr 2005, 2006; Haug, Haeringer and Mosca 2009). One can say that by creating their own public spaces, the movements are reacting not only to the democratic and the communication deficit of the EU, but also to the democratic deficit of the media, which give even less space to non-institutionalised actors at the European than at the national level (della Porta and Caiani 2006). The public spaces created by the movements are spaces where a European integration based on rights is debated as an alternative to the current market based integration.

Looking at the creation of transnational assembly publics (as opposed to looking at the content of established media) evokes the question of who creates and maintains these arenas, and what are the structural conditions that facilitate or constrain a Europeanisation of the communication within these spaces? Table 3.2 lists some dimensions that seem relevant here and tries to identify some of the important roles on each level of the public sphere: the *hosts* and/or *organisers* have a high importance in pre-structuring the communication that takes place in these assemblies, e.g., by inviting certain speakers, setting the agenda but also by inviting a certain (multi-national) audience. On the level of the mass media, the general policy of the *publisher* (i.e., owner) or the editorial statutes guiding the *editors* becomes comparable to the policy of the *organising committee* of an assembly or a conference.

Furthermore, when we look at roles structuring the ongoing communication in an arena, the role of a meeting *facilitator* becomes comparable to that of a *journalist*: just like the journalist is arranging the statements of various actors in a newspaper article (foregrounding some as opposed to others, raising certain questions, etc.), also the facilitator of a meeting gives speakers the floor, asks questions and juxtaposes their answers in a certain way. Perhaps he or she also provides a summary at the end. On the level of encounters, situational *leadership* roles might emerge, taking a similar functional role of structuring public communication.

Finally, we can also identify similar linking roles on each level. As Erbe (2005) has pointed out, the European public sphere (but also the national public spheres) consists of multiple arenas. This fragmentation of the public sphere is an obstacle in the formation of a European (or national) public sphere as long as these arenas are not interlinked. Erbe identifies various 'mechanisms' (ibid.: 77), which account for the linking of the arenas within national media systems, allowing us to speak of one public sphere instead of 'public sphericules', as Gitlin (1998) suggests in view of the plurality of public arenas. The most institutionalised of these mechanisms are the *news agencies*, which make the same information available to the various media arenas. Such linking roles can also be found on the level of assembly publics. People that take core positions in connecting previously unconnected arenas can be called '*brokers*' (Diani 2003).

Table 3.2. Functional Roles on the Three Levels of the Public Sphere

	Pre-structuring roles	Structuring roles	Linking roles
Mass media	*publisher/ editors*	*journalists*	*news agencies*
Assembly publics	*hosts/ organisers*	*facilitators*	*'brokers'*
Public Encounters	*none*	*situational leaders*	*travellers*

On the encounter level, linking roles are less pronounced, but people who move about between places (*travellers*) are most likely to provide links between various encounters.

For the sake of the argument, the roles described here remain somewhat simplistic. For one, roles connecting between different levels are not discussed here. More importantly, the focus on the roles of actors in Table 3.2 should not mislead us into believing that public communication is structured only by actors and their interaction. The important question when assessing the contribution of various public arenas to the creation of a democratic (European) public sphere is: what are the guiding norms and principles (pre-)structuring the communication in this arena, how are they realised, and in what way do they constitute a counter power to established institutions?, but also: which loci of power can be identified within these arenas and their organisational framework that might thwart the free flow of communication? This pertains not only to the norms and principles guiding the (pre-)structuring roles, but also to the speakers and – in many cases the most important form of pre-structuration – the public opinion (or *doxa*) established in a certain arena by previous communications.[5]

As we have seen, the media-content centred approach is concerned mainly with an EU-related top-down approach to the European public sphere and should be complemented by integrating organisationally less demanding levels of the public sphere into a wider research agenda. Including especially the level of assembly publics in EPS research makes it possible to trace the processes of alignment of the different communities mentioned above (nation, citizenry, audience and stake- or 'risk-holders') and thus identity formation at the European level (which might not (only) be directed at the EU, but also at other powerful actors). This perspective of looking at civil society and social movements not only as a set of *actors* (articulating certain interests and demands), but also to see the communicative *spaces* created by them, points to a neglected area of social movement research which will be dealt with in the next section.

Social Movements as Context

The limitations of the actor model of social movements are increasingly becoming evident, and the '"free spaces" in collective action' (Polletta 1999) are currently attracting the attention of scholars. The model of the unified collective actor has been challenged, at the latest, by the global justice movements (GJMs), which do not consider unity as a primary goal in order to be successful. Instead, they see the processes of communicative exchange and plurality as one of their highest values (Andretta et al. 2002: 85–87; della Porta and Mosca 2007). The most obvious expression of this tendency is the social forums, which have emerged all over the globe since the first WSF in 2001 in Porto Alegre. In fact, the idea of creating open spaces of discussion within movements and its possible incongruence with the idea of a unified, strong and effective movement is increasingly being debated with the movements themselves (see, for instance, Patomäki and Teivainen 2004; Reyes et al. 2004; Wallerstein 2004; Aguiton and Cardon 2005; Haug, Teune and Yang 2005: 87–89).

Reflecting on communicative processes within movements is adequate not just because of these recent developments, but it also means taking seriously the '[p]hases of self-reflection' (Rucht 1988: 313) within movements, which are characterised by extensive internal discussions. Moreover, there are whole movements that follow a rather 'expressive logic' (ibid: 317), i.e., they are 'concerned with the process of cultural rationalisation' (ibid.: 319) within the life-world as opposed to those 'fighting for the control of the systemic steering process [which] will be called "instrumental" (or power-oriented)' (ibid.). Internal public arenas are vital for expressive movements, while instrumental movements may operate with less or other forms of internal discussion. Rucht mentions the women's movement as an example of an expressive movement, which: 'concentrates its energies on methods of qualitative mobilisation: 1) On the one hand, the creation of autonomous cultural practices and the establishment of a specific feminist infrastructure; 2) On the other hand, the abolition of sexist institutions and modes of behaviour through techniques of provocation and ironic exaggeration and inversion of connotations' (ibid.: 321). It is not by chance that Freeman's (1970) classic text about internal structures of communication originated from the feminist movement. The political scope of such movements emphasising everyday practices as practices of subversion and resistance cannot be grasped by merely looking at their external behaviour, i.e., as actors in a larger context. And, even in instrumental movements, assembly publics can be highly relevant for the formation of common action frames.

Why have these '"internal" fields of action [where] organizations and groups within a social movement establish a daily routine that is not at all, or only indirectly, related to external conflicts' (Rucht 1988: 322) rarely been studied systematically? It might have been due to – as Snow and Benford (1988: 214) noted – movement scholars' preference to use archived material for their studies, but it might also have been due to a simple lack of access to such internal meetings. This situation, however, has changed in recent years, perhaps due to the spreading culture of openness, plurality and self-reflection in the GJMs. Accordingly, recent studies and research projects such as the DEMOS-project[6] have shown increased interest in examining contemporary movements' internal practices of democracy, seeing them as 'laboratories' in which new forms of (transnational) democracy (or collective decision-making) might emerge.[7]

So if, for all of the above-mentioned reasons, we want to study movements not *in context*, but *as context*, then we need an adequate conceptual framework to analyse the 'free spaces' (Poletta 1999) or 'internal fields of action' (Rucht 1988: 322). Organisational sociology might be a discipline to which to resort, but since it is widely rejected[8] to conceptualise movements as organisations (Endruweit 2004: 29–30; della Porta and Diani 2006: 25–29) we will need to look at other theoretical fields.

The field of (small) group research may be helpful when looking at individual movement groups, but when it comes to settings of mesomobilisation (Gerhards and Rucht 1992), where the gap between the micro-level of movement groups' mobilisation and the macro-level of movement campaigns is bridged, then the concept of group is soon overstretched because it tends to presuppose an identity that the mesomobilisation meetings are precisely set up to create (cf. Poletta 1999: 29 fn. 38). Although these groups share – to some degree – a common identity, seeing them as one group would risk overemphasising the aspect of unity rather than studying how it comes about through communicative processes.

Gerhards and Rucht (1992: 572ff.) focus on the cognitive function of master frames. Using the final result of such meetings (two leaflets signed by all groups), they analyse the master frames of the campaign, and how these comprise the frames of all participating groups. However, they do not analyse the communicative processes leading to these final results or the conditions under which the negotiations took place.

It will come to no surprise that our search for an adequate concept that helps us study these aspects of mesomobilisation settings leads to the concept of the public sphere, more precisely to the notion of assembly publics described above. Although social movements have mainly been seen as actors within the public sphere, the notion of public sphere has occasionally been used to refer to the communicative arenas created by or within social movements: Stamm (1988) speaks of 'alternative public spheres'; Wischermann (2003: 15) looks at 'movement public spheres' (*Bewegungsöffentlichkeit*) or 'internal public spheres' (*Binnenöffentlichkeit*); and – probably most prominently – Fraser (1992: 123) coined the term 'subaltern counter-publics'. Finally, Rucht (2002) writes about 'transnational public spheres within social movements' (all translations by the author).

Linking Transnational Movement Research to the European Public Sphere

So far, it was argued – in accord with the similar approach of Doerr (2005, 2006, chapter 4 in this volume) – that research on the European public sphere needs to be relieved of its media-content centred blinkers, and that social movement research might well look at communicative processes within movements using the concept of public sphere. In order to facilitate links between the two fields, a model (or a set of concepts) will be sketched that makes it possible to translate findings between both fields and make them relevant for each other.

Introducing the Arena Model of the Public Sphere

At the centre of the model is the concept of 'arena': a public arena is constituted by an audience observing the same communications at (roughly) the same time. Arenas exist on all levels of the public sphere, which means that they can be closely associated with a physical public space, but this need not be the case.[9] An arena can be a rather fixed framework of communication (such as *Financial Times* as a mass medium), a regular meeting (such as the Preparatory Assembly for the ESF), or a transient encounter of football fans in a bar during the FIFA World Cup. In other words, arenas exist on all three levels of the public sphere.

They are public because of the presence of an audience (as a third actor), which makes them fundamentally different to private situations between two actors. Strydom (2001: 176) stresses the vital difference between the 'problem of double contingency' that occurs whenever two actors A and B meet, and the 'problem of triple contingency' that occurs when C enters the scene: 'The inclusion of the third-person point of view, represented by C, means that the social situation in the case of triple contingency is very different and more complicated from the start. It is not simply a matter of aggregation of elementary interaction'.[10] It therefore makes sense to distinguish dyadic communicative relations as private from public ones which are triadic or even 'polyadic'.[11]

Having defined a public situation (or arena), it is important to note that one arena does not usually make a public sphere in the sense of being the shared communicative space of a collectivity. All members of a collectivity are rarely identical with the audience of one single arena.

EPS research has come to see the European public sphere as a network of interconnected public arenas, linked through flows of communication. Also Olesen (2005), who explores the infrastructure of transnational publics as 'new spaces for social movement activism', points in the same direction when he says that 'transnational publics are networks' (ibid.: 425). However, his concept remains somewhat unsatisfactory since he states that the nodes of these networks 'are usually social movements' (ibid.: 425), but then 'nodes of special influence may [also] be personalities' (ibid.: 427). Seeing 'social movements as agents', Olesen (2005: 425) fades out an important part of the transnationalisation of communication and thus the transnationalisation of public spheres – the transnationalisation of communication within the movements themselves,[12] and he confounds two analytical levels: networks of individuals ('personalities') and network of networks ('social movements').

Let us therefore take the network concept to an 'extreme' and examine the principle differences between communication in interpersonal networks and in an arena: both interpersonal networks and public arenas can serve the purpose of diffusing information. Networks, however, do not have the capacity for collective deliberation because the number of communicative acts necessary to spread all relevant elements of the discussion to everyone else in the network grows exponentially with every intervention. Considering that the passing on of information also takes time, it also becomes evident that it is rather difficult to keep a network-debate synchronised, i.e., to ensure that everyone has the same information before replying to previous interventions.

So, if we look at how a collectivity (e.g., a transnational social movement or the citizens of Europe) shares its communications, we can distinguish two basic modes of how information can be passed on and exchanged: private and public. The distinction between public and private communication allows us to conceptualise networks of (private) communication and arenas of (public) communication as two ideal typically opposed structures of communication, both – in principle – capable of diffusing and exchanging information.

In network communication, information is passed on bilaterally from one actor to the next and so on. In public communication, information is shared directly amongst several actors within an arena. If at least one actor from arena A is also in arena B, then these arenas are communicatively linked. If the link is only through one actor, it is a private link. If there is more than one connecting actor, the link is public.[13] This opposition between public and private communication is represented on the vertical axis in Figure 3.1. Both private and public channels contribute to the sharing of communication within a collectivity, so that they must be considered in our concept of the public sphere. However, since network communication is not public but private, the public sphere loses some of its 'publicness' if the share of networked communication increases. The con-

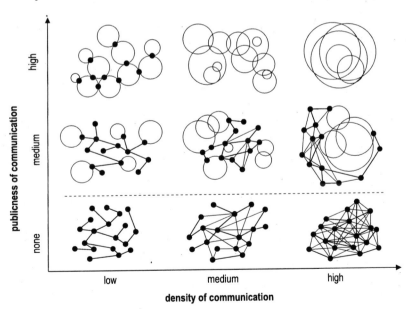

Figure 3.1. Two Parameters of the Public Sphere

cept of *publicness* allows us to grasp this dimension of a public sphere: the more communication takes place publicly, the higher the publicness of that space of shared communication.

As illustrated in Figure 3.1, there is another relevant dimension of the public sphere: its *density*. The density refers to the intensity in which communication is shared amongst the actors of that collectivity. In private networks, communication can be shared more intensely when more communicative links exist. This corresponds with the density concept in network theory. With increasing density of a network, the situation moves from double contingency toward triple contingency in the sense that the other members in the network tend to represent a kind of surrogate audience, even when they are absent. Social control not only takes place in public, but also occurs in dense private networks. In the public realm, the highest density is reached when all members of the collectivity assemble in the same arena, because then everything that is said directly reaches everyone else. The public sphere is then identical with one single arena.

Combining the dimensions of publicness and density, we can describe and compare public spheres: publicness is high, when most communication takes place in arenas, i.e., before an audience. The circles in Figure 3.1 represent the audience of public arenas: the density of the public sphere is high when there is a big overlap between the audiences of different arenas, and it is low when the connections between the arenas are only through small segments of the audience. Or more generally, the density of communication within a collectivity is higher when more actors are interlinked through communication. The 'base line' in Figure 3.1 with no publicness represents the ideal type of purely private networks, i.e., the absence of a public sphere.[14] The nodes (black dots) of the network are individual actors. It is here that the various linking roles mentioned in Table 3.2 become relevant.

The fact that the various arenas are actually located on different levels of the public sphere can be visualised as in Figure 3.2. The links, which appeared exclusively as 'horizontal' links in Figure 3.1, now turn out to be partly vertical ones, linking arenas on different levels of the public sphere. Depending on the research question, such links might be of particular relevance. Furthermore, clarifying the communicative structures on each level separately might help to explore the limitations and special capacities of each level of the public sphere in a transnational context.

Some limitations of this visualisation should be mentioned: since the images in Figures 3.1 and 3.2 represent snapshots of a public sphere at a particular moment in time, it is not able to depict very vibrant public spheres, where new arenas are constantly created and might or might not persist very long. These images should therefore be taken as a rough outline of a particular communicative space.

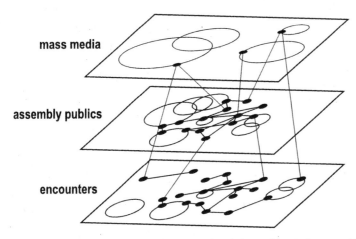

mass media

assembly publics

encounters

Figure 3.2. Arenas on Different Levels of the Public Sphere and Their Inter-connections

The idea of the model is to contextualise any arena under investigation in such a way that emerging processes of transnationalisation become traceable, and difficulties arising in such processes can be situated in a larger framework of the public sphere of the collectivity under investigation. It is, however, empirically difficult to fully map the complete space of shared communication of a larger collectivity. It therefore makes sense to limit the mapping of the communicative infrastructure to those arenas that are relevant for a particular communicative process, e.g., a certain controversial issue. In other words, looking, for example, at the public debate about the European Constitutional Treaty, arenas, where this issue was not debated, are irrelevant.

Another limitation of the model is that it does not account for external communicative relations, i.e., communications from within the public sphere of the observed collectivity to other public spheres. The openness of a communicative space to anybody has traditionally been made a decisive criterion to call it a public sphere. While such mix-ups of publicness with openness has led to much confusion, it can nevertheless be instructive to include openness as a further parameter of a public sphere. Openness would then have to be understood as 'porosity' (see chapter 6 in this volume) or permeability in order to refer to it as a property of letting information and people pass across its boundaries. By not making openness a *definiens* of the public sphere we acknowledge the possibility of a public sphere that is shielded off from outside communication, as, for example, the public sphere of a secret society. A public sphere is always connected to a certain collectivity. It makes sense to be explicit about whose public sphere we are talking about in our studies.

Conclusion: The Europeanisation of Debate within Social Movements

It was the aim of this chapter to suggest the arena model of the public sphere as a basic tool or developable conceptual framework to analyse transnational public spheres in movements and to challenge some of the elitist assumptions of common EPS research. Looking at the processes of transnationalisation or Europeanisation of communication within social movements, assembly publics are obviously central, although alternative media exist, and encounters do take place at transnational protest events and at the fringes of meetings. It is important to keep these arenas in mind as well. The creation of such transnational arenas is most prominently represented by the ESFs and the recurring preparatory assemblies preparing these forums (Doerr 2005, 2006; Haug, Haeringer and Mosca 2009), but anyone investigating the transnationalisation of social movements will be familiar with other similar arenas.

There is much to commend that such arenas are laboratories of democracy relevant for the construction of democratic transnational polities and public spheres. The principal arguments put forward here were thus:

1. The public sphere should be seen as a structured space and not be confused with the content of communication taking place within it (though a dynamic relationship between both is evident). It seems that much of what has been measured as a Europeanisation of the public sphere would be more adequately described as a Europeanisation of various discourses. The structural condition of their emergence and diffusion remains to be made explicit.

2. Public spheres and networks must be distinguished as different communicative structures, and their respective capacities for democratic debate should be assessed. Social movements are commonly conceptualised as 'networks', but they do also create and maintain deliberative arenas. This makes them an ideal site to explore both dimensions of the public sphere and their role in the democratic transnationalisation of communication.

3. Whether or not the space of shared communication of a collectivity is really one single space, or whether it is more appropriately described as a set of arenas, depends on how densely connected are the various arenas. For social movements in Europe, for instance, it is still a big challenge to connect social movement arenas in Western Europe with those in Central and Eastern Europe. Despite the efforts to include Eastern European activists into the ESF process, the communicative structures of east and west are still rather separate. However, apart from looking at the density of the public sphere, i.e., asking whether

there is one public sphere or several 'public sphericules', the publicness of this communicative infrastructure is another important criterion. With social movements relying highly on interpersonal networks to connect various arenas, the publicness of the movement public sphere is always at risk. The democratic accountability of social movement brokers connecting key arenas thus needs to be researched, especially when it comes to processes of transnationalisation.

4. The question of how various arenas are created and maintained is vital. Especially when looking at the level of mesomobilisation, it cannot be taken for granted that common arenas for inter-group co-ordination simply emerge and become institutionalised. Resources are needed to sustain them, and the question of ownership between those contributing more and those contributing less may be a source of conflict.

5. If the public sphere is supposed to contribute to the democratisation of Europe, then the framework of the public sphere itself needs to be democratised. This is not only a matter of democratising the mass media, but it also raises questions regarding how the various arenas on different levels should be interconnected (also to the so-called 'strong publics', i.e., those with decision-making power), and how debate within such arenas should be organised.

Notes

This chapter draws on a conference paper written with Nicole Doerr, whose contribution to this volume takes more of an empirical perspective on the issue, while this chapter concentrates on conceptual questions. The starting point for the original co-authored paper was our common criticism of the widespread media-centred approach to the European public sphere.

1. The academic debate referred to here is – amongst many others – reflected in Gerhards (1993, 2000, 2002); Grimm (1995); Eder and Kantner (2000, 2002); Eriksen and Fossum (2002); Risse (2002); van de Steeg (2002); Kantner (2004); Koopmans and Erbe (2004); Trenz (2004); Erbe (2006); Risse and van de Steeg (2007).

2. To assume that this common identity will necessarily be a European one would be short-sighted and does not account for the global interdependencies becoming more and more evident in everyday life. The relation between the global and the European dimension is also subject of an ongoing debate within social movements in Europe.

3. As Gerhards (2002: 154) rightly argued, the public sphere deficit on the European level is a result – not a cause – of the institutional democratic deficit at the European level.

4. The term 'public opinion' has been used in two different ways: one version signifies an aggregate of individual private (!) opinions, as in public opinion research; the other refers to the dominant or hegemonic opinion in public discourse. I use the term in the latter sense.

5. Tönnies (1922: 137–138, author's translation) has aptly described different 'states of aggregation' of public opinion – gaseous, liquid and solid – where the 'degree of cohesiveness is the degree of its uniformity'. In this sense, the crystallised parts of public opinion are part of the structural conditions of public communication. More recently, Hallin (1984: 21) has distinguished the 'sphere of consensus' and the 'sphere of legitimate controversy'. The first denotes opinions that are not regarded as controversial by journalists, so that they feel no urge to present opposing views, and the second refers to issues where different opinions seem legitimate so that norms of neutral and balanced journalism become vital when reporting on these. Since these spheres are constructed based on the journalists' observation of the public sphere, this is an example of how public communication can have a structuring effect on public communication.

6. DEMOS stands for 'Democracy in Europe and the Mobilisation of Society'; for details see http://demos.eui.eu.

7. In his Ph.D. project, the author of this chapter studied processes of discursive decision-making in social movement assemblies by following numerous movement meetings and mailinglists on the local (Berlin), the national (German) and transnational (European) level over a period of two to three years.

8. Nevertheless, just recently, there has been a first joint publication of organisational theorists and social movement researchers in the US (Davis et al. 2005); for an interesting use of organisational theory on movements see Leach (2005), but also Rucht (1999).

9. For the negligence with which physical (e.g., urban) spaces have been treated in public sphere research see Low and Smith (2006).

10. Strydom (2001) criticises Habermas' tendency 'to interpret the third point of view too strongly in terms of the idealised moral point of view' (ibid.: 166) instead of taking seriously 'the public in its inherent pluralism' (ibid.). He shows that this is due to Habermas' thinking remaining on the neoclassical level of double contingency even though his work points to the problem of triple contingency.

11. Eder et al. (2002: 106) define public situations slightly differently. They point out that '[t]he distinction between public and private should not be confused with the presence or absence of the addressed audience'. Instead, they distinguish public and private in relation to the presence or absence of a non-addressed audience. They are, however, not fully clear about how exactly we can tell a public from a private situation. First, they state that '[p]rivate situations consist of the direct communication between *two* persons or groups without an outside observer' (ibid.: 105), but later they say that private encounters are 'between *two or more* individuals' (ibid.: 109) (emphasis added in both citations). Also, while they define a private situation in terms of the factual absence of an outside observer, they use different categories for defining public situations as not being able to exclude 'the possibility that outside observers react to the form or content of the communication' (ibid.: 105f.).

12. For a similar criticism see Thörn (2007), though he, on the other hand, seems to equate face-to-face communication with private communication (ibid.: 904).

13. In relation to the creation of a unitary media public sphere, Erbe (2005: 77) called this linking mechanism 'overlapping media audiences'.

14. Perhaps the communicative structures of the Mafia are as close as you can get to purely private networks. In that case, the only way the collectivity remains capable of acting is through its hierarchical structure, i.e., centralised network.

References

Aguiton, C. and D. Cardon. 2005. 'Le Forum et le Réseau: Une analyse des modes de gouvernement des forums sociaux'. *Cultures et pratiques participatives: une perspective comparative, Paris, 20–21 January 2005.* Retrieved 3 September 2007 from http://mokk.bme.hu/centre/conferences/reactivism/FP/fpDC.

Andretta, M., et al. 2002. *No global – new global: Identität und Strategien der Antiglobalisierungsbewegung,* 2nd ed. Frankfurt am Main: Campus 2003.

Bobbio, L. 2003. 'Building Social Capital through Democratic Deliberation: The Rise of Deliberative Arenas'. *Social Epistemology* 17(4): 343–357.

Brüggemann, M. 2005. 'How the EU Constructs the European Public Sphere: Seven Strategies of Information Policy'. *Javnost – The Public* 12(2): 57–74. Retrieved 10 April 2008 from http://www.javnost-thepublic.org/article/pdf/2005/2/4/.

Commission of the European Community. 2001. 'European Governance: A White Paper'. Brussels, 25 July 2001. Retrieved 14 September 2006 from http://eur-lex.europa.eu/LexUriServ/site/en/com/2001/com2001_0428en01.pdf.

Davis, G.F., et al., ed. 2005. *Social Movements and Organization Theory.* Cambridge: Cambridge University Press.

della Porta, D. 2005. 'The Europeanization of Protest: A Typology and some Empirical Evidence'. In *Comparing European Societies: Towards a Sociology of the EU,* eds. G. Bettin Lattes and E. Recchi, 261–286. Bologna: Monduzzi.

della Porta, D. and M. Caiani. 2006. 'The Europeanization of Public Discourse in Italy: A Top-Down Process?' *European Union Politics* 7(1): 77–112.

della Porta, D. and M. Diani. 2006. *Social Movements: An introduction.* 2nd rev. ed. Oxford: Blackwell.

della Porta, D. and L. Mosca. 2007. 'In movimento: "Contamination" in Action and the Italian Global Justice Movement'. *Global Networks* 7(1): 1–27.

Diani, M. 2003. '"Leaders" or "Brokers"? Positions and Influence in Social Movement Networks'. In *Social Movements and Networks: Relational Approaches to Collective Action,* eds. M. Diani and D. McAdam, 105–122. Oxford: Oxford University Press.

Doerr, N. 2005. 'Sprache ist nicht das Problem: Die Sozialforen als Testfall für eine zukünftige europäische Öffentlichkeit'. *Berliner Debatte Initial* 16(4): 93–105.

———. 2006. 'Towards a European Public Sphere "from below"? The Case of Multilingualism within the European Social Forums'. In *Alternative Futures and Popular Protest,* eds. C. Barker and M. Tyldesley. Manchester, 19–21 April 2006.

Eder, K., et al. 2002. *Collective Identities in Action: A Sociological Approach to Ethnicity.* Aldershot: Ashgate.

Eder, K. and C. Kantner. 2000. 'Transnationale Resonanzstrukturen in Europa. Eine Kritik der Rede vom Öffentlichkeitsdefizit'. In *Die Europäisierung nationaler Gesellschaften (Kölner Zeitschrift für Soziologie und Sozialpsychologie special issue 40),* ed. M. Bach, 306–331. Wiesbaden: Westdeutscher Verlag.

———. 2002. 'Interdiskursivität in der europäischen Öffentlichkeit'. *Berliner Debatte Initial* 13(5/6): 79–88.

Eder, K. and H.-J. Trenz. 2003. 'The Making of a European Public Space: The Case of Justice and Home Affairs'. In *Linking EU and National Governance,* ed. B. Kohler-Koch, 111–134. Oxford: Oxford University Press.

Eliasoph, N. and P. Lichterman. 2003. 'Culture in Interaction'. *American Journal of Sociology* 108(4): 735–794.

Endruweit, G. 2004. *Organisationssoziologie.* 2nd ed. Stuttgart: Lucius & Lucius.

Erbe, J. 2005. '"What do the Papers Say?" How Press Reviews Link National Media Arenas in Europe'. *Javnost – The Public* 12(2): 75–92. Retrieved 13 April 2008 from http://www.javnost-thepublic.org/article/pdf/2005/2/5/.

———. 2006. 'Integration der politischen Öffentlichkeit in Europa durch Vernetzung: Der Fall der grenzüberschreitenden Presseschauen in Deutschland'. In *Europäische Öffentlichkeit und medialer Wandel: Eine transdisziplinäre Perspektive,* eds. W. Langenbucher, M. Latzer and W.R. Langenbucher, 156–178. Wiesbaden: Verlag für Sozialwissenschaften.

Eriksen, E.O. and J.E. Fossum. 2002. 'Democracy through Strong Publics in the EU?'. *Journal of Common Market Studies* 40(3): 401–423.

Ferree, M.M., et al. 2002a. 'Four Models of the Public Sphere in Modern Democracies'. *Theory and Society* 31(3): 289–324.

Ferree, M.M., et al. 2002b. *Shaping Abortion Discourse: Democracy and the Public Sphere in Germany and the United States.* Cambridge: Cambridge University Press.

Fossum, J.E. and H.-J. Trenz. 2006. 'The EU's Fledgling Society: From Deafening Silence to Critical Voice European Constitution-Making', *Journal of Civil Society* 2(1): 57–77.

Fraser, N. 1992. 'Rethinking the Public Sphere: A Contribution to the Critique of Actually Existing Democracy'. In *Habermas and the Public Sphere,* ed. C. Calhoun, 109–142. Cambridge: MIT Press.

———. 2005. *Transnationalizing the Public Sphere.* Vienna: European Institute for Progressive Cultural Policies. Retrieved 29 June 2006 from http://republicart.net/disc/publicum/fraser01_en.pdf.

Freeman, J. 1970. *The Tyranny of Structurelessness.* Retrieved 29 April 2007 from http://www.jofreeman.com/joreen/tyranny.htm.

Fung, A. and E.O. Wright. 2001. 'Deepening Democracy: Innovations in Empowered Participatory Governance'. *Politics and Society* 29(1): 5–41.

Gerhards, J. 1993. 'Westeuropäische Integration und die Schwierigkeiten der Entstehung einer europäischen Öffentlichkeit'. *Zeitschrift für Soziologie* 22(2): 100–110.

———. 2000. 'Europäisierung von Ökonomie und Politik und die Trägheit der Entstehung einer europäischen Öffentlichkeit'. In *Die Europäisierung nationaler Gesellschaften (Kölner Zeitschrift für Soziologie und Sozialpsychologie* special issue 40), ed. M. Bach, 299–305. Wiesbaden: Westdeutscher Verlag.

———. 2002. 'Das Öffentlichkeitsdefizit der EU im Horizont normativer Öffentlichkeitstheorien'. In *Transnationale Öffentlichkeiten und Identitäten im 20. Jahrhundert,* H. Kaelble, M. Kirsch and A. Schmidt-Gernig, 135–158. Frankfurt am Main: Campus.

Gerhards, J. and F. Neidhardt. 1990. 'Strukturen und Funktionen moderner Öffentlichkeit: Fragestellungen und Ansätze'. In *Öffentlichkeit, Kultur, Massenkommunikation,* eds. S. Müller-Dohm and K. Neumann-Braun, 31–89. Oldenburg: BIS der Uni Oldenburg 1991. Retrieved 29 June 2006 from http://oops.uni-oldenburg.de/volltexte/1999/685/pdf/kapii-1.pdf. [First published in 1990 as Discussion Paper FS III 90-101 at the Social Science Research Center Berlin].

Gerhards, J. and D. Rucht. 1992. 'Mesomobilization: Organizing and Framing in Two Protest Campaigns in West Germany'. *The American Journal of Sociology* 98(3): 555–596.

Gitlin, T. 1980. *The Whole World is Watching: Mass Media in the Making and Unmaking of the New Left*. Berkeley: University of California Press.

———. 1998. 'Public Spheres or Public Sphericules?' In *Media, Ritual and Identity*, eds. T. Liebes and J. Curran, 175–202. London: Routledge.

Goffman, E. 1963. *Behavior in Public Places: Notes on the Social Organization of Gatherings*. New York: The Free Press.

Grimm, D. 1995. 'Does Europe need a Constitution?' *European Law Journal* 1(3): 282–302.

Habermas, J. 1989. 'Volkssouveränität als Verfahren: Ein normativer Begriff von Öffentlichkeit'. *Merkur* 43(6): 465–477.

Hallin, D.C. 1984. 'The Media, the War in Vietnam, and Political Support: A Critique of the Thesis of an Oppositional Media'. *The Journal of Politics* 46(1): 2–24.

Haug, C., N. Haeringer and L. Mosca. 2009. 'The ESF Organizing Process in a Diachronic Perspective'. In *Another Europe: Conceptions and Practices of Democracy in the European Social Forums*, ed. D. della Porta, 26–45. London: Routledge.

Haug, C., S. Teune and M. Yang. 2005. 'Von Porto Alegre nach Berlin: Lokale Sozialforen in Deutschland'. *Forschungsjournal Neue Soziale Bewegungen* 18(3): 84–90.

Kantner, C. 2004. *Kein modernes Babel: Kommunikative Voraussetzungen europäischer Öffentlichkeit*. Wiesbaden: Verlag für Sozialwissenschaften.

Koopmans, R. and J. Erbe. 2004. 'Towards a European Public Sphere? Vertical and Horizontal Dimensions of Europeanized Political Communication'. *Innovation* 17(2): 97–118.

Leach, D.K. 2005. 'The Iron Law of what again? Conceptualizing Oligarchy across Organizational Forms'. *Sociological Theory* 23(3): 312–337.

Low, S. and N. Smith, eds. 2006. *The Politics of Public Space*. London: Routledge.

Neidhardt, F. 1994. 'Öffentlichkeit, öffentliche Meinung, soziale Bewegungen'. In *Öffentlichkeit, öffentliche Meinung, soziale Bewegungen*, ed. F. Neidhardt, 7–41. Opladen: Westdeutscher Verlag.

———. 2006. 'Europäische Öffentlichkeit als Prozess: Anmerkungen zum Forschungsstand'. In *Europäische Öffentlichkeit und medialer Wandel: Eine transdisziplinäre Perspektive*, eds. W. Langenbucher, M. Latzer and W.R. Langenbucher, 46–61. Wiesbaden: Verlag für Sozialwissenschaften.

Olesen, T. 2005. 'Transnational Publics: New Spaces of Social Movement Activism and the Problem of Global Long-Sightedness'. *Current Sociology* 53(3): 419–440.

———. 2006. '"In the Court of Public Opinion": Transnational Problem Construction in the HIV/AIDS Medicine Access Campaign, 1998–2001'. *International Sociology* 21(1): 5–30.

Patomäki, H. and T. Teivainen. 2004. 'The World Social Forum: An Open Space or a Movement of Movements?' *Theory, Culture & Society* 21(6): 145–154.

Polletta, F. 1999. '"Free Spaces" in Collective Action'. *Theory and Society* 28(1): 1–38.

Reyes, O., et al., eds. 2004. 'The European Social Forum: Debating the Challenges for its Future', (Euromovements Newsletter 1, December 2004). Retrieved 8 August 2007 from http://www.euromovements.info/newsletter/.

Risse, T. 2002. 'Zur Debatte um die (Nicht-) Existenz einer europäischen Öffentlichkeit. Was wir wissen, und wie es zu interpretieren ist'. *Berliner Debatte Initial* 13(5/6): 15–23.

Risse, T. and M. van de Steeg. 2007. *The Emergence of a European Community of Communication: Insights from Empirical Research on the Europeanization of Public Spheres* (Research Report). Utrecht and Berlin, 14 May 2007. Retrieved 5 April 2008 from http://www.atasp.de/downloads/eps_vandesteeg_risse_070513.pdf.

Rucht, D. 1988. 'Themes, Logics, and Arenas of Social Movements: A Structural Approach'. In *From Structure to Action: Comparing Movement Participation across Cultures*, eds. B. Klandermans, H. Kriesi and S.G. Tarrow, 305–329. Greenwich: JAI Press.

————. 1999. 'Linking Organization and Mobilization: Michels's Iron Law of Oligarchy Reconsidered'. *Mobilization* 4(2): 151–169.

————. 2002. 'Transnationale Öffentlichkeiten und Identitäten in neuen sozialen Bewegungen'. In *Transnationale Öffentlichkeiten und Identitäten im 20. Jahrhundert*, eds. H. Kaelble, M. Kirsch and A. Schmidt-Gernig, 227–251. Frankfurt am Main: Campus.

Sifft, S., et al. 2007. 'Segmented Europeanization: Exploring the Legitimacy of the European Union from a Public Discourse Perspective'. *Journal of Common Market Studies* 45(1): 127–155.

Snow, D.A. and R.D. Benford. 1988. 'Ideology, Frame Resonance and Participant Mobilization'. In *From Structure to Action: Comparing Movement Participation across Cultures*, B. Klandermans, H. Kriesi and S.G. Tarrow, 197–217. Greenwich: JAI Press.

Stamm, K.-H. 1988. *Alternative Öffentlichkeit: Die Erfahrungsproduktion neuer sozialer Bewegungen*. Frankfurt am Main: Campus.

Strydom, P. 2001. 'The Problem of Triple Contingency in Habermas'. *Sociological Theory* 19(2): 165–186.

Thörn, H. 2007. 'Social Movements, the Media and the Emergence of a Global Public Sphere: From Anti-Apartheid to Global Justice'. *Current Sociology* 55(6): 896–918.

Tönnies, F. 1922. *Kritik der öffentlichen Meinung*. Berlin: Julius Springer.

Trenz, H.-J. 2004. '"Quo vadis Europe?" Quality Newspapers Struggling for European Unity'. *One EU—Many Publics?, Stirling, 5–6 February 2004*. Retrieved 26 September 2006 from http://www.arena.uio.no/cidel/WorkshopStirling/PaperTrenz.pdf.

van de Steeg, M. 2002. 'Rethinking the Conditions for a Public Sphere in the European Union'. *European Journal of Social Theory* 5(4): 499–519.

Wallerstein, I. 2004. 'The Dilemmas of Open Space: The Future of the WSF'. *International Social Science Journal* 56(182): 629–637.

Wischermann, U. 2003. *Frauenbewegungen und Öffentlichkeiten um 1900: Netzwerke – Gegenöffentlichkeiten – Protestinszenierungen*. Königstein/Taunus: Helmer.

Chapter Four

Exploring Cosmopolitan and Critical Europeanist Discourses in the ESF Process as a Transnational Public Space

Nicole Doerr

Introduction

Genoa, July 2003: a meeting of activists in the arena of a public theatre. The air is full of voices and lively discussions in different languages. Activists from Europe's global justice movement (GJM) have returned to the place where the demonstrations against the G8 summit took place in 2001. In Genoa, they will discuss the future of 'another Europe' and the organisation of the second European Social Forum (ESF) in Paris. This is one of the many European Preparatory Assemblies (European Assemblies) for the ESF. Activists have travelled to participate in this meeting from places as distant as Moscow and Lisbon, Sofia and Stockholm, Glasgow and Istanbul. Hanna[1] from Attac Sweden is one of the few participants who have come from Scandinavia. She notes that:

> There is a space, but a space without a place. There are networks. It's a new place but the same scene for the same people. And I live a lot of my life inside.... That's the process, finding out who we are. ... It should be an arena but sometimes it has body-aspects. Anybody can come here.[2]

Here, Hanna talks about her experiences when participating in the preparatory process for the ESF and its transnational preparatory assemblies. Since the beginning of the ESF process, European Assemblies have taken place in various cities across Europe. The fact that she describes the European Assemblies as 'a space, but a space without a place' and an emerging transnational lifeworld for activists like herself ('I live a lot of my life inside') reveals the unfinished and open character of transnational network meetings in the ESF process. Considering that the participants in such novel transnational meetings still search for a collective identity ('That's the process, finding out who we are'), can we understand the European Assemblies as being part of the new 'proto-cosmopolitan public spheres' (Nash 2007: 56; see also Bell 2007: 3) initiated by social movements that provide room for the practice of democracy beyond the nation state?

This question is the starting point of this chapter: to what extent can the ESF process be considered as one of the new types of emerging 'transnational public spheres' (Fraser 2007:21) in which global struggles for democracy find their regional expression in the context of 'post-Westphalian states' as represented in the European Union (ibid.; della Porta 2009)? Against the background of a democratic deficit of EU institutions, there is a growing awareness of the political relevance of transnational public debates to include social movements (della Porta and Caiani 2007). As specified within deliberative and discursive theories on the public sphere, the presence of small, non-bureaucratically organised grassroots actors within social movements lies at the very heart of the question of a democratic public sphere in Europe (Habermas 1989; della Porta 2005a; Eder and Kantner 2000). However, there is little visibility of these groups in transnational media debates on the EU (Koopmans and Zimmermann 2004), and also legislative debates and institutional citizen arenas fail to include non-institutional actors in the deliberations on the future of the EU (see, for instance, Galligan and Clavero 2009; Kohler-Koch and Altides 2009; Wodak and Wright 2006). While much attention has been directed toward the mass media level of the public sphere and institutional arenas of deliberation, 'emerging transnational public spheres' within the internet and in face-to-face meetings of activists have been widely neglected (della Porta and Caiani 2009). The empirical analysis of public spheres emerging within movements could, to fill this gap, reveal details about processes of transnational identity formation and discursive practices of citizens' critical participation in EU politics 'from below' (della Porta et al. 2006; see also Olesen 2005; Doerr 2009; Mattoni 2009; chapter 3 in this volume). It is in exactly these new types of transnational public spheres that theorists of the public sphere hope to find 'solidarity that is built communicatively, across nation-states, linking various local events with the identification of a global system of injustice, namely neoliberal globalizing capitalism' (Bell 2007: 2; Fraser 2007). The case study presented in this chapter is used to bring together the recent critical thinking on emerging transnational public spheres as laboratories of democracy (Fraser 2007) with a 'bottom up' approach to European integration as seen from a social movements' perspective (see della Porta and Caiani 2009; Imig and Tarrow 2001; chapter 5 in this volume). To assess the democratic potential of the ESF process as a transnational public space, two aspects will be explored: the discursive constructions of 'another Europe' based on experiences and practices of radical democracy in the European Assemblies, and exclusionary moments alongside prevailing nationalist and material boundaries.

Case Study: Studying the Discourse on 'Another Europe' within the ESF Process

The idea of the social forum, namely, to build a public space at the transnational level where a radical democratic discourse on 'another Europe' finds a place, is of particular interest for the study of democracy, citizenship and participation in the broader context of the crisis of representative democracy and the democratic deficit of EU institutions (Manin 1995; Pizzorno 2001; Soysal 2001; Nanz 2006). Which kind of 'collective sentiments', cosmopolitan and tolerant patterns of global citizenship and activism (della Porta 2005a) or 'conceptions of Europeanness' (Schlesinger 2003: 21), develop in this diverse setting? What are the concrete empirically observable boundaries of participation in transnational public spaces for those who lack resources such as time, institutional funding (chapter 1 in this volume) and information, or for those who do not have an active command of foreign languages (Doerr 2009)?

Guided by these questions, this chapter will retrace the discourse of 'another Europe' in time and space, based on the experiences, discussions and narratives of activists in the transnationally travelling European Assemblies. Nancy Fraser has proposed, as a normative point of departure for assessing democracy and access to transnational public spheres, the 'all-affected principle' (Fraser 2007: 21). It holds that in a public sphere at the transnational level, 'what turns a collection of people into fellow members of a public is not shared citizenship, but their co-imbrication in a common set of structures and/or institutions that affect their lives' (Fraser 2007: 22).[3]

Emerging from the grassroots and being open to both citizens and denizens, individuals or group members who want to participate and who embrace the Porto Alegre Charter of Principles[4], the ESF process seems to be a case in point to explore the structurally unfinished open and hybrid features of participation, belonging and affectedness in transnational public spheres. On the one side, Europe and the EU[5] represent important reference points for the activists who created the ESF process under the slogan 'another Europe is possible' (della Porta 2005a). On the other side, the social forum concept emerged through practices of democracy at the global level, in Porto Alegre in February 2001, where activists held the first World Social Forum (Smith et al. 2007). Even if the origin of the GJM dates back earlier (see Rucht 2002a), Porto Alegre remains one of the foundational moments inspiring activists in Europe. This case study explores how activists frame the content of the double global and European discourse that scholars have conceptualised in the notions of 'deep-rooted cosmopolitans' (see Tarrow 2005: 43) or 'critical Europeanists' (della Porta 2005a; della Porta et al. 2006; chapter 5 in this volume). Both activists and scholars have cautioned against a possibly inherent Eurocentric bias and the problem of translatability of democracy in hybrid interaction sites beyond the nation state (Boéri 2006;

Doerr 2009). Transnational discourse practices require 'competent reflexive actors, engaging in demanding performances which do not presuppose understanding but take understanding as a rare and happy moment in a series of permanent misunderstandings' (Eder 2008: 16). Therefore, feminist discourse theorists and social movement scholars have urged researchers to empirically explore the inclusivity of (transnational) deliberative arenas (Young 2000, Fraser 2007; della Porta 2005b).

With a focus on both the mechanisms of inclusion and exclusion in transnational publics (Fraser 2007: 21–22), this analysis gives a central place to the voices of the (non-professional) grassroots activists among participants in the ESF process and those with scarce material resources such as non-Western European participants and migrants (Andretta and Doerr 2007). The experiences and discourses on 'another Europe' by these groups will be confronted with the conceptions of the relatively 'privileged' professional activists who organise the ESF events and the European Assemblies (Andretta and Reiter 2009; Maeckelbergh 2009). Different perspectives of these groups will be explored in the search of converging and diverging impressions, expectations and claims on democracy in the European Assemblies and the ESF process.

The discourses in the European Assemblies meetings constituting the political and social meaning of 'another Europe' are analysed combining a variety of different methods (i.e., triangulation, see Cicourel 1974). Gathering and analysis of data combined a survey, in-depth interviews, participant observation and Critical Discourse Analysis. First, the activists' perceptions of the practices of deliberative discussion, participation and accessibility in the European Assemblies were analysed using a survey and in-depth interviews among European Assemblies organisers and participants. Second, these data were complemented by the analysis of actual communicative practices in the assemblies. Both the survey (n: 100) and the qualitative in-depth interviews (n: 80) are based on a balanced sample, maintaining an equilibrium between activists' political orientation, organisational background, gender, nationality, time of participation and age. The questionnaires were distributed in preparatory meetings for the ESF taking place at both the European and national level (in Germany, Italy and the UK). Qualitative semi-standardised interviews were conducted with participants in the meetings under study, by approaching most interviewees to do face-to-face interviews in the breaks and social gatherings associated to the meetings. To explore experiences of inclusion and exclusion within a transnational public space such as the ESF process, the framework for the case study in this chapter is borrowed from Critical Discourse Analysis (CDA). CDA is a method of discourse analysis developed to explore the social context of deliberative arenas at the European or national levels in which culturally specific speech styles or (gendered) languages may be valorised and others devaluated (cf. Wodak 1996; Wodak and Wright 2006). In this case study, CDA was applied to explore the discursive interactions between the (often informally powerful) organisers and facilitators of the European Assemblies from Western Europe and other participants such as grassroots activists and members of resource-poor groups present in these meetings (cf. Doerr 2007). Discursive interactions were reconstructed using field notes of occurrences during the European Assemblies and transcripts of the discussions within the sessions. Discourse and communication of the European Assemblies were studied in eight meetings taking place from 2003 to 2006.

The European Assemblies – Transnationally Travelling Preparatory Meetings within the ESF Process

European Assemblies take place in different countries and occur several times each year.[6] These meetings represent a public space at the micro-level reflecting the spontaneous, informal and intercultural multi-level structure of the GJM in Europe (cf. della Porta et al. 2006). As an organisational microcosm, the institutionalisation of regular European Assemblies is novel and shows the proliferation of transnational exchange and the most recent opening of communication and participation to a wide number of grassroots activists (cf. Rucht 2002b). From a multi-level perspective, the European Assemblies represent a 'stage' at the regional level between national or local social forums on the one side, and the WSF process and the International Council (cf. Haeringer 2007; Smith et al. 2007) on the other.

A first interesting feature of the European Assemblies' cosmopolitan appeal is their transnational travelling. European Assemblies take place in EU countries and outside 'EUrope' including Turkish and Ukrainian host cities such as Istanbul and Kiev. The fact that the European Assemblies are rotating from one country to another reflects the organisers' wish for geographic diversity and the structural lack of resources. Through rotation, the financial weight of the ESF and its preparatory meetings is shared among different groups and hosts. Whether grassroots activists from different places are able to join the 'open space' that organisers wish to create within the European Assemblies depends on the venues for the meetings as well as their organisation. Regarding the first aspect, the venues for the meetings were chosen dependent on the political, ideological and financial backgrounds of the hosts. Reflecting the diversity of the involved movements and the resources available, the meetings studied took place in large assembly halls of parties' or unions' buildings[7] or in ideologically more 'neutral' public buildings such as the mentioned theatre in Genoa (July 2003). The hosts of the European Assemblies are mostly traditional left unions and parties (cf. Andretta and Reiter 2009). The second aspect influencing whether resource poor groups and grassroots activists could effectively access and participate in the European Assemblies varied strongly. Participation was encouraged or inhibited depending on the local context and the hosts' dealing with organisational matters. As an example, the European Assemblies studied varied considerably in their degree of openness toward activists who lacked resources or came from the *mouvements de sans* (i.e., movements of people without legal documentation, lodging and occupation).[8]

Discourses on 'Another Europe' – An Emancipatory Space for Social Learning?

A preliminary result with regard to the political motivation of activists' partici-pation in the ESF process arises from the evidence in the survey. Participants in the European Assemblies were neither euro-enthusiasts, nor eurosceptics. They saw 'another Europe' as the concrete local learning process and shared transna-tional experience made within a series of counter-summits and meetings in the GJM. Asked to describe their political concerns and engagement in the social forum process, participants within the European Assemblies and national pre-paratory assemblies seemed to be interested in global rather than in European politics: 77 per cent said their interest in global politics was 'very high', while interest accorded to European politics was lower (66 per cent). This is a very in-teresting finding: it confirms the emergence of multiple, tolerant identifications in the GJM (cf. della Porta 2005a). The struggle for 'another Europe' in the ESF process does not necessarily absorb activists' struggle for global justice. The sur-vey also indicates that participants increased their sensitivity toward the political struggles and problems in other countries through their experience of participa-tion in transnational preparatory meetings and ESF summits. When asked in the questionnaires about the effects that participation in the ESF process had for their own political interest and engagement, more than half of the respondents[9] (53 per cent) said that their 'sensitivity for the problems and political struggles in other countries' had increased through participation in the ESF process, while only 31 per cent stated that their political interest for European politics had gained an increased importance.

These results can be further contextualised by looking at the use of the no-tion 'another Europe' within public speech during the European Assemblies. As this concept was the official shared slogan for the ESF, it is interesting to trace back whether and to what extent this concept gained political meaning, attach-ment or critique for participants, dependent on their background. It is assumed that activists in the European Assemblies make sense of the idea of 'another Europe' in their personal stories and accounts that may 'reach out' or strategi-cally perform particular collective identities toward deliberative audiences (see Polletta 2006). Interestingly, the analysis of discourse in plenary assemblies in-dicates that activists mentioned the concept of 'another Europe' particularly in such moments in which conflict had emerged (e.g., when they were discussing the distribution of resources or the legitimate rules of working together). Using the concept within deliberations seemed to be a strategy to re-create solidarity among participants and at the same time make claims on behalf of specific issues or concerns. As will be explored in the following section, the mentioning of 'another Europe' related to the broader global inspirational sources of the GJM occurred also as a normative appeal to democratise the ESF process and to reveal internal contradictions between the ideal of an open, effectively inclusive space and the practice of discourse.

The findings from the interviews indicate that participants, independent of their national background, framed their experience of the European Assemblies in terms of learning and developing a kind of progressive 'critical Europeanism', beyond the limited version of 'Europeanisation from above' proposed by EU member states, as well as distinct (or different) from populist euroscepticism (cf. chapter 5 in this volume). To explore this ambivalence, the impressions of non-EU citizens among the participants are particularly interesting. These activists, who had to travel the longest distances to European Assemblies – often times with fewer resources – saw the ESF process as an important arena to reach and to exchange ideas with Western European progressive movements. The following account of a Turkish activist illustrates the intermingling of experiences of cosmopolitan solidarity in the European GJM with a rejection of top-down EU politics:

> I got affected by the Seattle process and then tried to organise demonstrations in parallel to the protests against the Prague summit of the WTO. I organised a small Turkish participation from Istanbul to Genoa.... Florence was marvelous and fantastic for all 40 of us from Turkey. Unbelievable. It was the first time in Europe for me and there were thousands of people in the Fortezza di Basso. 60,000 people. We attended a meeting with 5,000 people, incredible for all of us. With Susan George. The ESF process for me is learning. The first we learnt was what a social forum is. Then the slogans and the habits and the customs. We took them for our own policies in Turkey. ... Turkey is not seen as a European country. I still believe that each country in Europe is seen as a model for social rights and democracy, living standard. But on the other side there are the rulers like Berlusconi, Blair, their horrible policies.[10]

Here, as in other interviews with activists from non-Western European countries, the positively associated experience of learning through exchange with people from other countries is related to participation in the first ESF that took place in Florence in 2002. The starting point of the narrative, however, is 'Seattle', which relates to the globalist inspiration and experiences within the GJM that acquire a central political meaning for the interviewee. In this vein, the ESF process gains a subjective meaning as embedded in a multi-layered construction of global activism referring also to global protest events (Seattle, Prague) and intellectuals (Susan George). The findings of the interviews thereby reflect a socialisation process (cf. McAdam 1988: 51)[11] in which the idea of another, progressive Europe 'becomes real' and is related to the experiences of participation in transnational assemblies and protest events with people from many countries. In many of the interviews, this personal dimension is represented in narratives of counter-summits that symbolically give expression to participants' belief in the idea of 'another' community of communication and collective solidarity beyond the nation state. As a counter-narrative to official European integration, 'another Europe' is discursively constructed through personal experiences activists made through participation in the symbolically important places of protest summits and social forum events such as Genoa, Florence, Évian, Prague, London or Paris.

In the interview quoted above, 'another Europe' is thus associated to 'the people' in contrast to European political leaders (referring to 'rulers like Berlusconi, Blair, their horrible policies'). Interestingly enough, where non-EU citizens together with EU citizens participate in the European Assemblies, their narratives reflect a 'critical Europeanist' inspiration of protest. The narrative that the above interview constructs on Europe and the EU converges with the critical though pro-European framing that researchers also observed among global justice activists in Western Europe (see della Porta 2005a; della Porta et al. 2006). However, the activist sees herself as distant from 'Europe'. Discursively, this is derived from the outside-ascription of 'belonging', the fact that 'Turkey is not seen as a European country'. Where these activists, like their Western European colleagues, target EU policy-making on concrete policy goals, such as 'social rights and democracy', while rejecting official EU policy-making, their activism indeed gives an expression of the 'proto-cosmopolitan', and yet open and unfinished opportunities of participation in transnational publics (cf. Fraser 2007).

Furthermore, activists perceive their own participation in the European Assemblies as a supplementary window of opportunity (see Keck and Sikkink 1998) to build a new politics beyond the division of the left in a national political context. This was not only the case in countries such as the UK, where divides in the social forum process at the national level were particular virulent (Rootes and Saunders 2005; Kavada 2007; Doerr 2009). Activists from other countries also believed that the transnational level of the social forum process is an important signifier of solidarity beyond the nation state. Similarly to the above quoted activist from Turkey, a long-term participant in the European Assemblies points to the effect of a deliberative learning process that the ESF process engendered also in the place-specific context of Italy:

I think that we here in Italy are in a completely new process. We have to leave the political language of the nineteenth century. There is an emerging post-national subject, a new innovative process, a critique of the separatism of politics, or representative democracy and delegation, the demand for participative forms of democracy, of the facilitation of self-organisation, which leads to practices beyond the old separatist politics.[12]

In the view of many of the interviewed European Assemblies participants, the European layer of their activism represents a layer added to national, regional, local or, like in the quote from the above interviewee, multiple ideological identifications and political struggles. The identification with Europe takes place as a *bricolage* of multiple overlapping identifications (see Risse 2004) occurring in occasions of cross-fertilisation in transnational meetings (see della Porta and Mosca 2007). Consider, for example, the following interview with an activist from the Euromarches against unemployment, who was among the long-term participants of the European Assemblies:

> We founded the network against unemployment at the European level eight years ago, with the Euromarches against unemployment. We are a community; we have eaten together, we went together to the summits. … Some of us have learnt a new language and sometimes we communicate with hand and foot. The marching together creates our common feeling, the activity. … It started in 1997 with the march from Frankfurt/Oder to Amsterdam. … A bicycle tour, smaller marches. That unites, to be together, these collective experiences, and, also in daily life, not only marching. This accumulated for years creates communality.[13]

This extract illustrates two themes found in many interviews with long-time participants in the international ESF coordination. Activists report on the micro-mechanisms that occurred within socialisation in the social forum process: firstly, an important aspect that makes the emerging community of communication 'real' at the European level is its individual resonance and continuation in 'daily life' (see Favell 2008). After the common experience of participation in a transnational march, activists continue their exchange, probably via e-mail. Secondly, these experiences and slowly growing personal networks of people with an interest in politics facilitated people's engagement at the European level. The participant observation in this case study indicates that informal, personal networks indeed may have a very pragmatic organisational function to compensate for lacking material means: very often non-professional activists who participated in the European Assemblies, for instance, activists from local social forums or migrants networks, helped each other with free accommodation and inexpensive transport.

While all of these impressions indicate that the discourse on 'another Europe' and engagement in the European Assemblies emerged as an open-ended signifier that adds to multiple local, regional, national and rooted-cosmopolitan backgrounds, I will explore internal tensions and processes of exclusion within the European Assemblies and the discourses and narratives on 'another Europe' related to the (broader) meaning of global justice in the following section.

Limits of a Proto-cosmopolitan Public Space and the Problem of Exclusion

The findings up to this point indicate that a novel kind of discursive transnational community was effectively emerging in the European Assemblies. However, as will be argued in the following, parts of those who felt part of the 'imagined' transnational discursive community were effectively excluded from participating in the organisation of the ESF process and in the practice of decision-making that happened in the European Assemblies. The results gathered through participant observation, discourse analysis and interviews show that the European Assemblies remained structurally difficult to access for those who lacked material resources. Participant observation and the analysis of discussion in the meetings show that the facilitators within the European Assemblies represented host organisations financially supporting the ESF. They were mainly coming from Western Europe. Groups from Turkey or Central and Eastern Europe who were proposing themselves as hosts for the European Assemblies or the ESF reported little interest by their colleagues from Western Europe.[14] Interestingly, the former groups did not lack the material means or local mobilisation to host an ESF, but seemed to perceive a lack of recognition by their Western colleagues despite their long-lasting participation in the ESF preparatory process. Participant observation provides evidence for a subtle Eurocentric bias reflected in hidden internal hierarchies and struggles over power between different groups and individuals in the ESF process: in plenary sessions of the European Assemblies, these tensions coincided with organisational hierarchies in the chairing and facilitation of meetings and, partly also within the discursive setting. Firstly, if not in all situations in plenary discussions, it was particularly in strategically important moments within decision-making in which the unequal power relations among participants (dependent on various factors such as prestige, membership in transnational networks or organisational power) reproduced in the speech time and frequency of speaking turns allowed by facilitators. Secondly, the opportunities of participants to facilitate a session were distributed unequally. Central and Eastern European participants as well as activists from radically democratic, anarchist or autonomist groups and the local level of social forums hardly ever adopted this role.

The interviews and the survey show that the majority of the interviewees perceived the difficult geographic and material accessibility of the meetings to be the most crucial obstacle to internal democracy. Within the survey, activists participating in preparatory meetings at the national level were asked to specify all problems that restricted their participation in the European Assemblies. Several answers were possible. In the survey responses, 60 per cent of the respondents answered 'lacking financial resources and lacking time' as an obstacle to participation, followed by a 'lack of information' (24 per cent), with a comparatively smaller relevance of 'linguistic communication problems' (8 per cent) (Doerr 2009). When interpreting the findings, a potential non-response bias (see Klandermans and Smith 2002: 22) has to be considered because the respondents belonged to the most actively involved preparatory groups of the ESF (i.e., participants who were regularly participating in (national) preparatory assemblies of the ESF process).

To contextualise these results, a look at those interviewees who were not regularly participating in European meetings is needed. The interviews with participants in local social forums and other grassroots activists who were participating in European assemblies only occasionally show that high external hurdles of access implicitly lead to a perceived lack of legitimacy of the European Assemblies at the grassroots. Certainly, the initiators of the ESF process and organisers of European Assemblies continuously tried to balance material and gender inequalities between participants, for instance, through providing a solidarity funding for activists who lacked resources and introducing a parity rule for speakers in the assemblies (Doerr 2007). However, another challenge goes back to the diversity in organizational cultures and understandings of democracy (della Porta 2005b) that created a constant potential of misunderstandings and conflict in the pluralist European Assemblies. A participant from a local social forum said in an interview:

> I am an addict of the social forum process. The beauty in it is that you don't have to agree on everything. If it works, it can proceed across the boundaries that have always divided the European left. People have to grasp the concept of an open space, then it works. But here, within the preparatory meetings, people think they have to fight whose concept is best.[15]

The perceived conflict potential of varying understandings of democracy in the European Assemblies, as discussed by the interviewee, became a problem as soon as resources, for instance, the solidarity fund for Central Eastern Europeans and other materially less privileged participants, were distributed in an ad hoc manner or in a way that privileged certain groups.

Many grassroots activists also experienced the novel transnational setting as an incentive to reflect their own local cultures of organizing and practicing democracy with regard to the enlarged multi-level character of the social forum process:

> Some have the impression that the space is occupied by party connections. Decisions are made in the process, in an informal way. In the corridors, somewhere. … There is a lot of lack of transparency. But I come to appreciate the way it works. If we would make it more transparently we would lose the decentralised way. Though it should be more transparent. It should not be representative. Perhaps it has even more of a convergent strategy. 'We' need to have political discussions of what our priorities are.[16]

The above interview extract illustrates the ambiguities that participants reflect on with regard to mechanisms of exclusion and inclusion. European Assemblies are considered a hybrid institutional form that serves groups as an 'open space' for joint discussion *and* as an arena for decision-making that tends to be dominated by particular groups. Participants identify an organisational dilemma between strategic decision-making in the preparation of larger social forum events and the normative appeal of an open, deliberative space (cf. Whitaker 2004). However, it seems all the more interesting that a part of the grassroots activists, like the interviewee, coming from local groups or horizontal networks, perceived the European Assemblies as an inspiring space for transnational networking ('But I come to appreciate the way it works'). More studies indicate that the European Assemblies were perceived as a relatively more transparent, less dominated and more pluralist deliberative space than national social forum arenas in countries such as the UK or Germany (see, for instance, Maeckelbergh 2009; Doerr 2009; cf. Kavada 2007). A pattern to understand this is given by the comparatively high awareness of European Assemblies organisers and facilitators for the existing limitations of their discourse practices and their attempts to learn to work together more inclusively, which was (critically) supported by other groups of horizontal activists or activist interpreters (see, for instance, Boéri and Hodkinson 2004). To quote an interview from a facilitator who was part of the ESF organising committee from 2003 to 2006:

> For me, [another Europe] means that we French learn to break out of our belief in universalism, our 'universalist ghetto', to enlarge, to look elsewhere, to widen us. In [the first ESF in] Florence, we learnt that consensus is a process. Then, in Paris we fought for the inclusion of migrant organisations in the ESF, quite successfully, with a solidarity fund, for an enlargement of the groups so that the people who live in the *banlieue* and those from immigrant organisations were well included. After Paris this practice of inclusion unfortunately was falling into sleep again. The big organisations stopped giving money to pay migrant organisations the trip to participate in the European meetings. We have to get ordinary people included.[17]

The statement of this member of the organising committee of the ESF 2003, a long-standing European Assemblies facilitator, exposes a self-critical attachment to the making of 'another Europe' in the discourse practice of the ESF process. Similar to interviews with participants who were not an active part of the organisation, this insider also frames Europe as a learning process. Here, the ESF leads to the 'widening', the 'enlargement' of the national identity trying to 'break out of our "universalist" ghetto'. Interestingly, for the insiders, the attempt to build the ESF process as a transnational community of communication leads to the attempt to include different groups with less resources and ordinary people (e.g., the mentioned 'migrant organisations' and people from the *banlieue*). Yet, the narrative of enlargement implicitly seems to construct these groups as the 'Other' – as people and migrants located at the domestic level and yet conceived as different from the self. Considered the material asymmetries and mechanisms of exclusion observed and reflected equally in the above interview, it however remains an open question as to what extent these various constructed 'others' were effectively getting included within the open space of the European Assemblies.

Another Europe and Emancipatory Struggles for Inclusion within the ESF

As a matter of fact, both interviews and participant observation show that different disadvantaged groups were less present in the European Assemblies and participated less frequently. As a first cluster of groups, Central and Eastern European activists, migrants and Turkish participants effectively had the most material difficulties accessing meetings due to their lack of resources (Andretta and Doerr 2007). Secondly, radically democratic groups with fewer members, individuals from local social forums, anarchist, autonomist and other groups in Western Europe also had difficulties affording regular participation in European meetings (Doerr 2007; Haug 2007). A participant in the European Assemblies from the Istanbul Social Forum, who belonged to the former cluster of groups, describes activists' attempts to participate in European Assemblies and the difficulties they experienced as follows:

> I try to integrate in the European preparatory process, but it is difficult. This discussion here is not equally good for all. There is a hierarchy between the big countries, Germany and France, they count here. They are not interested in the problems we have here in Istanbul. They would not at all understand anything here. The local people from Istanbul, the poor, the women we work with will not get integrated here. ... They say we belong to Europe, but somehow this is not true. Yes, but we are different. We have different types of problems. Very different kinds

of problem, like poverty. Here is a hierarchy between the Europeans and us.[18]

The 'difference' that this interviewee perceives has to be contextualised within the discursive setting of the European Assemblies in general, and the assembly that took place in Istanbul in September 2005 in particular. In this distinct European Assembly in Istanbul, a few speakers, all experienced activists within the ESF process and coming from some Western European countries, presented their ideas as proposals by 'the Europeans'. Certainly, public statements such as 'the Europeans have decided' in the European Assembly in Istanbul can be contextualised as a double positioning of the ESF organisers to protect their proposals agreed upon in previous European Assemblies against the constant attacks and attempts of infiltration by Trotskyites and other extreme left parties to change the rules and strengthen the proposals of political parties informally active in the European Assemblies. Other local and Western European grassroots activists, however, perceived this wording as an 'exclusive framing'. Criticism against the exclusion of these groups came up not only in the Istanbul preparatory assembly, but also in several European Assemblies taking place in Paris, London or Berlin. Extracts from a group interview with several Western European local social forum activists after a European Assembly in Paris 2003 illustrate this:

> Interviewee 1: Today the Eastern countries have been completely ignored in what concerns the money, the long distances to participate in the meetings and the choice of the dates in which the decisions in this ESF preparatory meeting take place.
>
> Interviewee 2: In particular England! In terms of including them and making some steps towards them, if already they choose to do the next ESF in the UK.
>
> Interviewee 1: There is a podium which does not communicate with each other.
>
> Interviewee 2: My impression is that this is an assembly of people who know each other. It is the vanguard of the movement. They resemble each other in their political interests and opinions and their bureaucratic meetings in backrooms. But what happens is something else, because they can no longer decide in backrooms. They are divided, that is good.[19]

The extract from the group interview reflects the critical position of grassroots activists who were, by the time of the interview, getting involved in the internal organisation of the ESF. In this conversational interview, the ESF process is criticized for its 'vanguard' setting of 'people who know each other', 'bureaucrats' who are paid functionaries from trade unions or parties and who exclude 'the Eastern countries' as well as other non 'professional' activists. Interestingly though, the European process of the ESF with its transnational meetings brings with it at least some transgression: in the words of the second interviewee, 'they can no longer decide in backrooms' and 'They are divided'. More evidence confirms that particularly young interviewees with a 'horizontal' background were highly aware of the non-democratic decision-making processes in the European Assemblies. These activists were potential allies for those (non-EU) participants who lacked the money and the time to participate in all of the European Assemblies. The latter groups developed a number of tactics to struggle against (discursive and factual) exclusion, and they also developed their own enlarged 'critical Europeanist' viewpoint on what a public forum for 'another Europe' should look like.

For this, the evidence from interviews with migrants, Central and Eastern European, Kurdish and Turkish activists show two different related discursive strategies used to fight for equal recognition attached to the idea of 'another Europe': a first strategy of positioning in relation to the perceived exclusive discourse structure in European Assemblies, particularly of newcomers among this cluster of groups, was critical frame enlargement. We observe a critical frame enlargement when activists question the social setting of the European Assemblies perceived as unfair and exclusive without, however, rejecting the shared frame of 'another Europe' as such. In the interviews with newcomers, this strategy of critical frame enlargement manifested in a radical rejection of the undemocratic setting of meetings through the invoking of another, more inclusive vision of the concept of 'another Europe'. This is illustrated by an extract of an interview with an activist from Bulgaria after a decision within the European Assembly meeting in Paris in September 2003 that this newcomer perceived as unfair:

> This wasn't a 'European' assembly! Neither was this a consensus decision. It was not O.K. Many people have been simply overheard and ignored, not only those from Eastern Europe, but also from other delegations. There are a small number of people who have the power. They come from France, Italy, Great Britain and Greece. They make the decisions.[20]

According to the perception of the interviewee, the 'other Europe' that is represented in a hegemonic decision-making in the European Assemblies has not yet reached its full emancipatory potential of 'another' politics. On the contrary, in many ways it constructs boundaries between those 'who have' and those who 'have not'.

A second discursive strategy could be noticed among activists who had participated more than once in the European Assemblies, as a way to struggle for the effective inclusion of their groups. These activists, seeing the European Assemblies as a window of opportunity, tried to integrate or adapt themselves to the experienced power asymmetries in the European Assemblies for the sake of progress that they associated to the idea of 'another Europe' as a social transformative project for their own groups or networks. They used this notion by acting as brokers to struggle for an inclusion of groups that were not yet present or not sufficiently 'heard' when making claims in the European meetings. The latter strategy of discursive brokerage could be found both in the interviews with activists of the second generation of migrants living in Western Europe and with those non-EU citizens who had previously participated in transnational protest events of the GJM. An interview with a young activist from the Istanbul Social Forum illustrates this:

> This is not my first European preparatory assembly, so I see that the problem with a part of Turkish activists here is also that they victimize themselves. They don't see that it doesn't help if they tell everybody how many years they spent in prison if they want to get recognised as equals in the ESF process. ... On the other side there is a complete misunderstanding from the side of the so-called 'Europeans', including the Turkish elite people here. They see Turkey as if they lived in London. ... We all fight neoliberalism, but they come from the centre and we live in the periphery. However, this is an important opportunity for us.[21]

The comment of this activist reveals the challenges, but also the opportunities of the particular complex and interdependent transnational arena in the ESF process. The activist is conscious of the strong cleavage between what is framed here as 'centre' and 'periphery'. However, the activist takes a mitigated position on this, criticising Turkish activists who tell stories about European integration in front of the European Assembly in which they 'victimize themselves'. Her own (critical, reflexive) narrative of the European Assemblies also points at the change occurring through the ESF as a transnational arena: there are Turkish and Kurdish participants such as second generation migrants who are considered to become politically important mediators within the ESF process, the group to which the woman from Istanbul refers to as 'Turkish elite people'. This latter group is seen to be in-between the 'periphery' and the 'centre' and takes an interesting position of brokerage. The evidence from interviews and participant observation show that it was particularly women (migrants of the second generation or with transnational life trajectories) who were involved in a struggle for equal recognition for their groups in the European Assemblies and who took an important role also in the broader ESF process as part of the various networks of brokers for linguistic inclusion, gender equality and democratisation of the European Assemblies (see Doerr 2007, 2008). Another interview with a young Turkish migrant living in Germany illustrates the limits and difficulties in the political struggle for inclusion by these brokers:

> My proposals are rather not considered in meetings. For instance in the European preparatory meeting in Berlin I proposed together with

the Istanbul Social forum to host the next big ESF in Istanbul in 2004 or 2005, including finances, which would have been provided there. This proposal was completely ignored by the organisers of the European preparatory meeting. The French were very dominant in this preparatory meeting in Berlin in spring 2003. ... Then Kurdish speakers were a posteriori cancelled from the list of speakers between two meetings. I had to quarrel with the facilitator from the French Organisation Committee to put them on the list again.[22]

The above interview reflects the interviewee's experience with the 'other' side of power and decision-making in the transnational space of the European Assemblies: this activist – for some reason, maybe as an outsider to the influential 'national delegations' in the ESF process – was not heard. At first, the activist's proposals were 'ignored', though the interviewee does not give up and 'quarrel(s) with the facilitator from the French Organisation Committee' to put Kurdish speakers 'on the list again'. Such narratives by interviewees reflect the feature of constant learning and long-term political struggles for discursive inclusion of traditionally less advantaged groups that were not only observable in the European Assemblies, but also in other network meetings at the regional level of the GJM (Doerr 2008). The framing that interviewees used also reveals that the category of the nation state continues to play a role in the European Assemblies, where some national groups ('The French') are perceived as 'dominant' compared to others. And this ultimately points to the limits of the emancipatory discourse of 'another Europe' in the ESF process, reflecting the prevailing importance of what has been described as the possibly inherent nationalist limits of proto-cosmopolitan public spheres and progressive global activism (see Fraser 2007).

Conclusions

By departing from the concerns about the democratic deficit of the European Union, this chapter has tried to construct a bridge between critical social theories examining the transnationalisation of public sphere and social movement studies. It has explored the European experience of the global democracy initiative started in the WSF by looking at the role of 'new, emerging transnational public spheres' within the ESF. This empirical case study has asked to what extent the European Assemblies preparing the ESF event represent a 'proto-cosmopolitan' public space in which those, who are effectively affected and want to protest against patterns of neoliberal globalisation, may find a forum to express their claims and participate in deliberations on 'another Europe'.

From a meso-perspective on democracy and participation in the GJM, the findings give a complex picture of inclusion and exclusion at the European level. The fine-grained analysis of discourse, participation and stories about collective identifications in the European Assemblies shows that the abstract concept of 'another Europe' is filled with lively experiences of participation in a hybrid transnational 'space without a place'. The 'other Europe' that activists in the GJM are fighting for emerges in reflexive personal stories about participants' experiences and learning processes in 'other places' of European integration. Symbolic dates and places of the ESF process such as 'Genoa', 'Florence' or 'Paris' are explicitly defined in critical distance to the institutional context of the EU and associated to 'the people' of Europe, in opposition to 'the rulers'. However, the paradox of participation in the European Assemblies is their ambivalent inclusionary and exclusionary boundaries of discourse practice as manifested in personal narratives and identification. The findings show that many activists, independent of their origin, were identifying with the double idea of another world and another Europe. They acquired multiple and limited 'critical Europeanist' identifications within the GJM (see chapter 5 in this volume). The irony, however, lies in the fact that it was only a part of them, mostly Western European activists working for big social movement organisations, NGOs or political parties, who could afford participating in the European Assemblies on a long-term basis.

In the comparative perspective, it should be noted that the organisers of transnational meetings such as the European Assemblies have made important efforts to tackle a part of the ideological, gendered or informational hierarchies of discourse observable within social forum arenas at the national level, and they have been critically supported by activist-interpreters as far as the challenge of multi-lingualism is concerned (see, for instance, Boéri 2006; Doerr 2008). Nevertheless, transnational public spaces, due to their geographic and political boundaries, in many ways reflect the structural inequalities and trans-cultural discursive hierarchies within neoliberal globalisation that activists are fighting against.

There is, firstly, the relevant external aspect of exclusion limiting the open accessibility of the preparatory assemblies to the ESF due to lacking or unequally distributed resources or organisation (see Bédoyan, Van Aelst and Walgrave 2004). Secondly, the results have also illustrated that exclusion occurred within the discourse structure of the meetings, where less privileged activists in the context of a continuing thinking alongside 'national delegations' and 'vertical' participatory boundaries of discourse and decision-making found it difficult to get their claims included. Note that both (horizontal) Western European activists and migrants, Central and Eastern European, Kurdish and Turkish were critical about the cultural and material limits of discourse in the European Assemblies. This case study found two interesting tactics of these groups to struggle for effective inclusion. Firstly, a critical enlargement strategy, where the assembly of the European Assemblies is framed, particularly by newcomers or young (horizontal) activists as an incomplete project and activists imagine their own political struggle or conception of 'another Europe' beyond the limitations of the European Assemblies. Secondly, more experienced activists such as second generation migrants participating in the European Assemblies, tried to reach an effective inclusion through a continuous political brokerage for groups that were not present initially within these meetings.

Notes

The author would like to thank Simon Teune for his comments and ideas regarding this chapter.

1. The names of the activists are changed in order to ensure anonymity.
2. Interview, Genoa, July 2003.
3. As a proposal to assess democratic communication and discourse in transnational public spheres Fraser assumes that 'For any given problem, accordingly, the relevant public should match the reach of those life-conditioning structures whose effects are at issue' (Fraser 2007: 22).
4. See the Porto Alegre Charter of Principles (World Social Forum 2001).
5. The terms 'Europe' and the 'European public sphere' are considered as essentially contested political concepts without clear-cut geographical or political boundaries that allow for a multiplicity of interpretations.
6. See, for instance, Maeckelbergh 2009; Doerr 2005, 2007; Andretta and Doerr 2007; Haug 2007; Kavada 2007.
7. E.g., the European Assemblies studied in Berlin (June 2003) and Frankfurt (November 2006).
8. While in most cases meetings were open and there was a partly flexible entrance fee to pay dependent on the organisational and financial background of activists, in the case of an European Assembly taking place in London high entrance fees and security controls made it difficult for the 'have-nots' to access the meeting.
9. I.e., participants in preparatory meetings at both national and European levels.
10. Interview with an activist from the Coordination Global Peace and Justice of the Social Forum Turkey, Assembly for the Charter of Principles of Another Europe, Florence, November 2005.
11. I derive the concept of socialisation from Doug McAdam who defines socialisation as a process of transformation in which people's ideas and interests change over different stages through participation in activism, for instance, from occasional apolitical attitudes to strong political commitment (McAdam 1988:51). I assume that in the European Assemblies and the ESF process, socialisation took place as a process of collective learning in a participative democracy setting in which the ideas and interests of the participants were positively attached to the idea of another Europe in the social forums, adding to the activists' pre-existing place specific, national and ideological backgrounds.
12. Interview with an activist from Transform, Florence, Assembly for the Charter of Principles of Another Europe, November 2005.
13. Interview with an activist from Euromarches, Social Forum in Germany, Erfurt, July 2005.
14. Result of the interviews.
15. Interview with a participant from Attac Sweden, Istanbul, September 2005.
16. Interview with a participant from a local Attac network, European Assembly, Genoa, July 2003.

17. Interview with an ESF organiser from FSU/ Attac France, Florence, November 2005.
18. Interview with an activist from Istanbul Social Forum within the European Assembly, Istanbul, September 2005.
19. Interview with two activists from the Irish Social forum (interviewee 1), and the organisation team of the ESF (interviewee 2). Interview conducted after the European Assembly, Paris Bobigny, September 2003.
20. Interview with a participant from Bulgaria after the European Assembly, Paris Bobigny, September 2003.
21. Interview with an activist from an organisation for poor people's housing, conducted after the European Assembly, Istanbul, September 2005.
22. Interview with an activist from a network of Kurdish migrants, conducted in the context of the European Assembly, Berlin, June 2003.

References

Andretta, M. and H. Reiter. 2009. 'Parties, Unions and Movements. The European Left and the ESF'. In *Another Europe: Conceptions and Practices of Democracy in the European Social Forums,* ed. D. della Porta, 173–203. London: Routledge.

Andretta, M. and N. Doerr. 2007. 'Imagining Europe: Internal and External Non-State Actors at the European Crossroads'. *European Foreign Affairs Review* 12(3): 385–400.

Bédoyan I., P. Van Aelst and S. Walgrave. 2004. 'Limitations and Possibilities of Transnational Mobilization: The Case of EU Summit Protesters in Brussels, 2001'. *Mobilization* 9(1): 39–54.

Bell, V. 2007. 'The Potential of an "Unfolding Constellation": Imagining Fraser's Transnational Public Sphere Theory'. *Culture and Society* 24(4): 1–5.

Boéri, J. 2006. 'The role of Babels in the ESF in London 2004'. *Alternative Futures and Popular Protest,* Manchester, 19–21 April 2006.

Boéri, J. and S. Hodkinson. 2004. 'Babels and the Politics of Language at the Hearth of Social Forum'. *Euromovements Newsletter,* December 2004. Retrieved 1 January 2007 from http://www.euromovements.info/newsletter/babel.htm.

Cicourel, A. 1974. *Methode und Messung in der Soziologie.* Frankfurt: Suhrkamp.

della Porta, D. 2005a. 'Multiple Belongings, Tolerant Identities, and the Construction of "Another Politics": Between the European Social Forum and the Local Social Fora'. In *Transnational Protest and Global Activism,* eds. D. della Porta and S. G. Tarrow, 175–202. Lanham: Rowman and Littlefield.

———. 2005b. 'Deliberation in Movement: Why and How to Study Deliberative Democracy and Social Movements'. *Acta Politica* (40)3: 336–350.

———. 2009. "Social Movements and Multilevel Governance: The External Dimension of Democracy". In *Democracy in Social Movements,* ed. D. della Porta, 100–126, Houndsmill, Palgrave.

———, ed. 2007. *The Global Justice Movement. Cross-national and Transnational Perspectives.* Boulder: Paradigm.

della Porta, D. et al. 2006. *Globalization from below: Transnational Activists and Protest Networks.* Minneapolis: University of Minnesota Press.

della Porta, D. and M. Caiani. 2007. 'Europeanization from below? Social Movements and Europe'. *Mobilization* 12(1): 1–20.

—————. 2009. *Social Movements and Europeanization*. Oxford: Oxford University Press.

della Porta, D. and L. Mosca. 2007. 'In movimento: "Contamination" in Action and the Italian Global Justice Movement'. *Global Networks* 7(1): 1–27.

Doerr, N. 2005. 'Sprache ist nicht das Problem: Die Sozialforen als Testfall für eine zukünftige europäische Öffentlichkeit'. *Berliner Debatte Initial* 16(4): 93–105.

—————. 2007. 'Is "another" Public Space actually Possible? Deliberative Democracy and the Case of "Women Without" in the European Social Forum Process'. *Journal of International Women's Studies* 8(3): 71–87.

—————. 2008. 'Deliberative Discussion, Language, and Efficiency in the WSF Process'. *Mobilization* 13(4): 395–410.

—————. 2009. 'Language and Democracy in Movement. Multilingualism and the Case of the European Social Forum Process'. *Social Movement Studies* 8(2): 149–165.

Eder, K. and C. Kantner. 2000. 'Transnationale Resonanzstrukturen in Europa. Eine Kritik der Rede vom Öffentlichkeitsdefizit'. In *Die Europäisierung nationaler Gesellschaften (Kölner Zeitschrift für Soziologie und Sozialpsychologie* supplement 40), ed. M. Bach, 306–331. Wiesbaden: Westdeutscher Verlag.

Galligan Y. and S. Clavero. 2009. 'The Quality of Gender Democracy in the European Union: A Study of Two Legislative Processes'. *First European Conference on Politics and Gender,* Belfast, 22–23 January 2009.

Favell, A. 2008. *Eurostars and Eurocities: Free Movement and Mobility in an Integrating Europe*. Oxford: Blackwell.

Fraser, N. 2007. 'Transnationalizing the Public Sphere – On the Legitimacy and Efficacy of Public Opinion in a Post-Westphalian World'. *Theory, Culture and Society* 24(4): 7–30.

Habermas, J. 1989. 'Volkssouveränität als Verfahren: Ein normativer Begriff von Öffentlichkeit'. *Merkur* 43(6): 465–477.

Haeringer, N. 2007. 'Participating in the Social Forums' Process – Plasticity, Cohesion and Democracy of an Open Space'. *ECPR Joint Sessions of Workshops,* Helsinki, 7–12 May 2007.

Haug, C. 2007. 'Meta-Democracy? Practices of Public Decision-Making in the Preparatory Process for the European Social Forum 2006'. *ECPR Joint Sessions of Workshops,* Helsinki, 7–12 May 2007.

Imig, D.R. and S.G. Tarrow, eds. 2001. *Contentious Europeans: Protest and Politics in an Emerging Polity*. Lanham: Rowman and Littlefield.

Kavada, A. 2007. 'The "Horizontals" and the "Verticals": Competing Communicative Logics in the 2004 European Social Forum'. *ECPR General Conference,* Pisa, 6–8 September 2007.

Keck, M.E. and K. Sikkink. 1998. *Activists beyond Borders: Advocacy Networks in International Politics*. New York: Cornell University Press.

Klandermans, B. and J. Smith. 2002. 'Survey Research: a Case for Comparative Designs'. In *Methods in Social Movement Research,* eds. B. Klandermans and S. Staggenborg, 3–43. Minneapolis: University of Minnesota Press.

Kohler-Koch, B., and C. Altides. 2009. 'Bringing Civil Society in: The European Union and the Rise of Representative Democracy'. *Multi-level Accountability via Civil Society Associations?* Florence, 13–14 March 2009.

Koopmans, R. and A. Zimmermann. 2003. *Internet: A New Potential for European Political Communication?* Discussion Paper SP IV 2003-402, Social Science Research

Center, Berlin. Retrieved 1 January 2008 from http://skylla.wz-berlin.de/pdf/2003/iv03-402.pdf.

Maeckelbergh, M. 2009. *The Will of the Many. How the Alterglobalisation Movement is Changing the Face of Democracy*. London: Pluto.

Manin, B. 1995. *Principes du gouvernement representative*. Paris: Flammarion.

Mattoni, A. 2009. 'Organisation, Mobilisation and Identity. National and Transnational Grassroots Campaigns between Face-to-face and Computer-mediated Communication'. In *Political Campaigns on the Web*, eds. S. Baringhorst, V. Kneip and J. Niesyto, 199–232. Bielefeld: Transcript.

McAdam, D. 1988. *Freedom Summer*. Oxford: Oxford University Press.

Nanz, P. 2006. *Europolis: Constitutional Patriotism beyond the Nation State*. Manchester: Manchester University Press.

Nash, K. 2007. 'Transnationalizing the Public Sphere – Critique and Critical Possibilities'. *Theory, Culture and Society* 24(4): 53–57.

Olesen, T. 2005. 'Transnational Publics: New Spaces of Social Movement Activism and the Problem of Global Long-Sightedness'. *Current Sociology* 53(3): 419–440.

Pizzorno, A. 2001. 'Natura della disugualianza, potere politico e potere privato nella società in via di globalizzazione'. *Stato e Mercato* 2(62): 201–236.

Polletta, F. 2006. *It Was Like a Fever: Storytelling in Protest and Politics*. Chicago: Chicago University Press.

Risse, T. 2004. 'European Institutions and Identity Change: What Have We Learned?' In *Transnational Identities: Becoming European in the EU*, eds. R.K. Herrmann, T. Risse and M. Brewer, 247–271. Lanham: Rowman and Littlefield.

Rootes, C. and C. Saunders. 2005. '*The Global Justice Movement in Britain. Demos Working Paper No. 2/2005*'. N.p. On the Demos project see (http://demos.iue.it).

Rucht, D. 2002a. 'The EU as a Target of Political Mobilization: Is there a Europeanization of Conflict?' In *L'action collective en Europe*, eds. R. Balme and D. Chabanet, 163–194. Paris: Presses de Sciences Po.

———. 2002b. 'Transnationale Öffentlichkeiten und Identitäten in neuen sozialen Bewegungen'. In *Transnationale Öffentlichkeiten und Identitäten im 20. Jahrhundert*, eds. H. Kaelble, M. Kirsch and A. Schmidt-Gernig, 227–251. Frankfurt am Main: Campus.

Smith, J., et al. 2007. *Global Democracy and the World Social Forums*. Boulder: Paradigm.

Soysal, Y. 2001. 'Postnational Citizenship: Reconfiguring the Familiar Terrain'. In *The Blackwell Companion to Political Sociology*, eds. K. Nash and A. Scott, 333–341. Oxford: Blackwell.

Tarrow, S. 2005. *The New Transnational Activism*. Cambridge: Cambridge University Press.

Whitaker, C. 2004. 'The WSF as an Open Space'. In *The World Social Forum: Challenging Empires*, eds. J. Sen et al, 111–121. New Delhi: The Viveka Foundation.

Wodak, R. 1996. *Disorders of Discourse*. London: Longman.

Wodak, R. and S. Wright. 2006. 'The European Union in Cyberspace: Multilingual Democratic Participation in a Virtual Public Sphere?' *Journal of Language and Politics* 5(2): 251–275.

Young, I.M. 2000. *Inclusion and Democracy*. Oxford: Oxford University Press.

Macro-Level

Protest and Societal Systems

Chapter Five

Reinventing Europe
Social Movement Activists as Critical Europeanists

Donatella della Porta

Social Movements and the European Union:
An Introduction

Social movement studies, as other areas of the social sciences, have been late to address the phenomena of Europeanisation, and are still in search of adequate theories, concepts and methods to analyse them. There are several reasons for this. First, not exceptionally, most scholarship has, time and again, confirmed the important role that national political opportunities play in influencing social movement mobilisation, its scope, duration and forms. Protest event analysis time and again indicated that most contentious actions address the national, if not the local level. Second, and again not exceptionally, social movement studies (as well as research on other political actors) considered European institutions as un-welcoming for social movements and similar actors. The democratic deficit of European institutions, the depoliticisation of a 'legitimation by the output', the lack of transparency of the Eurocracies, the constraints (among others, linguistic) on the development of a European public sphere, the lack of a European demos (or, at least, identity): all of these characteristics of EU politics produced, at the best, a very selective integration of a few, 'polite' and tamed civil society organisations, which had to renounce protest in favour of lobbying. On its side, for a long time, research on European integration privileged intergovernmental, neorealist visions that focussed on states as the only actors and on their interests as the only relevant motivations. A regulatory approach to the EU helped keep politics (and social movements) outside of the picture. Additionally, when social movement organisations were perceived as relevant players, they tended to be considered as eurosceptic, fundamentally opposed to EU institutions (often protecting national welfare state and national privileges). This image was especially strengthened when the French electorate blocked the constitutional treaty, and the call for a 'no' vote was made by some influential movement organisations (such as Attac).

As this chapter argues, many social movement activists and organisations are instead *critical Europeanists* – promoting other visions of Europe, but not a return to the nation states, as well as getting involved in multi-level protest. Counter EU-summits as well as European Social Forums (ESF) represented occasions for social movement organisations belonging to different countries, movements and ideological traditions to meet and develop a critique of the actual form of Europeanisation and a vision of 'another Europe' as well as constructing loose organisational networks across borders.

This 'long march' started in Amsterdam, in June 1997, when the coalition European Marches against Unemployment, Job Insecurity and Social Exclusion mobilised 50,000 people from all over Europe to contest the Amsterdam Reform Treaty. Three years later, another important step in European integration, the Treaty of Nice, was met by protest. On 6 December 2000, 80,000 people gathered in Nice, calling for more attention to social issues. The event was called for by an alliance of 30 organisations from all over Europe, including associations of the unemployed, immigrants, environmentalists, feminists and ethnic minorities. In the following days, 'street parties' were staged by peaceful demonstrators, while street battles involved the more radical groups and the police. In June 2001, the protest escalated in Gothenburg, where tens of thousands marched 'For another Europe', contesting yet another EU summit, while a Reclaim the City party escalated in street battles that ended up with three demonstrators heavily wounded by police bullets. In the following year, three EU summits were met by protest. On 14 to 16 March 2002, three days of protest targeted the EU summit in Barcelona, whose main focus was market liberalisation and labour flexibility. On Saturday, 16 March, 300,000 people followed the slogan 'Against a Europe of capital, another Europe is possible', marching from Placa de Catalunya to the Mediterranean harbour front in the largest demonstration against EU policies. Initially called by the Confederation of European Trade Unions, with representatives from the 15 EU countries, the event was joined by new unions, environmentalists, anarchists and independentists, anti-capitalists and different civil society organisations. Protesters called for full employment and social rights against free market globalisation (Timms 2003: 399). A few months later, on the occasion of the EU summit held in Seville on 20 to 22 June, a counter-summit mobilised about 200,000 people, marching 'against the Europe of capital and war' (Timms 2003: 402). Six months later, in Copenhagen, the Initiative for a different Europe (a coalition of 59 Europe grassroots movement organisations, social and students' organisations, trade unions and left wing political parties from all over Europe) protested against a Europe that 'does not like democracy'. Activists asked for a Europe without privatisation, social exclusion, unemployment, racism and environmental destruction, calling for a right to free movement and dissent (Timms 2003: 410).

Side-by-side with the counter-summits, ESFs brought together thousands of groups and tens of thousands of activists in open spaces for encounters among civil society organisations and citizens. Using the example of the World Social Forum (WSF), which had started to meet in January 2001 in Porto Alegre,[1] the European activists imported the idea of constructing arenas for discussion that were not immediately oriented to action and decisions (Schoenleitner 2003; Rucht 2005: 294–295). Since 2001, social forums were organised also at the macro-regional, national and local level. Among them, the ESF played an important role in the elaboration of activists' attitudes toward the European Union, as well as the formation of a European identity. The first ESF took place in Florence on 6 to 9 November 2002. Notwithstanding the tensions before the meeting,[2] the ESF in Florence was a success. Not only was there not a single act of violence, but also participation went beyond the most optimistic expectations. As many as 60,000 participants – more than three times the expected number – attended the 30 plenary conferences, 160 seminars and 180 workshops that were organised at the Fortezza da Basso; even more attended the 75 cultural events in various parts of the city. About one million participated in the march that closed the forum. More than 20,000 delegates of 426 associations arrived from 105 countries – among others, 24 buses from Barcelona, a special train from France and another one from Austria, and a special ship from Greece. Up to four hundred interpreters worked without charge in order to ensure simultaneous translations. A year later, as many as a thousand Florentines and 3,000 activists from the rest of Italy went to Paris for the second ESF.

Since 2002, activists have met yearly in ESFs to debate Europeanisation and its limits. The second ESF in Paris in 2003 involved up to 60,000 individual participants, 1,800 groups, 270 seminars, 260 working groups and 55 plenary sessions (with about 1,500 participants each). Three hundred organisations, among them 70 unions, signed the call. Some three thousand volunteers and 1,000 interpreters made the event possible. According to the organisers, 150,000 participated in the final march. The third ESF, in London in 2004, involved about 25,000 participants and 2,500 speakers in 150 seminars, 220 working groups and 30 plenary sessions, as well as up to 100,000 participants at the final march. The fourth one in Athens in 2006 included 278 seminars and workshops, plus 104 cultural activities listed in the official program, 35,000 registered participants and up to 80,000 at the final march.[3]

The success of the ESF is the result of networking between groups and individuals with, at least, partly different identities. The multi-form composition of the Global Justice Movement (GJM) is reflected in a differentiated attention paid to how 'globalisation' affects human rights, gender issues, immigrant conditions, peace and ecology. However, the different streams converged on their demands for social justice and 'democracy from below' as the dominant interpretative scheme recomposing the fragments of distinct cultures. Both a multi-level public intervention aimed at reducing inequalities produced by the market and the search for a new democracy are in fact the central themes of the emerging European movement.

As we are going to see in this chapter, during these events, a European social movement emerged and developed ideas for 'another Europe'. In what follows, I am going to look at the ESFs as emerging structures of a European social movement, which is made up of loosely coupled networks of networks of activists endowed with multiple associational memberships and experiences, who embrace various forms of political participation (part 2). Looking at the frames and discourses of these activists, as well as their organisations, I shall discuss the development of a form of 'critical Europeanism', which is fundamentally different from the populist euroscepticism on which research focussed in the past (part 3). As we shall discuss in the conclusions, protestors expressed strong criticism of the forms of European integration, but no hostility to the building of supra-national European identities and institutions. They can therefore be seen as a critical social capital for the emerging of a European polity.

The European Social Forums: the Organisational Dimension[4]

The common basic feature of the social forum is the conception of an open and inclusive public space. Participation is open to all civil society groups, with the exception of those advocating racist ideas and those using terrorist means, as well as political parties as such. The charter of the WSF defines it as an 'open meeting place'.[5] Its functioning, with hundreds of workshops and dozens of conferences (with invited experts), testifies for the importance given, at least in principle, to knowledge. In fact, the WSF has been defined as 'a market place for (sometime competing) causes and an "ideas fair" for exchanging information, ideas and experiences horizontally' (Schoenleitner 2003: 140). In the words of one of its organisers, the WSFs promote exchanges in order 'to think more broadly and to construct together a more ample perspective' (Schoenleitner 2003: 141).

The ESF is, however, also a space of networking and mobilisation. The spokesperson of the Genoa Social Forum (who organised the anti-G8 protest in 2001), Vittorio Agnoletto, describes the ESF as a 'non-place':

> It is not an academic conference, even though there are professors. It is not a party international, even though are party members and party leaders among the delegates. It is not a federation of NGOs and unions, although they have been the main material organisers of the meetings. The utopian dimension of the forum is in the active and pragmatic testimony that another globalization is possible. (Il manifesto, 12 November 2003)

Activists referred to the ESF as an 'academic seminar' in their comments online. Writing on the ESF in Paris, the sociologists Agrikoliansky and Cardon (2005: 47) stressed its plural nature:

Even if it re-articulates traditional formats of mobilizations, the form of the 'forum' has properties that are innovative enough to consider it as a new entry in the repertoire of collective action. ... An event like the ESF in Paris does not indeed resemble anything already clearly identified. It is not really a conference, even if we find a program, debates and paper-givers. It is not a congress, even if there are tribunes, activists and mots d'ordre. It is not just a demonstration, even if there are marches, oc-cupations and actions in the street. Neither is it a political festival, even if we find stands, leaflets and recreational activities. The social forums concentrate in a unit of time and space such a large diversity of forms of commitment that exhaustive participation to all of them is impossible.

What unifies these different activities is the aim of providing a meeting space for the loosely coupled, huge number of groups that form the archipelagos of the GJM. Its aims include enlarging the number of individuals and groups involved, but also providing a ground for a broader mutual understanding. Far from aim-ing at eliminating differences, the open debates should help increasing aware-ness of each other's concerns and beliefs. The purpose of networking (through debating) was in fact openly stated already in the first ESF in Florence, where the Declaration of the European Social Movements read:

We have come together to strengthen and enlarge our alliances because the construction of another Europe and another world is now urgent. We seek to create a world of equality, social rights and respect for diver-sity, a world in which education, fair jobs, healthcare and housing are rights for all, with the right to consume safe food products produced by farmers and peasants, a world without poverty, without sexism and oppression of women, without racism, and without homophobia. A world that puts people before profits. A world without war. We have come together to discuss alternatives but we must continue to enlarge our networks and to plan the campaigns and struggles that together can make this different future possible. Great movements and struggles have begun across Europe: the European social movements are repre-senting a new and concrete possibility to build up another Europe for another world.

Democracy in the forum is an important issue of discussion, with tensions be-tween different models (horizontal versus vertical) testified for by the different structures present within the forums. In fact, social forums belong to emerging forms of action that stress, by their very nature, plurality and inclusion. Similar forms of protest that favour networking and successively 'contamination' (or cross-fertilisation) are the 'solidarity assemblies', a series of assemblies where multiple and heterogeneous organisations active on similar issues are called to participate with their particular experiences,[6] or, the 'fairs on concrete alternatives' whose aim is to link together various groups presenting alternatives to the market economy, ranging from fair trade to environmental protection (della Porta and Mosca 2007). Degrees of structuration, inclusivity and representation are always at the centre of the discussion about internal democracy.

The networking capacity of counter-summits and social forums is reflected in the overlapping membership of its participants. According to a survey at the first ESF,[7] participants are deep-rooted in dense organisational networks. The activists were well grounded in a web of associations that ranged from Catholic to Green, from voluntary social workers to labour unions, from human rights to women's organisations: 41.5 per cent are or have been members of NGOs, 31.8 per cent of unions, 34.6 per cent of parties, 52.7 per cent of other movements, 57.5 per cent of student groups, 32.1 per cent of squats, 19.3 per cent of religious groups, 43.1 per cent of environmental associations, 51.3 per cent of charities and 50.9 per cent of sport and recreational associations (see della Porta et al. 2006: 47).

While respecting existing differences, participants to the forum share a common set of values. If doubts about the liberalisation of markets and cultural homogenisation are also expressed in religious fundamentalism or conservative protectionism, these expressions of anti-globalisation are not, however, present in the movement, which has a clearly left wing profile. Significantly, activists interviewed at the first ESF in the main defined themselves as 'left' (della Porta et al. 2006: 211), with a large component saying 'extreme left', and limited acceptance of the category 'centre-left'. With the exception of British activists, the great majority of whom were extreme left (67.2 per cent, followed at a distance by the French at 37.1 per cent), placement on the left wing ranges from 44.3 per cent among the Germans to 53.4 per cent of Spaniards and confirmed at around 50 per cent of Italians. This is the background in the various countries for a critique of national governments' policy choices – including left wing governments – as well as of intergovernmental organisations.

Critical Europeanists?[8]

The Declaration of the Assembly of the Movements of the fourth ESF, held in Athens on 7 May 2006, addresses the European Union:

> Although the EU is one of the richest areas of the world, tens of millions of people are living in poverty, either because of mass unemployment or the casualization of labour. The policies of the EU based on the unending extension of competition within and outside Europe constitute an attack on employment, workers and welfare rights, public services, education, the health system and so on. The EU is planning the reduction of workers' wages and employment benefits as well as the gen-

eralization of casualization. We reject this neo-liberal Europe and any efforts to re-launch the rejected Constitutional Treaty; we are fighting for another Europe, a feminist, ecological, open Europe, a Europe of peace, social justice, sustainable life, food sovereignty and solidarity, respecting minorities' rights and the self-determination of peoples.

This statement does not reject the need for a European level of governance, nor the development of a European identity (that goes beyond the borders of the EU), but criticises the EU policies asking for 'another Europe'. It also links different specific concerns within a common image of a feminist, ecological, open, solidary, just Europe. Many issues are indeed bridged in the process of the ESFs, which we shall address here as an illustration of the development of a European social movement. The document approved by the Assembly of the Movements, held at the third ESF, stated:

We are fighting for another Europe. Our mobilizations bring hope of a Europe where job insecurity and unemployment are not part of the agenda. We are fighting for a viable agriculture controlled by the farmers themselves, an agriculture that preserves jobs, and defends the quality of environment and food products as public assets. We want to open Europe to the world, with the right to asylum, free movement of people and citizenship for everyone in the country they live in. We demand real social equality between men and women, and equal pay. Our Europe will respect and promote cultural and linguistic diversity and respect the right of peoples to self-determination and allow all the different peoples of Europe to decide upon their futures democratically. We are struggling for another Europe, which is respectful of workers' rights and guarantees a decent salary and a high level of social protection. We are struggling against any laws that establish insecurity through new ways of subcontracting work.

Similar attitudes are widespread among activists. Previous surveys have indicated that activists internalised the criticism of representative democracy. Among the participants in protest against the G8 in Genoa, trust in representative institutions tended to be low with, however, significant differences regarding the single institutions (see also della Porta et al. 2006: 202). In general, some international organisations (especially the EU and the UN) were seen as more trustworthy than national governments but less so than local bodies. Research on the first ESF confirmed that diffidence in the institutions of representative democracy is cross-nationally spread, although particularly pronounced where national governments were either right wing (Italy and Spain at the time), or perceived as hostile to the GJM's claims (as in the UK). Even national parliaments, supposedly the main instrument of representative democracy, were not trusted, while there was markedly greater trust in local bodies (especially in Italy and France), and, albeit somewhat lower, in the UN. The EU scores a trust level among activists barely higher than national governments (except, in this case, for the more trustful Italians). A low trust in the EU reflects the growing criticism of EU policy and institutions, with a politicisation and polarisation of positions during and after the French referendum on the European constitutional treaty (della Porta and Caiani 2006, 2007). Similar data on the second and the fourth ESF confirm the general mistrust in representative democratic institutions, although with some specification (della Porta 2007a). Among other actors and institutions, we might notice a strongly declining trust in the church and mass media, as well as in the unions in general and a stable (though low) trust in the judiciary and (even lower) in political parties. Instead, activists continue to trust social movements (and less, NGOs) as actors of a democracy from below.

The activists mistrust the EU, which is accused of using competences on market competition and free trade to impose neoliberal economic policy, while the restrictive budgetary policies set by the Maastricht parameters are stigmatised as jeopardising welfare policies. Privatisation of public services and flexibility of labour are criticised as worsening citizens' well-being and job security. Under the slogan 'another Europe is possible', various proposals were tabled at the first ESF, including 'taxation of capital' and, again, the Tobin Tax. Demands were also made for cuts in indirect taxation and assistance for weaker social groups, as well as for a strengthening of public services such as education and health care. At the second ESF, the European Social Consulta stated:

> We have learnt to recognize the strength of coordinated action and the vulnerability of the 'untouchable' organisations of capitalism. We need to deepen our contact and communication with society, decentralizing our struggle and working in local and regional context in a coordinated way with common objectives. ... The European Union is being shaped under the neoliberal politics. The European constitution comes to reinforce it and next year it will be our main goal to fight it.

The constitutional treaty is feared as 'constitutionalisation of neoliberalism'. A participant at the second ESF seminar 'Pour une Europe démocratique, des droits et de la citoyenneté', referring to the constitutional treaty, claims that: 'The first part of the text is similar to a constitution. But the third one, which focuses on the implementation of concrete policies, goes beyond the normal frame of a constitution. It constitutionalizes competition rights. Making rigid the policies to be followed, it takes away from the citizens all possibilities to change the rules. It is an unacceptable practice because it is anti-democratic. Anyway, all changes are made impossible by the need to obtain a unanimous vote by 25 states'. In the third part, the participant states, 'everything is subordinated to competition, including public services, the relations with the DOM-TOM [French overseas territories, DdP], and the capital flow (something that, by the way, makes any Tobin Tax impossible)'.

In particular, the lack of democratic accountability is criticised: 'at the local level we have very low influence in the decision-making process, but our influence becomes null in questions as the European constitution or the directives of the WTO or the IMF. We are even criminalized when we attempt it'. The Women in Development (WIDE) network together with the German Rosa Luxemburg Foundation ask for basic services and goods, such as education, health and water, to be subordinated to democratic decisions, involving the local community. Stating that public services are the bases of fundamental rights, the need to democratise the provision of public services is stressed.

Criticism of conceptions of democracy at the EU level is also addressed toward security policies, with a call for a Europe of freedoms and justice against a Europe 'sécuritaire et policière'. In the first ESF, EU stances in foreign policies are considered as subordinated to the US, environmental issues as dominated by the environmentally unfriendly demands of corporations and migration policy as oriented to build a xenophobic 'fortress Europe'. In the Paris ESF, the construction of a European judicial space is considered as a way to control police power. In particular, EU legislation on terrorism is criticised as criminalising such categories as young, Muslim and refugee. EU immigration policies are defined as obsessed with issues of security and demographic needs. While terrorism is stigmatised, there is a call to 'take a clear stand for international law, including the right of people's to fight occupation', but also to 'defend national sovereignty'. As for the EU foreign policy, there is criticism of the subordination of humanitarian politics and developmental help to commercial and security aims. Instead, the important role of the local population is recognised. Solidarity groups denounce the role or European states and corporations in Haiti, Latin America, Africa and the aggressive EU trade policies, including asymmetric negotiations of commercial treaties. In terms of defence policies, proposals range from 'a Europe without Nato, EU-army and US bases' to multi-lateralism and the refusal of a nuclear Europe. Furthermore, an increase in the resources allocated to the UN is demanded as well as the introduction of an article to the European constitution that 'Europe refuses war as an instrument of conflict'.

Activists present at the various ESFs share these criticisms of EU politics and policies. Interviewees from different countries stated, in fact, that the European Union strengthens neoliberal globalisation. They shared mistrust in the capacity of the EU to mitigate the negative effects of globalisation and to safeguard a different social model of welfare (della Porta et al. 2006: 207). The data from a survey at the demonstration in Rome in 2005 against the EU Bolkestein directive confirm this image (with even stronger disagreement on the capacity of the EU to mitigate the negative consequences of economic globalisation). Italian respondents at the first ESF in Florence expressed greater trust in the EU, and British activists were more eurosceptic (followed by French and Spanish activists). The differences were, however, altogether small. Respondents in Athens confirmed a widely shared scepticism that strengthening the national governments would help to achieve the goals of the movement: only about one-fifth of the activists responded positively (della Porta 2007b).

In general, the movement seems, in fact, aware of the need for supra-national (macro-regional and/or global) institutions of governance. At one of the plenary assemblies of the second edition of the ESF, Italian activist Franco Russo stated: 'There is a real desire of Europe … but not of any Europe. The European citizens ask for a Europe of rights: social, environmental, of peace. But does this Constitution respond to our desire for Europe?' And the representative of the French union federation G10 Solidaires, Pierre Khalfa, declared that the Constitutional treaty 'is a document to be rejected … [but] the discussion of the project is the occasion for a Europe-wide mobilization' (*Liberazione,* 14 November 2003).

The image of 'another Europe' (instead of 'no Europe') is often stressed in the debates. During the second ESF, the Assembly of the Unemployed and Precarious Workers in Struggle stated:

> For the European Union, Europe is only a 'large free-exchange area'.
> We want a Europe based upon democracy, citizenship, equality, peace,
> a job and a revenue to live. Another Europe for another world. … To
> build another Europe imposes to put the democratic transformation
> of institutions at the centre of elaboration and mobilization. We can,
> we should have great political ambition for Europe … *Cessons de subir
> l'Europe: prenons la en mains.*

Unions and other groups active on public services proclaim 'the European level as the pertinent level of resistance', among others against national decisions. The 'No to the Constitutional draft' is combined with demands for a legitimate European constitution, elaborated in a public consultation, 'a European constitution constructed from below'. And many agree that 'the Europe we have to build is a Europe of rights, and participatory democracy is its engine' (http://workspace.fse-esf.org/mem, accessed 20 December 2006). In this vision, 'the European Social Forum constitutes the peoples as constitutional power, the only legitimate power'. In a report on the seminar 'Our vision for the future of Europe', we read:

> Lacking a clear and far reaching vision the EU-governments are stum-
> bling from conference to conference. In this manner the EU will not
> survive the challenges of the upcoming decades! Too many basic prob-
> lems have been avoided for lack of a profound strategic position. In our

vision we outlined an alternative model for the future of Europe. It contains a clear long range positioning for Europe making a clear choice for the improvement of the quality of life for all and for responsible and peaceful development.

Moving from the assessment of existing institutions to the imagined ones, the activists of the first ESF expressed strong interest in the building of new institutions of world governance: 70 per cent of the respondents are quite or very much in favour of this, including strengthening the UN, an option supported by about half of our sample (della Porta et al. 2006: 207). Statistic analyses show that opinions about the strengthening of different institutions are not much influenced by gender, age or occupation (although support for the EU declines among manual workers and employees, trust in Europe and attachment to Europe among unemployed, attachment to Europe again among workers). However, the younger activists and the more educated are more in favour of the building of alternative institutions of world governance. Activists who locate themselves at the radical left are more sceptical about the utility of strengthening the EU as a way to reach the movement's aims (the same applies to the option to strengthen national governments), and are more convinced that the EU strengthens neoliberal globalisation, trust less the EU, and feel less attached to Europe. Significantly, according to the data on the anti-Bolkestein protest in Rome, the belief that the EU strengthens neoliberalism and does not defend the social model is especially widespread among those who work in education and in the third sector.

Moreover, the activists at the first ESF expressed quite a high level of affective identification with Europe: about half of the activists feel a (partly strong) attachment to Europe, with, also in this case, less support from British and Spanish activists and more from French, Germans and Italians. ESFs participants therefore do not seem to be eurosceptics, who want to return to an almighty nation state, but 'critical Europeanists' (or 'critical globalists'), convinced that transnational institutions of governance are necessary, but that they should be built from below.

These positions are in line with the debates in the ESFs. Already in the first ESF in Florence, specific policy proposals for the EU level were made by networks of social movement organisations and NGOs, often already active on specific issues. For instance, the European Assembly of the Unemployed and Precarious Workers in Struggle stressed the importance of developing claims at the EU level (e.g., a minimal salary of 50 per cent of the average revenue); groups involved in the promotion of Esperanto as well as associations from ethnic minorities made proposals for linguistic and cultural rights; the European Social Consult asked to 'strengthen and widen the European social fabric in a network that should be participatory, horizontal and decentralized, as much in the taking of the decisions as in the realizations of actions' (Llana, Fresnillo and Lago 2003). Concrete proposals to improve the quality of democracy were also suggested during the second ESF and Europe remained similarly central at the fourth edition of the forum. Beyond the concrete policy choices, criticism was also addressed at the secretive, top-down ways in which these policies are decided. The Assembly of the third ESF asked, among others, for more participation 'from below' in the construction of 'another Europe':

> At a time when the draft for the European Constitutional treaty is about to be ratified, we must state that the peoples of Europe need to be consulted directly. The draft does not meet our aspirations. This constitutional treaty consecrates neoliberalism as the official doctrine of the EU; it makes competition the basis for European community law, and indeed for all human activity; it completely ignores the objectives of ecologically sustainable society.

A European Social Movement? Some Conclusions

> One can be against a Europe that supports financial markets, and at the same time be in favour of a Europe that, through concerted policies, blocks the way to the violence of those markets. ... Only a social European state would be able to contrast the disaggregative effects of monetary economy: so one can be hostile to a European integration based only upon the Euro, without opposing the political integration of Europe. (Bourdieu 1998: 62)

More and more Europeanised protests address the lack of concerns at the EU level for social equality: they ask, as Bourdieu put it, for a social Europe that can contrast the negative effects of 'a Europe that supports financial markets'. In this sense, they point at a weakness in a European integration that has advanced more by taking away economic borders, than by building new identities. Since its origins, the EU has been a reaction to the weakening of the European nation state in certain key areas: from the military defence of the frontiers to the expansion of markets. As Stefano Bartolini (2002; see also Bartolini 2005) put it, the process of territorial de-differentiation that is at the base of European integration was pushed by the evidences of the intolerable consequences of historical rivalry between the European states as well as the growing risks of an economic marginalisation of Europe in the world economy. The deepening of this process demands, however, the creation of cultural identity and citizenship that can sustain the social sharing of risks and legitimate political decisions (Bartolini 2002). One of the main features in the construction of the nation state – citizens' rights – is, though, still weak at the EU level. The process of European integration advocated primarily economic policy tools. Although these are necessarily linked to social policies, the latter have hardly been a priority at the EU level. The ideology of a regulatory Europe, as legitimised by good performances, appears less and less convincing: producing policies, the EU became a target of claims and protest. In this process, national actors of different types started to address the EU. If those richer in resources have been the first to open headquarters in Brussels, resource-poor actors have also started to network supra-nationally (della Porta and Caiani 2006) and to frame European issues. Vertical integration created horizontal processes that, while legitimising the European institutions by recognising them, also politicised the debate on the EU and contributed to the development of a European public sphere by contesting public decisions (see also chapter 3 and 4 in this volume).

The European movement I have addressed asks for a 'Europe of rights', addressing the fundamental importance of the recognition of citizens' rights for the construction of a polity. Support for Europe emerges therefore as a polymorphic term that refers not only to different processes, but also to different 'Europes'. The social forum process focussed criticism against a certain vision of Europe, but at the same time helped to network at the European level and to frame 'another Europe'. The social movement activists referred to in this chapter appear, in fact, as critical Europeanists, in favour of deeper integration but with policies very different from those that have thus far characterised the 'negative integration' dominant in the EU. In line with the results of other research – departing from an analysis of party positions based on expert evaluations – our data confirms that a call for more attention on environmental, labour and cohesion policies can be bridged with demands for more European integration (Hooghe, Marks and Wilson 2004). Social movement criticisms are in fact directed toward what is perceived as the survival of the prevalently economic nature of European integration, as well as toward an idea of Europe as emphasising Western values. They do not call, however, for a return to the nation state, but for a process of Europeanisation from below.

Although critical of the European institutions, activists promote a European identity through their actions and campaigns. Looking at the frames and discourses of these activists, as well as of those of their organisations, we have observed the development of a form of 'critical Europeanism', which is fundamentally different from the traditional 'nationalist' euroscepticism on which research on Europeanisation has focussed so far. According to our survey data, activists from different countries express strong criticisms of the actual politics and policies of the EU, but they also show a high identification with Europe and a certain degree of support for the European level of governance.

As occurred during the construction of the nation state, the focussing of protests at the national level followed the centralisation of decisional power (Tilly 1978). Social and political actors also moved on multiple territorial levels: alliances with the state builders targeted local governors, but there were also alliances among the periphery against the centre (Tarrow 2005). The construction of the nation state has, however, been a conflictual process: citizens' rights are the results of social struggles (Marshall 1950; Bendix 1964). Democracy emerged with the contestation of public decisions: criticism of national governments contributed to legitimising the state as the main decisional level. Even avoiding pushing too far the parallel between nation building and the construction of peculiar and anomalous supra-national institutions, such as the European Union, our research appears to confirm the development of a 'Europeanisation by contestation'.

Similarly, support for the process of European integration cannot be measured in terms of (more or less permissive) consensus toward the decisions of European institutions. To the contrary, as Thomas Risse (2003) observed, contestation appears as a crucial pre-condition for the emergence of a European public sphere rather than as an indicator for its absence. The more contentious European policies and politics become, the more social mobilisation occurs on European issues, the more likely is the development of truly European public debates. If political issues are not contested, if European politics remain the business of elites, the attention level for Europe and the EU will remain low. European issues must become salient and significant in the various public debates so that a European public sphere can emerge (ibid.).

It is indeed not a silent consensus with the governors that signals a democratic process, but instead a submittal of their decisions to the 'proof of the discussion' (Manin 1995). It is not the agreements upon borders, ideologies and various cleavages, but the public debate about them that indicates the existence of a European public sphere (Habermas 1981; Risse 2003: 6–7).

Notes

I am grateful to Massimiliano Andretta, Manuela Caiani and Lorenzo Mosca for their help with data collection and data analysis.

1. The WSF was held in Porto Alegre (2002 and 2003), Mumbai (2004), Porto Alegre (2005), Caracas, Karachi and Bamako (2006), Nairobi (2007) and substituted by a global day of action in 2008.
2. Centre-right politicians but also many opinion leaders expressed a strong fear of violence in a city considered particularly fragile because of its cultural heritage (as a result they suggested limitations to the right of demonstration in the *città d'arte*).
3. Data on participation are from the entry 'European Social Forum' in Wikipedia (http://en.wikipedia.org/wiki/European _social_forum, accessed 12 July 2008).
4. This part draws upon my introductory chapter in the volume 'Another Europe' (della Porta 2009).
5. http://www.forumsocialmundial.org.br/main.php?id_menu=4&cd_language=2, accessed 12 July 2008.
6. An Italian activist defined these solidarity assemblies as 'a "logistical pot" in which everyone puts their ingredients' (interview 20, in della Porta and Mosca 2007: 3).
7. During the ESF, the Gruppo di Ricerca sull'Azione Collettiva in Europa (GRACE) interviewed 2,384 activists using a semi-structured questionnaire that had been

translated into Italian, French, Spanish, English and German. Questionnaires were distributed randomly at various events at the ESF (for more information see della Porta et al. 2006: ch. 1).

8. This part develops ideas presented in Social Movements and Europeanisation, co-authored with Manuela Caiani (della Porta and Caiani 2009: ch. 4).

References

Agrikoliansky, E. and D. Cardon. 2005. 'Un programme de débats: forum, forms et formats'. In *Radiographie du movement altermondialiste*, eds. E. Agrikoliansky and I. Sommier, 45–74. Paris: La Dispute.

Bartolini, S. 2002. 'Lo stato nazionale e l'integrazione europea: un'agenda di ricerca'. *Quaderni di Scienza Politica* 9(3): 397–414.

———. 2005. *Restructuring Europe*. Oxford: Oxford University Press.

Bendix, R. 1964. *Nation Building and Citizenship*. New York: Wiley & Sons.

Bourdieu, P. 1998. *Acts of Resistance. Against the New Myths of our Time*. Cambridge: Polity Press.

della Porta, D., ed. 2007a. *The Global Justice Movement. Crossnational and Transnational Perspectives*. Boulder: Paradigm Publishers.

———. 2007b. 'Global Activists: Conceptions and Practices of Democracy in the European Social Forums'. *ECPR Joint Sessions of Workshops*, Helsinki, 7–12 May 2007.

———, ed. 2009. *Another Europe: Conceptions and Practices of Democracy in the European Social Forums*. London: Routledge.

della Porta, D., et al. 2006. *Globalisation from below*. Minneapolis: University of Minnesota Press.

della Porta, D. and M. Caiani. 2006. *Quale Europa? Europeizzazione, identità e conflitti*. Bologna: Il Mulino.

———. 2007. 'Europeanization from below? Social Movements and Europe'. *Mobilization*, 12(1): 1–20.

———. 2009. *Social Movements and Europeanization*. Oxford: Oxford University Press.

della Porta, D. and L. Mosca. 2007. 'In movimento: "Contamination" in Action and the Italian Global Justice Movement'. *Global Networks: A journal of transnational affairs* 7(1): 1–28.

Habermas, J. 1981. *Theorie des kommunikativen Handelns*. Frankfurt am Main: Suhrkamp.

Hooghe, L., G. Marks and C.J. Wilson. 2004. 'Does Left/Right Structure Party Position on European Integration?' In *European Integration and Political Conflict*, eds. G. Marks and M.R. Steenbergen, 120–140. Cambridge: Cambridge University Press.

Llana, M., I. Fresnillo and R. Lago. 2003. *Presentation of the Seminar*. Retrieved 12 July 2008 from http://workspace.fse-esf.org/mem/Act2303/doc448.

Manin, B. 1995. *Principes du gouvernement representative*. Paris: Flammarion.

Marshall, T.H. 1950. 'Citizenship and Social Class'. In T.H. Marshall and T. Bottomore, *Citizenship and Social Class*, 3–51. London: Pluto Press.

Risse, T. 2003. 'An Emerging European Public Sphere? Theoretical Clarifications and Empirical Indicators'. *Annual Meeting of the European Union Studies Association*, Nashville, 27–30 March 2003.

Rucht, D. 2005. 'Un movimento di movimenti? Unità e diversità fra le organizzazioni per una giustizia globale'. *Rassegna italiana di sociologia* 46(2): 275–306.

Schoenleitner, G. 2003. 'World Social Forum: Making Another World Possible?' In *Globalising Civic Engagement,* ed. J. Clark, 127–149. London: Earthscan.

Tarrow, S. 2005. *The New Transnational Activism.* Cambridge: Cambridge University Press.

Tilly, C. 1978. *From Mobilization to Revolution.* Reading: Addison-Wesley.

Timms, J. 2003. 'Chronology of Global Civil Society Events'. In *Global Civil Society Yearbook 2003,* eds. M. Kaldor, H. Anheier and M. Glasius, 395–410. Oxford: Oxford University Press.

Chapter Six

Porous Publics and Transnational Mobilisation

Thomas Olesen

Introduction

When people in Denmark speak about the Muhammed cartoons protests in early 2006, they often use the adjective 'hit': Denmark was hit by protests in the Muslim world, by a massive consumer boycott, by international criticism and so on. This way of phrasing the event reflects the shocked surprise that most Danes felt in the hectic period in late January/early February 2006. In a display of anger and protest normally reserved for mightier nations, Danish flags were trampled on, the Prime Minister burned in effigy and official representations attacked and set on fire. All because of twelve satirical cartoons of the prophet Muhammed published months earlier, on 30 September 2005, in *Jyllands-Posten,* a large Danish liberal-right newspaper. That Danes felt hit and under siege, then, is probably understandable. But the 'folk wisdom' of the metaphor is misleading. It depicts the protests, to use another metaphor, as a swarm of meteors crashing through the greenhouse of the Danish public sphere from outer space. What this account misses is the dialectic of the protests. It paints a portrait of simple and unidirectional causality in which the protests are seen as a direct and instant reaction to the cartoons. Regrettably, this folk wisdom also surfaces in many scholarly and journalistic accounts. It is more accurate to analyse the conflict and protests as a dynamic interaction between the national level of Denmark and the world around it. To capture this situation, this chapter employs the twin concepts of the porous public and the transnational dialectic.

In simple form, the theoretical argument offered is this: public spheres undergo important transformations in the process of globalisation, but this should not lead us to conclude that they cease to be national. What should interest us, instead, are two things: how national public spheres are penetrated by issues and information from areas outside it, and how issues and information in national public spheres 'migrate' or are 'lifted out' in a way that ends up affecting politics in other national contexts. This openness in both directions is the defining characteristic of the porous public. Clearly, the two statements are logically connected. We could not have one without the other. It is an observation that actively breaks down the outside-inside dichotomy that permeates much of the current debate on globalisation. The problem has two interrelated dimensions. First, globalisation tends to be viewed as a condition where events in one locale affect events in other locales and vice versa. This definition is on the right track but stops, so to speak, when the fun begins. What it fails to acknowledge is how local or national events do not simply wield influence across space in a unidirectional manner, but how distant events in fact produce each other dialectically.[1] Second, many studies work with a problematic conception of causality in which globalisation is seen as an almost extra-social force that causes things to happen at the local and national level. In contrast, it is proposed that we see globalisation as both cause and outcome of social and political phenomena. These two points place the interaction between the local, national and transnational level at the heart of analysis. The twin concepts of the porous public and the transnational dialectic consequently advocate a definition of globalisation, which does not privilege the national or transnational level of analysis, but rather sees them as mutually constitutive.

What is the relevance of these observations for the study of transnational mobilisation? If the national public sphere is indeed becoming increasingly porous, we are likely to see a growing number of 'scale shifts' (Tarrow 2005). A transnational scale shift occurs when a local or national protest event becomes the centre of attention in distant localities.[2] This is precisely what happened in the Muhammed cartoons protests. The protests were initially confined to the national level in Denmark, but during the following months, they spread to the transnational level. Tarrow also suggests that the scale shift is not always 'upward', but that events at the transnational level can also move in the opposite direction, from the transnational to the local or national. This way of conceptualising the dynamic corresponds well with what was referred to above as the transnational dialectic. But the scale shift model lacks a historical and sociological theory of the public sphere. Because scale shift, at least at the transnational level, presupposes porous publics and what could be termed *communicative visibility*. The latter concept simply suggests that for a scale shift to occur, groups and individuals need to be able to see and hear what is being said and done in other geographical settings than in their own. The extent to which communicative visibility is present at the global level has undergone momentous historical change. To put it more directly: we seem to be getting more and more of it. This development is central to a social (as opposed to an economic) definition of globalisation. It is this broad historical and sociological framework that seems to be missing from the concept of scale shift. This reflects a general problem in the current and constantly expanding literature on transnational mobilisation: the lack of a macro-theoretical and sociological framework that can guide discussions of what transnational mobilisation has to tell us about the current character and direction of our rapidly globalising world. Since the public sphere is a decidedly historical and sociological category, the concept of the porous public developed in this chapter might help establish a more firm sociological foundation for the discussions of transnational mobilisation.

The aim of the chapter is consequently primarily theoretical. The first part of the chapter develops the concepts of the porous public and the transnational dialectic. In the second, the utility of these concepts is illustrated through an analysis of the Muhammed cartoons protests, and, in the third part, the relationship between the porous public concept and that of the transnational public sphere is briefly addressed.

Porosity and Dialectic

To elaborate on the arguments briefly presented in the introduction, this section proceeds through three theoretical steps. First, it elucidates in what way it still makes sense to think of the public sphere as national. It then discusses how this 'nationality' is increasingly shot through with inbound and outbound influences. It concludes with the argument that these opposite influences dialectically constitute each other to produce globalisation.

The National Dimension

Although public spheres rest on the same set of values (at the most basic level, freedom of speech and critique of authority), these values are differently interpreted and practised from one national context to the next. The differences are the result of distinct historical experiences closely linked to the formation of nation states. In fact, the development of the public sphere cannot be separated from the nation state. This is because the public sphere pre-supposes, first, a shared language, and, second, a constitutional status in which a state guarantees the autonomy of the public sphere. Both of these preconditions still apply. Even in our supposedly globalised age, public spheres continue to reflect a shared cultural and language community, which are constitutionally guaranteed by a state. This is perhaps most evident if we look at the media. The essence of the public sphere is debate and communication (Habermas 1962/1989). In the imagined community of the modern public sphere it is the media that create what we might call its communicative infrastructure (Anderson 1983; Taylor 1992). Even a cursory glance at the world's media landscape reveals that the large majority of media are still tied to a specific national and language context. In a similar vein, Koopmans and Erbe's (2004) analysis of the Europeanisation of the German public sphere and media point to the discrepancy between the advanced state of political interaction at the European level and the absence of genuine European media of some importance.

Increasing Porosity

However, this national public sphere is increasingly porous. The adjective 'porous' is preferred because it is theoretically sterile to debate whether the public sphere today is mainly national or transnationalised. The dichotomy is artificial. Historically, the national public sphere has always been subject to external influences. We need only think about the way the European revolutions of the mid nineteenth century became the subject of debate in every public sphere around Europe. The porosity metaphor avoids this dichotomy. Rather than saying that the public sphere is either mainly national or transnational, it suggests that it is both. It is more precise, then, to speak about *degrees of porosity*. This way of thinking about the public sphere enables us to make important distinctions without falling into the dichotomous trap. First, it makes it possible to examine historically how public spheres have generally become increasingly porous over time, and, second, to conceive of contemporary public spheres as porous in varying degrees (for example, the Danish public sphere is more porous than the Iranian counterpart). The degree of porosity can be measured along two interconnected parameters: media and people.

The media, as noted above, constitute the communicative infrastructure of the public sphere. In their analysis of the Europeanisation of the German public sphere, Koopmans and Erbe (2004) focus on the presence of European elements in selected German newspapers. Varying across issues they find a considerable influence of European issues. Importantly, this indicates that national newspapers and news channels today have more transnational orientations and routines than previously. They are increasingly interconnected transnationally through inter-media monitoring (facilitated by online versions), co-operative arrangements and the use of the same sources (press agencies and major transnational news channels) (Holm 2006). This development evidently reflects the process of globalisation in which events outside of the local and national context come to have an ever greater effect on these contexts and therefore attain increasing news value.

While it is true, as stated above, that the majority of media are still directed toward a specific national audience, there has also been a noteworthy growth in the last decades of what we might term *transnational media*. Well-known empirical examples are news channels, such as CNN and BBC World. Even if their headquarters are nationally located, their intended audience is transnational. This transnationality is reflected in the issues they take up (and in the commercials they show!). CNN and BBC World do strive to present a global outlook, but their use of the English language and their anchoring in a Western context restricts significantly the potential audience. However, since the mid 1990s, Western dominance in the area of transnational broadcasting has been challenged by the emergence of Arab-language transnational media such as *Al-Jazeera*, which caters for a broad transnational Arab and Muslim audience (Lynch 2005; Seib 2005).

The national and transnational newspaper and news channel media described above are normally placed under the rubric of mass media. Here, they will be referred to jointly as macro-media. Macro-media are macro in the sense that their news production is aimed at a broad and relatively abstract public audience. One of the major media developments in recent years is the increasing importance and accessibility of what we could call micro-media. Micro-media, as the term suggests, are different from macro-media in that they are more private and direct. They may include a variety of media, such as phone, fax, letters, e-mail, listservs, weblogs, websites and so on. Micro-media, obviously, are not of a kind. Inspired by Diani's (2001) distinction between public and private communication, it is possible to single out three types: phone, fax and letters are mainly used in what we might term private one-to-one communication; e-mail and SMS can be used in this way, but may also be involved in semi-private communication between a sender and an audience connected to that sender through an already established inter-personal network (in some cases the audience is so large that the communication blurs the boundary between public and private; hence the term 'semi-private'); listservs, weblogs and websites, in contrast, are more genuinely public forms of communication in that they are accessible to all.[3] However, because they are often used by individuals or groups who work with different news criteria (and budgets!) than macro-media, they are categorised as micro-media. Importantly, micro-media often blur the distinction between national and transnational, which is more easily made in relation to the macro-media. We might even say that they often dissolve the very distinction: a weblog written in English by an Egyptian may be categorised as 'Egyptian', but its audience will typically be transnational; and a Thai human rights group may maintain a website in both Thai and English and thus communicate simultaneously with national and transnational audiences.

All of these types of media, as summarised in table 6.1, increase the porosity of national public spheres. The distinction allows us to discuss how porosity can differ over time and space. For example, public spheres in the mid nineteenth

Table 6.1. Media and Porosity

	National	*Transnational*
Macromedia	**Box A** National newspapers and news channels with transnational content.	**Box B** News channels catering to a transnational audience.
Micromedia	**Box C** Personal or activist group-based media working on a private, semi-private or public basis (phone, fax, letters, e-mail, listservs, weblogs, websites); typically blur the national-transnational distinction.	

century may have had elements of box A, but not B and C. Similarly, some contemporary states regulate news flows by restricting the accessibility of the media in box B and C. To repeat what was said above, porosity, then, is not a fixed state of affairs. It makes more sense to speak about degrees of porosity and consequently of variations across historical time and between countries.

The porous public is not just about media, macro or micro. The multi-cultural societies that have emerged in Europe in the last 50 years or so also provide a more physical dimension. As a result of increased immigration, most Western European countries (including the Nordic countries, but most notably Sweden and Denmark) have become 'tied' to other countries via personal networks. As demonstrated in the sociological and anthropological literature (see for example Sheffer 2003) on diaspora networks, immigrants and refugees usually maintain a degree of contact with friends and family in their country of origin and consequently come to serve as brokers between this country and their 'new' country. They will have a sense of what goes on in the public sphere of each country and will distribute this information in both directions. This exchange takes place when they travel 'home' or when they receive visitors from the 'old' country. Primarily, however, it happens via the micro-media already described (the distinction made between media and people is thus partly artificial). SMS, mobile telephony, cheap long-distance phone cards and e-mail make it possible to maintain a stable flow of communication across space.

There is another and more cognitive aspect of the people factor that cannot be reduced to multi-culturalism. This is the rather abstract notion of a global consciousness identified by various, usually sociologically inclined, authors as a central element in globalisation processes (e.g., Robertson 1992; Rosenau 1997; Shaw 2000). Rosenau (1997) has couched this discussion in terms of a skill revolution that is taking place in the decades since World War II. What he suggests is that people today are increasingly capable of analysing apparently singular, local and national issues and events in an abstract and transnational context.[4] This development is greatly dependent on media technologies. As demonstrated by Dayan and Katz (1992), the media, especially satellite television, facilitate the creation of shared transnational experiences that become part of people's cognitive reservoirs. This situation radically increases the degree of a public sphere's porosity because people in other settings will be inclined to interpret events within it as relevant in relation to their own social and political realities.

National-Transnational Dynamics

The discussions above have concentrated on identifying conditions that facilitate porosity and have not touched directly on the types of social and political phenomena that these conditions can actually set in motion. In the introduction, it was argued that porosity can only be understood in relation to the concept of the transnational dialectic. The core idea of the porosity concept is precisely to emphasise the simultaneous presence of inbound and outbound influences in the public sphere. These influences constitute each other in a dialectical spiral process whose end result is typically 'more' globalisation. Rather than outbound and inbound arrows, these are consequently better understood as part of the same movement. A theoretical example: something happens in country A involving a citizen from country B. The issue then becomes a theme in the public sphere in country B. This debate, in turn, is closely followed in country A, affecting the public understanding and decisions regarding the problem in this country and so on. Obviously the country A and B example is the simplest possible example. In most cases, numerous public spheres are simultaneously involved and the complexity is correspondingly higher (this dynamic in relation to the Muhammed cartoons protests is illustrated in Figure 6.1 below).

The Muhammed Cartoons Protests[5]

The debate about the Muhammed cartoons was a national Danish issue long before it became a transnationally contested issue. The infamous cartoons were published already on 30 September 2005, but it was not until January and February of the following year that it erupted on a transnational scale. It is not the ambition here to reconstruct how and why this escalation occurred, although some causal claims will be made in the analysis. The aim is rather to describe elements from the case that empirically illustrate the theoretical arguments in the preceding section. In other words, it is not claimed that the elements discussed in the following are what caused the protests to escalate. Porosity, in other words, does not mean that every issue more or less automatically transcends national borders. In fact, due to the continuing national character of public spheres pointed out in the theoretical section, most issues never cross national boundaries. The conditions described below therefore only *facilitate* what Tarrow (2005: ch. 8) calls the externalisation of domestic issues.

In the following, it is argued that the porosity of the Danish public sphere during the cartoons protests was visible in the role played by: (1) transnational news channels; (2) Danish media acting transnationally; (3) non-Danish media acting transnationally; (4) Danes or people living in Denmark with a Muslim background; and, (5) transnationally shared events. The section closes with a discussion of these elements in relation to the concept of the transnational dialectic.

Methodology

The data for the analysis below is drawn from a data set developed elsewhere (Olesen 2007). The set is based on a coding of news items in the Danish centre-left newspaper, *Politiken*. The electronic newspaper archive, *Infomedia*, was used to collect the news items. A wide net was cast by extracting all items containing the search words 'Muhammed' and '*tegninger*' (cartoons). The search period ran from 30 September 2005 when the cartoons were published to 31 March 2006 when protests were on the wane. The search turned up a total of 923 news items. A number of these were not relevant. Removing them reduced the data set to 716. The remaining news items were read and coded to yield information on these questions (inspired by Koopmans 2002): 1) who is making a claim? 2) to whom is the claim addressed? 3) what is the purpose and content of the claim? and 4) how and through what channels is the claim expressed? These questions enable the identification of the central actors and their claims in the protests and let us draw a precise map of the debate surrounding the cartoons. With such a map at hand, it is possible to extract a number of empirical observations allowing us to analytically reflect on porosity and dialectic in the Muhammed cartoons protests.[6]

The choice of source needs some explaining. First, it might be objected that using only one newspaper, *Politiken,* creates a biased view of the issue. The point is valid, but because of its salience, drama and novelty, the cartoons protests received extensive coverage in all Danish newspapers. It is a reasonable assumption, therefore, that any Danish newspaper provides a broad and representative view of public debate on the issue. However, *Politiken* was chosen because it had a critical stance toward *Jyllands-Posten* and the Danish government in its coverage. This, combined with the fact that it is considered a serious newspaper with a large and diverse readership, has resulted in a broad coverage that has given voice to numerous different actors. This broadness is important when we want to use a newspaper to draw a public map of debate on an issue. Second, it may seem odd to base the analysis on one national newspaper and it obviously creates a somewhat national bias in the data selection. Two things justify this choice. First, the analysis is primarily concerned with an analysis of the porosity of the Danish public sphere. Second, since Denmark was at the eye of the storm during the protests, Danish newspapers are where the most extensive coverage is found.

The Porous Public

As mentioned in the theoretical section, the last decade has seen a surge in transnational satellite television channels catering mainly for Muslim audiences. In the Muhammed cartoons protests, the satellite television channels *Al-Jazeera* and *Al-Arabiya* played a pivotal role in the diffusion of the protests. Their ability to reach a large audience and create awareness about the Muhammed cartoons intensified the porosity of the Danish public sphere. What was essentially a national event was exposed on a transnational level. On 1 February 2006, as the protests were gathering full force, Naser Khader, a Lebanon born Danish MP and co-founder of the association *Demokratiske Muslimer* (Democratic Muslims), thus remarked that the protests had escalated when *Al-Jazeera* and *Al-Arabiya* started giving the issue attention on 26 January (Nielsen and Flensburg 2006). The day after, he said, the cartoons were a major theme in Friday prayers in Egypt, Saudi Arabia and Iraq. Khader's observation (though not necessarily his causal inference!) is supported by a search in *Al-Jazeera's* archive, which reveals that the issue was reported only twice prior to 26 January on the channel's website. In the following two weeks, it was reported 36 times. Outside of the Muslim world, news channels also contributed to porosity. A search on CNN's website reveals that the issue only started attracting attention on 2 February, that is, a little later than what was found with *Al-Jazeera*. Of the 51 times the issue is mentioned, 45 date from the period between 2 February and 19 February (CNN 2006). A somewhat similar picture materialises when searching the BBC website, the main difference being that the BBC seemed to be earlier in directing attention to the protests (most likely because of the protests' European angle). Here, the issue was mentioned four times prior to 26 January. In the following fortnight, the number rose to 67 (BBC 2006).

The cartoons protests began with the publication of twelve satirical cartoons of the prophet Muhammed in *Jyllands-Posten,* a liberal daily with a large circulation. When the protests escalated in January/February 2006, the newspaper found itself under heavy cross-fire. Muslims expressed anger at what they saw as blasphemous publications, and non-Muslim politicians, media and organisations criticised it for wilfully insulting Muslim religious sentiments. In terms of porosity, it was rather actors outside of Denmark (including the transnational news channels discussed under point 1) creating porosity by referring to the actions of a Danish newspaper. However, during the protests, *Jyllands-Posten* went from being a passive object of criticism to becoming an active player in the debate. On 30 January, the newspaper issued a statement through the Jordanian news agency in which it apologised for having hurt Muslim sentiments (Ritzau 2006). This statement was also published on the newspaper's website in English and Arabic. The use of websites by national newspapers to communicate with audiences outside of their national context is a novel development, which leads to increasing porosity. The possibilities, of course, are still limited because, as noted in the theoretical section, national newspapers still cater for national language audiences. Porosity via online versions thus requires that texts are translated or that the newspaper's main language has significant global distribution. The upshot of this observation is that some publics are less porous than others as a result of language barriers. For example, online versions of US newspapers will be more widely 'visible' to non-national audiences than, say, Russian online newspapers.

National newspapers and news channels outside of Denmark also contributed to porosity. These can roughly be grouped into two categories: (1) those with a negative position toward *Jyllands-Posten* and the cartoons, and, (2) those with a supportive position. Critical articles, op-eds and commentaries were present in national newspapers and news channels all over the world (but concentrated in Europe and the Muslim world). There is as yet no hard evidence to provide a clear picture of the pattern of this critical coverage (its geographical distribution and concentration, its main claims, its distribution according to newspapers' and news channels' political positions and so on). In relation to supportive coverage, there are, however, some preliminary data that also give us an idea of the general extension of coverage outside of Denmark. Numerous newspapers in Europe, and to a lesser extent in the USA and the Muslim world, provided varying degrees of support for the right of *Jyllands-Posten* to publish the cartoons. According to a survey conducted by the Danish School of Journalism, all or some of *Jyllands-Posten's* cartoons were published in at least 143 newspapers in 56 different countries (eJour 2006; the survey was concluded on 27 February 2006). The majority of these reprints were aimed at supporting the publication, placing the defence of freedom of expression at the heart of the argument. Perhaps the most visible involvement on the part of European newspapers came through a continent-wide and apparently coordinated display of solidarity in late January and early February, which included the publication of the cartoons in a number of European newspapers (Munck 2006). In a telling illustration of the transnational dialectic discussed in the theoretical section, this solidarity display itself became a topic for debate and protests in the involved public spheres and, later, in Denmark. The cartoons were also published in a number of Arab and Muslim countries (see eJour 2006). In many of these cases, the responsible editors and journalists were fired and sued for defamation (see, for example, Al-Khalidi 2006).

Porosity, as argued in the theoretical section, does not only have a mediated dimension; it also has a more physical aspect resulting from the multi-culturalism of many of today's societies. Denmark has a Muslim population of about 200,000 (approximately 3.8 per cent of the total population). This sector of Danish society obviously took a special interest in the cartoons and in many cases came to serve as brokers between Denmark and their countries of origin, relaying information about debates in the Danish public sphere to recipients in other public spheres. This took place on a personal level and through micro-media. Precisely for this reason, we do not have any hard data on the extent of such communication and its importance. The role of Muslims living in Denmark in creating porosity is clearer in some of the more organised and publicly visible attempts to generate awareness. In Denmark, early protest against the cartoons was mainly voiced by *Det Islamiske Trossamfund* (the Islamic Faith Community), an umbrella organisation for Muslims in Denmark. In December 2005, the organisation toured parts of the Arab world, bringing with it material to document what they considered a generally hostile climate for Muslims in Denmark (see 'Delegationens mappe', Politiken, 26 February 2006, for this material). On their tour, the delegation met with Egyptian government and Arab League representatives (Exner 2006). During January, and especially as the protests escalated, the delegation became the target of harsh criticism in Denmark, accused of contributing to the transnationalisation of the protests (Sørensen 2006). The spokesmen of *Det Islamiske Trossamfund* became visible public figures in as well as outside of Denmark and were often used in a brokerage function by non-Danish media, especially those from Arabic countries, to comment on the situation.

The transnationalisation of media and people described earlier reflect a growing global consciousness. There is a dialectical causality at play here. Media become more transnational because of increasing global consciousness (people need and demand more transnational news), but in that very process they also produce more of it, so to speak. This dialectic is important to understand what was referred to in the theoretical section as the cognitive aspects of porosity. In this light, the events on 11 September 2001 (9/11) can be identified as a transnationally shared event that has increased the porosity of national public spheres. In another article on the cartoons protests (Olesen 2007), it is argued that the transnational resonance of the cartoons was partly due to the new world political climate created after 9/11. In terms of porosity, this means that local and national events with a conflictive Muslim aspect are more likely to be 'lifted out' of that context. The events on 9/11 have thus politicised religion, and especially Islam, and provide claims-makers, Muslim as well as non-Muslim, with new opportunities for framing and legitimising claims. In the same article, it was consequently suggested that media, politicians, institutions and corporations were more inclined to politicise the cartoons than they would have done under different conditions; some because they emphasised the need for cross-cultural understanding in a post-9/11 world and others because they were eager to draw a clear line between Western and Muslim conceptions of society and democracy.

The Transnational Dialectic

The concept of porosity is important because it enables a more precise formulation of what has been referred to throughout the chapter as the transnational dialectic. Many, if not most, events and issues emerge at the local and national level and stay there. But once an event, perhaps facilitated by some of the factors discussed above, migrates out of its local or national context to create scale shift and externalisation, it sets in motion a dialectical dynamic that is difficult to control and predict. Stated in a rather unscientific manner, it acquires a life of its own and when it has run its course, it leaves behind social, cultural and political experiences that proceed to shape future events. Viewed in this way, the transnational dialectic is very much an active learning process.

It is probably safe to say that no one predicted the mobilisation of the cartoons protests that occurred during January and February 2006. For a long time during October, November, December and most of January, this meant that the Danish government and media were expecting the smouldering protests quietly to die out. Apparently unaware of the potentially explosive character of the cartoons, both the Danish government and *Jyllands-Posten* adopted a quite unconditional stance toward the first rounds of criticism from actors in and outside of Denmark (these early criticisms came primarily from *Det Islamiske Trossamfund* and from the ambassadors to Denmark of a number of Muslim countries; see Letter from Ambassadors 2005). For many Muslims and non-Muslims concerned with inter-religious and inter-cultural respect (including representatives of international institutions and Western governments), this represented a display of arrogance that fuelled further contention. As anger and frustration began to build up, the Danish government and *Jyllands-Posten* felt forced to change tactics toward at least partial concessions. In late January and early February, statements were issued that expressed regret (but not outright apology) over the effect of the cartoons (conciliatory statements directed to the Muslim world were also issued by Danish corporations, such as Arla, who were beginning to feel the effects of consumer boycotts). While this dampened some groups, others were infuriated by the lack of an unconditional apology. The change of tactics also motivated a heated debate in Denmark on democracy, freedom of speech and the appropriate response by the government and *Jyllands-Posten* to the protests. Domestic politicians, media, corporations and the public were deeply divided on the issue, some calling for an unconditional defence of the freedom of expression and others for greater cross-cultural understanding. The protests, in other words, were coming home to roost and left a lasting mark on Danish politics and society. It seems reasonable to say that the result of the protests has been an increased global consciousness across the spectrum in Danish society, an awareness, to put it banally, that we are not alone in the world. This experience, as briefly discussed in the introduction, may have come rather late to Denmark. Even if Denmark in many respects is a highly globalised society, it has rarely experienced national events to take on such a highly politicised and transnational dimension as in the cartoons protests. Figure 6.1 illustrates the transnational dialectic of the protests.[7]

A Transnational Public Sphere?

The porous public is still a national public, although, as the chapter has sought to demonstrate, one increasingly penetrated by inbound and outbound influences. Even if one accepts this argument, it begs the following question: does the plurality of national porous publics mean that we cannot also speak of a transnational public sphere in the singular? This question cannot be given sufficient attention here, but it is important to at least sketch the theoretical differences between the two concepts.

The two concepts are not mutually exclusive, but rather closely interconnected. Because, to put it banally, porosity enables a situation in which different

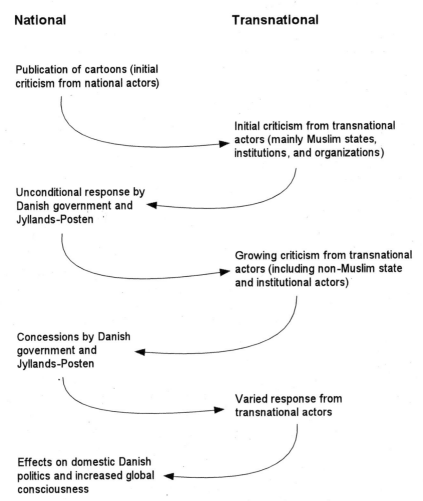

National   **Transnational**

Publication of cartoons (initial criticism from national actors)

Initial criticism from transnational actors (mainly Muslim states, institutions, and organizations)

Unconditional response by Danish government and Jyllands-Posten

Growing criticism from transnational actors (including non-Muslim state and institutional actors)

Concessions by Danish government and Jyllands-Posten

Varied response from transnational actors

Effects on domestic Danish politics and increased global consciousness

Figure 6.1. The Transnational Dialectic in the Muhammed Cartoon Crisis

publics debate the same issues at the same time. When this happens, we can meaningfully speak of a transnational public sphere. To be sure, it is something that only happens relatively rarely on a genuinely transnational scale. The Muhammed cartoons protests are one example of a full-blown transnational public sphere (another example might be the debate and protests surrounding the impending war in Iraq in early 2003). In these situations, the transnational flow of information is significantly concentrated. It does not necessarily mean that there is more information in circulation, but that a large number of people are aware of and are interested in the same issue. In line with what has been said earlier, this flow of information is still to a considerable degree carried by national media. Importantly, this also indicates that a transnational public sphere cannot usefully be conceptualised simply as a national public sphere writ large. The concept of the transnational public sphere does not, in other words, necessarily suggest a situation where the world's people speak directly to each other across geographical and cultural differences or use the same media as sources of information. Of course, there is genuinely cross-national debate, and as discussed earlier, the world is witnessing a growth in transnational news channels, but these forms of information flow and exchange continue to be dwarfed by those that occur in national media and public spheres. To repeat, if it makes sense to speak of a transnational public sphere, it is as a social space created when individuals, organisations, media, politicians and officials at local and national levels around the world, aware of voices in other places, debate the same questions at the same time with reference to the same events, statements and actions. The term 'social space' is a key point in the definition of a transnational public sphere. It suggests that it is a space with no permanence or concrete form or to use Scholte's (2000) term, a 'supraterritorial' phenomenon. The transnational public sphere is not something constantly 'out there', it comes and goes because it always emerges on the back of specific issues that for one reason or the other acquires transnational resonance.

There are many reasons to believe that we will see more examples of an activated transnational public sphere in the future. The conditions that increase the porosity of national public spheres are likely to progress, and since the transnational public sphere, as argued above, is largely a result of national porosity, this phenomenon will tend to become more common. The point is strengthened if we view such developments as active learning processes. Every time the transnational public sphere is activated, it leaves behind a set of experiences that can be drawn on by activists in subsequent episodes. In other words, there is a continual build-up of cognitive, technological and organisational infrastructures that can facilitate future mobilisations.[8]

Conclusion

There are two main implications of the preceding discussion for the study of transnational protest. First, the Muhammed cartoons protests underline the importance of taking seriously the transnational dialectic. One way of doing this is to direct more attention to the way national and transnational dynamics shape each other in instances of protest. From a practical research point of view, of course, dialectical dynamics can be problematic. They make it difficult to propose clear-cut causalities and tend to blur conclusions. This is no excuse. We need to devise more sophisticated theoretical and methodological tools that can help us to analyse such processes with scientific rigor. Second, the community of transnational mobilisation scholars should confront the sociological challenge more directly than they do at present. The study of transnational mobilisation has many insights to contribute to those broad sociological debates that want to say something about the kind of societies in which we live today. To mention just one example, Ulrich Beck's (2005) recent work is deeply inspired by transnational mobilisation and activism. He could certainly benefit from some of the fine-grained theoretical tools developed in social movement theory, but it is also evident that many transnational mobilisation scholars could find important inspiration in his work to engage in broader sociological and intellectual debates about transnational mobilisation and globalisation. One of the strengths of the social movement field (something that is also reflected in the study of transnational mobilisation) is its anchoring in a political science/political sociology tradition that rewards empirical analysis and theoretical and methodological rigor. But there is also a tendency to professional parochialism in this tradition: we study mobilisation and provide detailed accounts of it, but we often fail to relate this research to broader debates about the societies in which mobilisations occurs. At the same time, much macro-sociological analysis often suffers from the opposite problem, making sweeping and often undocumented statements about the character of today's world. Hopefully, the attempt in this chapter to discuss transnational mobilisation in the light of one of the classical sociological categories, the public sphere, has demonstrated how the two traditions could potentially benefit each other.

Notes

This is a revised version of an article printed in *Acta Sociologica* 50(3) (2007). The author is grateful to the publishers of *Acta Sociologica* for allowing him to reprint parts of that article in the present volume.

1. But see Robertson (1995) and Rosenau (2003) for more dialectical conceptions of globalisation.
2. Tarrow and McAdam (2005) do not confine scale shift to the transnational level, but mention, for example, the US civil rights movement as an instance of scale shift from the local to the national level.
3. In this sense, they also straddle the boundary between macro-media and micro-media. Most television channels today have websites with additional and supplementary information. These websites, then, are logically part of the macro-media. On the other hand, websites belonging, for example, to activist organisations are more correctly placed in the micro-media category. I thank Simon Teune for alerting me to this distinction.
4. That people have a global consciousness does not necessarily mean that they are also political cosmopolitans. As discussed by Tarrow (2005: ch. 4), most people still overwhelmingly self-identify with their country.
5. This section adopts some phrases and arguments from Olesen (2007).
6. Although this method is clearly inspired by the so-called political claims analysis (Koopmans and Statham 1999; Koopmans 2002), it does not, as political claims analyses typically do, provide quantitative measures of the coding results. The cod-

ing of the questions has mainly been used to draw a map of the development and chronology of the cartoons protests.

7. Readers familiar with the work of Thomas Risse and Kathryn Sikkink (see especially Risse and Sikkink 1999) will recognise that the model draws inspiration from the spiral model developed by these authors to conceptualise the interaction between transnational human rights activists and human rights violating states.

8. This argument in many ways echoes those made by social movement scholars studying the importance of mobilising structures (e.g., McAdam 1982; McCarthy 1996). Authors in this tradition contend that pre-existing organising experiences are important to the success of subsequent rounds of mobilisation.

References

Al-Khalidi, S. 2006. 'Tegninger udløser endnu en fyreseddel'. *Politiken,* 4 February.

Anderson, B. 1983. *Imagined Communities: Reflections on the Origins and Spread of Nationalism.* London: Verso.

Beck, U. 2005. *Power in the Global Age: A New Global Political Economy.* Cambridge: Polity Press.

BBC. 2006. Search for the combination of 'cartoons' and 'Denmark' on the BBC website. Retrieved 14 May 2006 from http://search.bbc.co.uk/cgi-bin/search/results .pl?tab=ns&q=cartoons+denmark&edition=i&recipe=all&scope=all&start=.

CNN. 2006. Search for the combination of 'cartoons' and 'Denmark' on the CNN website. Retrieved 14 May 2006 from http://search.cnn.com/pages/search.jsp?currentPage =1&query=cartoons+denmark&sortby=Date.

Dayan, D. and E. Katz. 1992. *Media Events: The Live Broadcasting of History.* Cambridge: Harvard University Press.

Diani, M. 2001. 'Social Movement Networks: Virtual and Real'. In *Culture and Politics in the Information Age: A New Politics?,* ed. F. Webster, 117–128. London: Routledge.

eJour. 2006. '143 aviser viser tegningerne'. Retrieved 16 January 2008 from http://www .djh.dk/ejour/52/52Tegninger1.html.

Exner, P. 2005. 'Danske muslimer opfordrer til global protest'. *Politiken,* 10 December.

Habermas, J. 1962/1989. *The Structural Transformation of the Public Sphere.* Cambridge: Polity.

Holm, H. 2006. 'De lokale-globale danskere: En journalistisk udfordring'. *Journalistica* 2: 5–26.

Koopmans, R. 2002. 'Codebook for the Analysis of Political Mobilisation and Communication in European Public Spheres'. Retrieved 16 January 2008 from http://europub .wzb.eu/Data/Codebooks%20questionnaires/D2-1-claims-codebook.pdf.

Koopmans, R. and Statham, P. 1999. 'Political Claims Analysis: Integrating Protest Event and Public Discourse Approaches'. *Mobilisation* 4(2): 203–222.

Koopmans, R. and J. Erbe. 2004. 'Towards a European Public Sphere?' *Innovation: The European Journal of Social Science Research* 17(2): 97–118.

Letter from Ambassadors. 2005. Retrieved 16 January 2008 from http://gfx.tv2.dk/images /Nyhederne/Pdf/side1.pdf and http://gfx.tv2.dk/images/Nyhederne/Pdf/side2.pdf.

Lynch, M. 2003. 'Beyond the Arab Street: Iraq and the Arab Public Sphere'. *Politics and Society* 31(1): 55–91.

McAdam, D. 1982. *Political Process and the Development of Black Insurgency, 1930–1970.* Chicago: University of Chicago Press.

McCarthy, J.D. 1996. 'Constraints and Opportunities in Adopting, Adapting, and Inventing'. In *Comparative Perspectives on Social Movements: Political Opportunities, Mobilising Structures, and Cultural Framings,* eds. D. McAdam, J.D. McCarthy and M.N. Zald, 141–151. Cambridge: Cambridge University Press.

Munck, A. 2006. 'Aviser over hele Europa trykker tegningerne'. *Politiken,* 2 February.

Nielsen, H.F. and T. Flensburg. 2006. 'Khader i fortrolige samtaler med statsministeren'. *Politiken,* 1 February.

Olesen, T. 2007. 'Contentious Cartoons: Elite and Media Driven Mobilisation'. *Mobilisation* 12(1): 37–52.

Risse, T. and Sikkink, K. 1999. 'The Socialization of International Human Rights Norms into Domestic Practices: Introduction'. In *The Power of Human Rights: International Norms and Domestic Change,* eds. T. Risse, S.C. Ropp and K. Sikkink, 1–38. Cambridge: Cambridge University Press.

Ritzau. 2006. 'Boykot mod Danmark: Undskyldende artikel fra Jyllands-Posten'. *Jyllands-Posten,* 31 January.

Robertson, R. 1992. *Globalisation: Social Theory and Global Culture.* London: Sage.

———. 1995. 'Glocalization: Time-Space and Homogeneity-Heterogeneity'. In *Global Modernities,* eds. M. Featherstone, S. Lash and R. Robertson, 25–44. London: Sage.

Rosenau, J.N. 1997. *Along the Domestic-Foreign Frontier: Exploring Governance in a Turbulent World.* Cambridge: Cambridge University Press.

———. 2003. *Distant Proximities: Dynamics beyond Globalisation.* Princeton: Princeton University Press.

Scholte, J.A. 2000. *Globalisation: A Critical Introduction.* Houndmills: Palgrave Macmillan.

Seib, P. 2005. 'Hegemonic No More: Western Media, the Rise of Al-Jazeera, and the Influence of Diverse Voices'. *International Studies Review* 7(4): 601–615.

Shaw, M. 2000. *Theory of the Global State: Globality as an Unfinished Revolution.* Cambridge: Cambridge University Press.

Sheffer, G. 2003. *Diaspora Politics: At Home Abroad.* Cambridge: Cambridge University Press.

Sørensen, A.M. 2006. 'Politisk flertal truer imamerne'. *Politiken,* 4 February.

Tarrow, S. 2005. *The New Transnational Activism.* Cambridge: Cambridge University Press.

Tarrow, S. and D. McAdam. 2005. 'Scale Shift in Transnational Contention'. In *Transnational Protest and Global Activism,* eds. D. della Porta and S. Tarrow, 121–150. Lanham: Rowman and Littlefield.

Taylor, C. 1992. 'Modernity and the Rise of the Public Sphere'. *The Tanner Lectures on Human Values,* Stanford University. Retrieved 16 January 2008 from http://www.tannerlectures.utah.edu/lectures/documents/Taylor93.pdf.

Chapter Seven

Thinking about Transnational Diffusion and Cycles of Protest:

The 1996–2005 Wave of Democratisation in Eastern Europe

Tsveta Petrova

Introduction

The Soviet block collapsed amid an epic wave of contention. Some of the former Soviet Union republics (Latvia, Lithuania and Estonia) and some of the Central European former Soviet satellites (the Czech Republic, Hungary and Poland) quickly entered the ranks of capitalist democracies. The remaining majority of Eastern European post-socialist states transitioned to 'hybrid regimes' (Carothers 2002; Diamond 2002) or autocracies with mixed marketisation records (Dawisha and Parrott 1997; Offe 1997).

Then, in the mid 1990s and later in the early 2000s, another wave of democratisation through the so-called electoral revolutions swept through post-socialist Central Europe, the Balkans and the Soviet successor states. The cycle began with three overlapping and interconnected struggles in Bulgaria, Romania and Serbia from November 1996 to March 1997. In those campaigns, upcoming elections became the focal point of a growing conventional and extra-institutional cooperation between civil society groups and opposition parties in the name of regime change. Moreover, those struggles produced a set of injustice, agency and identity frames,[1] which subsequently diffused to other countries in the region with the help of personal contacts between Eastern European activists, Western donors and the mass media. Slovakia followed in 1998 and Croatia in 2000. In 2000, Serbia, where the 1996 campaign had been unsuccessful, managed to bring down one of the most authoritarian orders in the region. After that, the electoral revolution model spread to the generally more illiberal Eurasian countries of the post-Soviet Union space. There, it was successful in Georgia in 2003, Ukraine in 2004 and Kyrgyzstan in 2005, but it failed in Azerbaijan in 2003 and 2008, Armenia in 2004 and 2008, Belarus in 2001 and 2006 and Kazakhstan in 2005.

The 1996–2005 wave of democratisation in Eastern Europe is not only an important case to be accounted for by current theories of transnational diffusion, but also a crucial one: one that 'must fit a theory if one is to have any confidence in the theory's validity' (Eckstein 1975: 118; Gerring 2007). The region is particularly well suited for transnational diffusion because of the many similarities among the hybrid democracies in this region and the perception of these similarities by the political and civic elites as well as the citizenry (Bunce and Wolchik 2006a). Thus, the 1996–2005 Eastern European wave of democratisation presents a good opportunity for re-examination and re-adjustment of some recent theories of transnational diffusion.

Moreover, the wave also features some interesting characteristics, which allow for further theoretical development. First, it spanned a decade and is thus an example of medium-term diffusion. Second, the cycle began with a simultaneous ideological and tactical experimentation within a set of three connected and overlapping struggles. And third, it further depended on feedback effects in developing the diffusion items and consolidating their effects, as some countries that were unsuccessful at first carried out electoral revolutions more than once.

In its attempt to re-examine and to further develop recent theories of transnational diffusion, this chapter uses the case study method. Case studies are particularly well suited for developing and generating theoretical propositions because they highlight the relationships between different social phenomena and the processes linking them (Brady and Collier 2004). However, because a single case study can not both generate theoretical propositions and test them, the case presented in this chapter is offered more suggestively than definitively. Therefore, the suggestions of this chapter should be taken with caution, but will hopefully be revisited and tested by scholars of contentious politics in the future.

Based on the 1996–2005 wave of democratisation, this chapter offers two suggestions: 1) since ideological and tactical diffusion can have expressive (as well as instrumental) significance, innovations can spread within and between movements even if they are or seem to be ineffective in immediately affecting change; and 2) the later in the cycle, the less dynamic, ambiguous and malleable the innovations will be, since late-comers are more likely to need to compensate for their relative structural disadvantages by legitimating their actions through conformity with the core of the innovation as it has evolved through the customisations of the early adopters.

A Look at the Literature: Transnational Diffusion and Contentious Cycles

Sidney Tarrow (1989), in his theory of 'protest cycles'[2], first formulated the idea that collective dissent comes in waves of contention encompassing the actions of ecologically interdependent contenders (and authorities). A protest cycle, Tarrow holds, is a period of heightened conflict across the social system: a rapid diffusion of collective action from more mobilised to less mobilised sectors, the invention of new forms of collective action, the creation of new mobilisation master frames of meaning, a combination of organised and unorganised participation, and sequences of intensified interactions between challengers and authorities (Tarrow 1994: 153). An opening of new political opportunities triggers collective action, which exposes the authorities' points of weakness that might not have been evident until challenged and reveals allies within or outside of the system. Such a demonstration of elite vulnerability thus expands not only the group's own opportunities for mobilisation, but also the opportunities for competitive- and counter-mobilisation. At the same time, opportunities also open up for the authorities to repress the movement and for elites to advance their own policies and careers by aligning themselves with or against particular mobilised groups. The iterative interaction of challengers, and challengers and authorities eventually leads to the gradual institutionalisation of some demands and the radicalisation and subsequent marginalisation of other groups, that is, it leads to the routinisation of the relations between a majority of the actors in the polity.[3]

McAdam (1995) further argued that it is theoretically important to distinguish between two classes of movements: 1) initiator movements or early-risers, which signal or otherwise set in motion a protest wave by seizing expanding political opportunities; and 2) spin-off movements or late-comers, which draw their impetus and inspiration from the original initiator movement(s). Expanding political opportunities facilitate collective action by early-risers by seriously undermining the stability of the entire political system and/or by increasing the political leverage of the single challenging group. Whether or not that leverage is exercised may depend on the organisational and ideational resources available to the movement. However, in the absence of expanding opportunities, it matters little how resource-rich or aggrieved is the group. Still, the spread of the cycle, according to McAdam, owes to cognitive and cultural processes rather than political ones. To the extent that early-risers are 'clusters of new cultural items – new cognitive frames, behavioural routines, organisational forms, tactical repertoires etc.' (McAdam 1995: 231), late-risers become the creative adapters and interpreters of the cultural lessons of early-risers. Most importantly, spin-off movements appropriate the early-risers' master frame, which provides the ideational and interpretative anchoring necessary for the development of 'insurgent consciousness' around some aspect of life portrayed as illegitimate but subject to change through group action. As a result, spin-off movements also borrow the repertoire of early-risers. Such frame and tactical diffusion is mediated by direct or indirect ties linking a potential adopter to an early-riser.

While research on transnational protest cycles (Tarrow 1989; Soule and Tarrow 1991; Beissinger 2002) relies on an acknowledgment of diffusion dynamics, it was an article by McAdam and Rucht (1993) that stimulated explicit theorisation of transnational diffusion between social movements in general. These authors imported from classical diffusion theory the understanding that transnational diffusion involves four essential elements: '1) a person, group, or organization that serves as the emitter or transmitter; 2) a person, group, or organization that is the adopter; 3) the item that is diffused, such as material goods, information, skills, and the like; and 4) a channel of diffusion that may consist of persons or media that link the transmitter and the adopter' (McAdam and Rucht 1993: 59).

McAdam and Rucht (1993) also built on Meyer and Strang's (1993) work on structural equivalence and competition as contributing to global isomorphism by pointing to the role of: 1) direct relational ties – in encouraging an initial identification of activist-adopters in one country with activist-transmitters in another; and 2) non-relational channels – as the principal means of information transmission once this initial identification is established. Further improvements on Meyer and Strang included examining the role of previously overlooked non-relational or indirect pathways and logics: the role of social categories (McAdam and Rucht 1993), mass media (Myers 2000) and brokers (Bunce and Wolchik 2005).

In addition to specifying the structural mechanisms – characteristic relations between source and adopter – that promote diffusion, further theoretical development in transnational diffusion also focussed on the interpretive work and the discourse that catalyse the flow as well as the cultural status of the diffusing item. Snow and Benford (1995) presented a typology of diffusion based on the passivity of the transmitter and/or the adopter in accomplishing the interpretive work. Strang and Meyer (1993) discussed how practices are theorised in terms of general models and causal relationships and suggest that the more successfully theorised a diffusing practice is, the less its diffusion will be relationally structured. Lastly, resonance with the adopters' experience (Bunce and Wolchik 2006a) and/or with elements of salient world culture models (Strang 1990) as well as perceived success (Soule 2004) have been suggested to account for why certain innovations travel.

A Brief Overview of the 1996–2005 Eastern European Democratisation Wave

Having reviewed the recent literature on transnational diffusion and cycles of protest, this chapter now turns to a short overview of the 1996–2005 East European wave of democratisation, against which these theories can be re-evaluated. A word on the limitations of the empirical presentation in this chapter is in order. This chapter is not based on any systematic empirical investigation, but rather on a thorough reading of the empirical literature on the electoral revolutions in the region.[4]

Defining the Phenomenon: Content in Time and Space

The democratising campaigns at the turn of the century have especially captured the imagination of practitioners and academics, who saw in them a sign that 'democracy gained new dynamism in the region in unexpected ways and places' (McFaul 2005: 5). Most analysts study the contentious episodes centred around fraudulent national elections in the early 2000 wave of regime change in Eastern Europe.[5] These studies agree that such campaigns share the following features: 1) a fraudulent national election, provoking 2) mass protests meant to defend the existing, democratic constitution and 3) resulting in a victory for the challengers. Where the term 'revolution' is used, it does not imply that these events will end up either being revolutionary or leading to successful democratic consolidation in the long run (Tucker 2007), but rather that 1) challengers and incumbents make competing and simultaneous claims to hold sovereign authority (McFaul 2005); and/or 2) that 'the pro-democracy movement in each case was in fact successful in overthrowing the current regime' (Tucker 2007: 2).

An exception to such a spatially and temporally narrow understanding of these democratisation campaigns is Bunce and Wolchik's (2006a: 5) definition. These authors' interpretation of the second wave of democratisation through electoral revolutions in Eastern Europe includes not only the campaigns in Serbia, Georgia, Ukraine and Kyrgyzstan at the turn of the century, but also those in Bulgaria, Romania, Slovakia and Croatia in the late 1990s, where opposition movements with substantial popular involvement also transformed certain elections into genuinely competitive and fair processes with long-term democratisation consequences. Electoral revolutions are described as 'attempts by opposition leaders and citizens to use elections, sometimes in combination with political protests, to defeat illiberal incumbents or their anointed successors; to bring liberal oppositions to power; and to shift their regimes in a decidedly more democratic direction' (Bunce and Wolchik 2006a: 5).[6]

This chapter adopts Bunce and Wolchik's definition because: 1) it unites campaigns in which elections served as focal points of broad social electoral and/or extra-institutional mobilisation for regime change; and, 2) because these campaigns were interconnected by the conscious decision of their participants to associate themselves with and learn from past electoral revolutions. The Serbian, Bulgarian and Romanian actors of 1996–1997 all drew ideas from each other. The campaign in Slovakia benefited from the experience of the Romanian and Bulgarian opposition leaders, and Slovak activists in turn played a crucial role in coaching the Croatian and Serbian coalitions of 2000. Then, Serb student leaders assisted the Georgian ones, and the Slovak, Georgian and Serb campaigners advised the Ukrainian ones. Lastly, Kyrgyz student organisers came to Ukraine in 2004 as election observers and returned home to create a movement modelled on the Serbian and Ukrainian ones.

Why consider those campaigns as episodes of contentious politics rather than of electoral politics? The electoral revolutions were the work of broad social movements that were driven by more than support for an opposition party. The growing cooperation between civil society, especially student groups, and opposition parties was in the name of regime change. Moreover, all movements availed themselves to unconventional tactics to a lesser or a greater degree – whether as a disruption of a challenged order or in ritualistic support of the opposition parties.

A Chronology of a Revolutionary Cycle

The 1996–2005 wave of democratisation in Eastern Europe began with three overlapping and interconnected struggles in the Balkans, tacitly supported by the West, but especially by the US. There were presidential elections in Bulgaria and in Romania.[7] Bulgaria elected a pro-Western reformer, but his victory was symbolic since the country is a parliamentary republic. Nevertheless, while civic groups mobilised the citizenry into protest against the incumbents, the opposition parties managed to unite and to articulate accession to the EU as a credible alternative to the anti-reform rule of the former communists. Romania followed suit, creating in the local and international media a sense of a pro-democratic flow of events in the Balkans. The Romanian liberal political elite came together to defeat the incumbent, who was a former communist and whose authoritarian leadership and ambivalence toward democratic principles and human rights were undermining the country's transition. The opposition ran a sophisticated political campaign, including massive rallies and demonstrations in favour of a pro-reform and pro-Western democratic future for Romania. Given this popular mandate, the victory of the opposition candidate with far stronger liberal credentials and commitments was not just a regular turnover in power, but a radical break with the past (Mungiu-Pippidi 2006).

On the day of the presidential elections in Romania, there were local elections in Serbia. They were rigged by the incumbents, who had been suffering from their defeat in the Bosnian war and the resultant international isolation and economic difficulties. Civic, but especially student, groups and opposition parties called for daily protests against the regime until the electoral victories of the opposition coalition were recognised. Because fraud occurred throughout Serbia, the protests quickly spread across the country, even if they remained somewhat poorly coordinated (Bieber 2003). Foreign media carried accounts of the impressive struggle of the Serbian opposition movement against Slobodan Milosevic's rule to every corner of the post-communist region.

The Bulgarian media not only picked up the story, but, in editorials, was also calling on the opposition to learn from their counterparts in Serbia. Much inspired by the protests there and emboldened by the victory of their presidential candidate, the Bulgarian opposition parties began co-operating with the protesting labour unions. Student associations, also inspired by their Serbian counterparts, emerged as a third pillar of the campaign that mobilised demonstrators. The coalition sought to capitalise on the macro-economic crisis in the country to de-legitimise the unreformed incumbents; the demand by the coalition was for pre-term elections toward democratic consolidation through economic reform and EU accession. Following the Serbian example, in late December 1996, the opposition movement declared that they would protest peacefully until their demands were met.[8] The campaign spanned 51 days of massive protests, which paralysed the country and forced the socialists to concede (Petrova 2010).

By that time, the massive Serbian struggle was winding down as well. The opposition's demands had never gone beyond the correction of the electoral fraud. By eventually conceding in just a few municipalities, the regime fulfilled these demands without surrendering broad political powers. Because it was fragmented and enmeshed with the regime, the political opposition was unable to successfully challenge the regime on the basis of the protests even after three months of ambitious contentious mobilisation (Bieber 2003).

Learning from the struggles in the Balkans, the leaders of the Slovak opposition were already devising a strategy for unseating their Prime Minister, Vladimir Meciar. His nationalist and semi-authoritarian leadership had compromised the democratisation and EU accession of the country. Some US ambassadorial officials helped to arrange a meeting between the Slovak opposition leaders and key campaign organisers from Bulgaria and Romania. In addition to appreciation for unity among opposition parties and for joint political and civic extra-institutional mobilisation, the Slovaks benefited from voter registration, election monitoring and polling programs developed, with US assistance, by the Romanian but especially by the Bulgarian campaigners (Bunce and Wolchik 2006b). The Slovak opposition improved on such programs and combined their deployment with large-scale non-partisan grassroots mobilisation. Such civic mobilisation not only forced the regime onto the defensive, but also compelled the opposition parties to reject cooperation offers by Meciar, who won just 27 per cent of the 1998 vote (Forbrig and Demes 2007).

The very next year, the long-serving dictator, Franjo Tudjman, passed away, weakening the governing party in Croatia. Coached by the Slovaks, the Croatian opposition faithfully followed the Slovak 'recipe for success'. A new president was voted in, in the name of the democratisation and Europeanisation of the country. This was a symbolic achievement, since real power in Croatia is vested in parliament, but it was an achievement, which was cemented by the return of the opposition coalition to power in parliament three years later (Bunce and Wolchik 2006a).

Later in 2000, the electoral revolution wave returned to Serbia, where Milosevic had continued to rule with a heavy authoritarian hand. The media was closely controlled by the regime, the opposition was often harassed and the external election monitors as well as some of the international and regional actors assisting the opposition were kicked out of the country right before the elections. However, the opposition had learned from its 1996 campaign and from the Bulgarian, Romanian and especially the Slovak electoral revolution graduates. The political parties united. They also worked closely with civil society on voter mobilisation behind the little known Vojslav Kostunica and on hammering out his pro-reform platform. The opposition coalition also prepared to expose electoral fraud by developing – with Slovak help – civic election monitoring and polling programs. The elections occurred shortly after the Serbian capitulation to the 1999 NATO air campaign and amidst corruption scandals and economic decline. The Yugoslav Election Commission declared that although Kostunica had gained the most support, neither candidate had received the necessary 50 per cent of the vote to be declared the winner. The opposition coalition, however, announced that by the count of its 25,000 election monitors, Kostunica had won 55 per cent of the vote. Kostunica refused to participate in the run-off. A well-prepared, broad coalition of student groups, the oppositional parties coalition, regional government heads, union leaders and other civil society organisers co-ordinated their efforts. When the Serbian Constitutional Court annulled the election results, effectively denying Kostunica his victory, over a million people marched on Belgrade and quickly seized control of the parliament and the Serbian state-run television. The following day, overwhelmed by resistance and lacking the full support of the repressive apparatus, Milosevic resigned (Birch 2002; Bieber 2003; Bujosevic and Radovanovic 2003; Thompson and Kuntz 2004).

The Serbian victory, in bringing down one of the most authoritarian orders in the region, helped to spread the model among the generally more illiberal Eurasian countries of the post-Soviet Union space. The US government and NGOs (mainly the Soros Foundation) supported the process by funding Serbian exchanges with other opposition activists from the region. Moreover, local and international media were closely following the flow of the model. The coverage of the electoral revolutions in Radio Free Europe – Radio Liberty and even in mainstream media, such as CNN and the BBC, reverberated back in domestic sources, amplifying its impact.

The last three successful electoral revolutions closely resembled the Serbian one and each other in that they all centred around a fraudulent national election, which occurred in the context of incumbent failures to set the economy on a sound course and to curb corruption. In addition to borrowing the Serbian injustice, agency and identity frames, all of the countries adopted the protest strategy and tactics[9] of the Serbian opposition campaign. All of the campaigns also built upon earlier rounds of protests and recent successes in local elections and reached out to a diverse set of civic groups, especially young people. Modelled after the Serbian youth movement, a Georgian and a Ukrainian one were set up. These students groups closely co-operated with opposition parties, especially on popular mobilisation before and after the elections. Also, all of the Election Commissions handed the victory to the illiberal incumbents, but all of the oppositions were armed with proof of electoral fraud and with non-partisan exit polls from election monitoring and polling programs, modelled on the ones fine-tuned in Slovakia and then in Serbia. Lastly, all of the campaigns featured joint political and civic protests for regime change during which the repressive apparatus was present but internally split and unwilling to move; the break-throughs in Georgia and Ukraine additionally benefited from defections from the ruling circles (Bunce and Wolchik 2006a).

Georgia's regime was the least illiberal one among the cases in which electoral fraud occurred. Independent media and a fairly democratic civil society had developed and a significant number of local and international media and election monitoring groups had moved in. Moreover, Western governments, especially the US, made their most consistent attempt ever in any ex-Soviet republic (Fairbanks 2004) to improve the quality of the elections by international pressure and hands-on assistance in reforming the process. At the same time, however, the Georgian ruling party as well as the opposition remained most disunited, so that the ruling party committed electoral fraud anyway. The student movement, as trained by their Serbian counterparts, took the lead in contesting the election results through protest. When the incumbent president, Eduard Shevardnadze, tried to address the inaugural session of the newly 'elected' Georgian parliament, protestors stormed the parliament demanding Shevardnadze's resignation. Since the police was unable and unwilling to move against the protesters, Shevardnadze resigned (Kandelaki 2005; Karumidze and Wertsch 2005; Wheatley 2005).

By 2004, the Ukrainian regime had grown corrupt and violent in suppressing the media and the opposition. Moreover, the ruling circle had help from Russia in rigging 'Ukraine's dirtiest election' (Kuzio 2005). To stand up for the pro-reform and pro-European governance, more than a million protesters turned up in the dead of winter. Trained by Slovak and Georgian graduates, the student movement played nearly as important a role as the one in Serbia. Moreover, central control over the media broke down during the campaign. Although, the repressive apparatus was divided, the EU, Poland and Lithuania intervened to ensure a peaceful outcome of the crisis. The international community appealed to both Parliament and the Supreme Court (Karatnycky 2005). Amidst continuing massive protests, the Parliament accepted a resolution declaring the results of the presidential elections invalid and then gave the government a vote of no confidence. Following this, the Supreme Court declared the second round of election results to be invalid and ordered that the round be run again. The second run-off was a much more fair election, which sealed the victory of the opposition led by Victor Yushchenko (Kubicek 2005; Kuzio 2005; Way 2005; Wilson 2005).

Finally, the Kyrgyz President Askar Akayev stacked the parliamentary elections by changing the composition of parliament and the election rules used to select its members and then proceeded to buy votes, de-register candidates and interfere with the media. Consequently, various groups joined together to protest the electoral fraud as a coalition. However, few of these groups existed prior to the election. Moreover, the opposition remained largely disunited. And, despite studying from the Ukrainian campaign, the Kyrgyz opposition could not keep its struggle peaceful. Unable to contain the protests, Akayev fled to Russia two weeks after the start of the demonstrations. Although the opposition leader was subsequently elected to replace Akayev, the fraudulently elected parliament was allowed to continue to operate without new elections as part of the negotiations among the various opposition figures (MacWilliam 2005; Tucker 2007; Beissinger 2007).

In the meantime, however, the model had suffered defeats in Belarus in 2001, in Azerbaijan in 2003 as well as in Armenia in 2004. The wave died out with the unsuccessful revolutions in Belarus and Kazakhstan in 2005 and the second attempts in Belarus in 2006 and in Azerbaijan and Armenia in 2008. Political and civic actors in Russia and Moldova never carried out campaigns, but they entertained the idea. Uzbekistan, Tajikistan, Turkmenistan and Mongolia were the only countries not swept by the wave. It should also be noted that these failed attempts were despite training by previous electoral revolutions graduates and exposure to the model in the mass media (Mendelson and Gerber 2007).[10] All unsuccessful cases featured more repressive regimes, divided oppositions and only sporadic protests, the combination of which allowed incumbents to maintain power. By the time the model arrived in those countries, their incumbents had learnt from the repeated successes and failures of past electoral revolutions. The regimes responded to the threat of the model by moving aggressively to prevent challengers from rising, repressing them forcefully and raising the institutional constraints that they face. Illiberal rulers also turned to manipulating elections without engaging in outright fraud, thereby avoiding aspects of the model that might fuel opposition mobilisation (Beissinger 2007). They also established their own pro-regime youth movements to counteract the influence of the model-driven transnational youth movements (Deheryan 2005). Moreover, such autocrats established closer relations with Russia as a way of providing their own regimes with international support against the threat of transnational revolution (Torbakov 2005).

Lessons of the 1996–2005 East European Wave of Democratisation

Having briefly reviewed the merits and limitations of previous studies of diffusion within protest cycles in the second section in this chapter, this discussion proceeds by identifying some lessons this cycle, as summarised in the third section, carries about these theories.

Political Opportunities, Movement Success and Diffusion

The beginning of the 1996–2005 East European wave of democratisation presents an opportunity to rethink the relationship between political opportunities, movement success and diffusion. Scholars of contentious politics traditionally argue that early adoption depends on the success of the innovation, which in turn depends on favourable political opportunities (Koopmans 2005). In the words of Mayer Zald (1996: 271), 'failing movements are less likely to provide ideological and symbolic models but they do provide … reservoirs of experience drawn on by later movements with loose similarities'. Others, however, point out that success or failure may not always be easy to determine, especially at the time of a movement's campaign (Soule 1999). The spread of the electoral model in 1996–1997 began even before the relevant actors could obtain much information about it and its effectiveness. The question then becomes: given how much was at stake for the opposition movement in Bulgaria, why was it borrowing Serbian strategy and tactics, if their effectiveness was at best unknown? Studying the diffusion of unsuccessful tactics, Soule (1999) points out that they spread quickly because the media portrayed them as successful and because they resonated with the life experiences of potential adopters. The tactical diffusion from Serbia to Bulgaria allows us to build on that explanation and to take it one step further to acknowledge the expressive importance of tactical diffusion. Such an extension echoes McAdam's point that the spread of the cycle owes more to cognitive and cultural processes rather than to political ones.

Soule studies the spread of shantytowns among US universities' campuses despite their ineffectiveness in getting universities to divest from apartheid South Africa. The author argues that the innovation fit with existing student tactical repertoires and resonated with student perceptions of South Africa, because it evolved from the familiar tactic of the sit-in to sit-out (waiting outside), then to camp-out (a longer sit-out) and eventually to shantytowns, which also came to provide a symbolic representation of ghetto life in South Africa. In other words, one of the broader points Soule is making is that a movement's tactics are chosen in part because they are appropriate to the opportunity, the movement and the goal.

Back to the beginning of the 1996–2005 East European wave of democratisation, the Serbian protests inspired the Bulgarian campaign to borrow both strategy (daily protests) and tactics (peaceful, theatrical, etc.). These innovations were familiar to elites and the population in Bulgaria because the domestic and foreign media had been paying close attention to the protest in neighbouring Serbia. It should be noted, however, that the domestic independent newspapers and radio stations were not just channels linking the two campaigns; they also served as brokers, who were pointing out the similarities between the two struggles and calling to the Bulgarian opposition to learn from their counterparts in Serbia (Petrova 2010). The movement in Bulgaria could and did identify itself with their Serbian counterparts because they too saw themselves as fighting the last remnants of the old communist order in their country, as the Serbs were in theirs. This collective identity of the Bulgarian opposition had already been articulated in the preceding few months during the presidential race (Petrova 2010). Consequently, the Serbian strategy and tactics seemed relevant and appropriate to the Bulgarian goals and borrowing them was borrowing legitimacy and a further validation of the Bulgarian movement. Indeed, strategies, tactics and organisational forms are not only means to other ends, but also ends in themselves, that is, ways of communicating the identity of the movement (Gamson 1992; Morris and Mueller 1992; Jasper 1997). Therefore, if they serve such expressive purposes, innovations might diffuse, even when they are or seem to be ineffective in immediately affecting change.

Moreover, such expressive adoption can also serve functional purposes in the long run. Tactical anchoring can express the identification of early-risers with each other and signal to the authorities and the public a more inclusive and broader definition of the emerging struggle – a challenge to all illiberal orders in the region by pro-reform movements in the case of the 1996–2005 East European wave of democratisation – which consequently also becomes more difficult to suppress. The message might multiply participant numbers and resolve and eventually compel the regime to concede.

A related question is about the hypothesised importance of expanding opportunities for the beginning of a protest wave. Some scholars emphasise favourable political opportunity for the innovators in a cycle, because they see expanding opportunities as increasing the chances for movement success and the consequent diffusion of its innovations (Koopmans 2005). However, as discussed above, even 'unsuccessful' movements can become diffusion sources. Does this mean that expanding opportunities are not a necessary condition even for early-risers? Not necessarily. McAdam's (1995) original emphasis seems to be on the necessity of favourable political opportunities for the emergence of, and not the success of, a movement. The author further looks to broad social change processes – wars, economic or political crises, political realignments/succession crises, etc. – to undermine the stability of the entire political system or to increase the political leverage of a challenger. Such opportunities were in fact present in both the Serbian and the Bulgarian contexts: the Milosevic regime had lost the war in Bosnia the year before and there was a severe macro-economic crisis in Bulgaria. (For further discussion of the relationship between national political opportunities and transnational mobilisation, see chapter 8 in this volume).

Early and Late Adoption and the Customisation of the Diffusion Item

Relevant to the role of political opportunity in diffusion is the question of the interpretation and implementation of the adoption. McAdam (1995: 224) points out that there is not only no increase in the system vulnerability with regards to subsequent spin-off movements, but that such movements are further disadvantaged by the necessity of having to confront a state, which is already preoccupied with and has acquired some experience in dealing with similar movements in the face of early-risers. However, other scholars of protest cycles argue that early diffusion itself creates expanding political opportunities for collective action. Tarrow (1989), for example, suggests that early challengers signal the vulnerability and responsiveness of elites, thus increasing them. Similarly, Koopmans (2005: 26) describes how diffusion produces 'opportunity cascades' because the authorities are 'no longer able to scare regime opponents from the streets'. Lastly, Beissinger (2002) points to the fact that early protests create a sense of flow and direction of events, which has an empowering effect. When studying the 1996–2005 wave of democratisation in Eastern Europe, Bunce and Wolchik (2006a) and Beissinger (2007) document that the spread of electoral revolutions is shaped across space and time by certain pre-existing structural conditions: even though ideas out-race capabilities and preparation, examples raise the expectations of both incumbents and challengers that state authority could be successfully challenged through similar means, thus facilitating such action and increasing the odds of its success. It seems, however, that structural factors might impact not just movement success, but also how the diffusion item is defined and implemented. The 1996–2005 East European cycle of electoral revolutions suggests that, due to permissive opportunity structure, early adopters might be able to experiment with and 'customise' the innovation. Late-comers, on the other hand, draw legitimacy from and take advantage of the opportunities created by the actions of early-risers and consequently mostly conform to an increasingly less and less dynamic, ambiguous and malleable innovation.

What all adopters of the electoral revolution model shared was: 1) an injustice frame – an unrepresentative and unresponsive, anti-reform and corrupt regime, i.e., a distortion of the will of the people; 2) an identity frame – pro-reform and pro-Western (European) movements;[11] 3) an agency frame – transforming certain elections into genuinely competitive and fair processes with long-term democratisation consequences; and, 4) a 'democratisation' master frame that unites all three previous elements and resonates well exactly what the international norms the Eastern European illiberal regimes had been paying lip service. However, the electoral revolution model that spread early on throughout the Balkans and Central Europe was so much in flux that it is not recognised as such by many scholars. It was mostly the interpretation of the injustice frame and the implementation of the organisational (political and/or civic actors) and tactical (conventional/electoral and/or extra-institutional) interpretations of the agency frame that differed. (For a discussion of cross-national frame differences during episodes of transnational mobilisation, see chapter 8).

The injustice frame centred on the fraudulent election in Serbia in 1996, a macro-economic crisis in Bulgaria, and a political one, related to EU accession, in Romania and Slovakia. Moreover, in Serbia in 1996, there was civic and political extra-institutional mobilisation (massive daily protests) to defend the existing democratic constitution; while in Romania, there were primarily electoral political mobilisation and occasional marches and rallies expressing ritualistic support and a mandate for a radical break with the past. In Bulgaria, joint civic and political protests were meant to bring about pre-term elections, in preparation for which a political strategy for electoral mobilisation (voter registration, 'get out the vote', election monitoring and polling programs) was also devised. Lastly, in Slovakia, the electoral mobilisation was non-partisan and predominantly civic with some ritualistic extra-institutional mobilisation in the process as well.

Croatia, while borrowing much of Slovakia's interpretation of the model, implemented it mostly symbolically: mobilisation occurred around the presidential election, but it is parliament that is vested with power in the country. A hint of this decoupling of elections as a symbol of a break with the past and as a mechanism for turnover in real power in the country was also present in the Bulgarian struggle. This recombination of customisations of earlier struggles suggests that the model was beginning to become more rigid than malleable and that capabilities and preparation were falling behind as the cycle unfolded more and more due to diffusion effects. Indeed, the same year Serbia carried out a successful electoral revolution, which was modelled after the unsuccessful 1996 one and after all of the efforts of successful recent graduates in other countries, which featured joint civic and political electoral and extra-institutional mobilisation.

As discussed in 'Defining the Phenomena' section above, many academics and practitioners only recognise the electoral revolution model as the model 'hardened' with the campaign in Serbia in 2000. Whether there was decoupling of elections as symbols of or real opportunities for defeating illiberal incumbents or their anointed successors, as in Georgia and the Kyrgyz Republic or not as in Serbia and Ukraine, the injustice frame exploited the contradiction between a hybrid regime's claim of legitimacy through electoral political competition and the reality of elections that were rigged in various ways to favour illiberal candidates. Moreover, in all of the post–2000 cases – both successful and unsuccessful – there was civic and political electoral and extra-institutional mobilisation. Given their relative structural disadvantage, later adopters seem to have been more likely needing to compensate for it by legitimating their actions by closely conforming to the increasing less dynamic model. The later the adoption in the cycle, the greater the level of conformity to the core of the innovation, as it had evolved through the customisations of the early adopters.[12]

It should be noted that Chabot and Duyvendak (2002) have expressed their concern about the treatment of the diffusion item as a pre-given, fixed and coherent entity rather than as an emergent dynamic and relational process. They argue that the innovation may be dynamic, ambiguous and malleable, both in the transmitting and receiving context. These authors, however, opt to offer a completely new model of diffusion, in that they differ from this chapter, which proposes instead that the fluidity of the innovation – as so many other aspects of diffusion – might be related to the timing of the adoption within the cycle.

Conclusion

The 1995–2006 East European wave of electoral revolutions is a useful reminder that 'the most fundamental fact about collective action is its connectedness, both historically and spatially, and both with other instances of collective action of similar kind, and with the actions of different claim-makers such as authorities and counter-movements' (Koopmans 2005: 19). In other words, treating campaigns or movements as independent, related, interchangeable or comparable instances of general classes of events, understandable on their own, misses the dynamic interactions among the multitude of contenders within a contentious cycle that shapes the face of protest. This chapter attempts to contribute to a better understanding of transnational activism by using the 1996–2005 wave of democratisation in Eastern Europe to generate two suggestions about diffusion within contentious waves to be explored further in future research: 1) ideological and tactical innovations can diffuse within and between movements for expressive purposes despite a real or perceived ineffectiveness in immediately affecting change; and 2) the fluidity of such innovations might be related to the timing of their adoption within the cycle: the later in the cycle, the less dynamic, ambiguous and malleable the innovations become, because in their attempt to compensate for their relative structural disadvantage, late-comers seek to legitimate their actions by closely conforming to the core of the innovation as it has evolved through the customisations of the early adopters; this consequently additionally hardens this core.

Notes

The author wishes to express her gratitude to Sidney Tarrow, Valerie Bunce, Sarah Soule, Christopher Anderson, Jenifer Hadden and Lucia Seybert for their comments on the early drafts of this chapter. The author also acknowledges the financial and intellectual support of the Cornell Mellon-Sawyer group on 'Social Movements and Regime Change in Latin America and Postcommunist Eurasia'.

1. On those different types of frames, see Gamson (1992).
2. The term 'cycle' might imply a periodically recurring sequence of phenomena, but the concept of a protest cycle is not meant to; that is why some prefer to use protest wave instead of protest cycle (Koopmans 2005), but this chapter uses both interchangeably without suggesting that either is a periodically recurring set of events.
3. Building on Tarrow's work, Koopmans (2005) theorises the three fundamental features, universal to all protest cycles: 1) *expansion* of contention across social groups and sectors or the destabilisation of social relations in a polity resulting from expanding opportunities, diffusion and reactive mobilisation; 2) *transformation* of

contention in terms of changes in the strategies, alliance structures and identities in the interaction of challengers, and challengers and authorities, depending on feedback processes involving several actors simultaneously; 3) *contraction* of contention through re-stabilisation of social relations in the polity, such that they converge on a new equilibrium in which neither party can hope to make substantial gains by continuing to raise the stakes of contention.

4. The events in the 1996–2005 Eastern European wave of democratisation through electoral revolutions have been documented in detail, mostly in single country studies of the factors contributing to the success or the failure of a particular revolution there. There are also comparisons of some of the successful episodes in the region (McFaul 2005; Tucker 2007) or contrasts between successful and failed/unattempted cases of electoral revolutions (Herd 2005; Silitsky 2005). Lastly, Bunce and Wolchik (2006a) and Beissinger (2007) study the 1996–2005 democratisation campaigns as a transnational protest cycle. Beissinger's goal is to examine the effects of structure and example not only on those who would look to support change, but also on elites who potentially oppose it. Bunce and Wolchik's goal is to explain why electoral revolutions in the region succeeded in spreading from state to state in greater numbers than in other regions.

5. Most analysts refer to the phenomena as 'electoral revolutions' (Herd 2005; Silitski 2005; Bunce and Wolchik 2006a; Tucker 2007), as 'modular democratic revolutions' (Beissinger 2007), and more generally, as a 'second wave of democratisation in the post-communist world' (McFaul 2005; Bunce and Wolchik 2006a). Some of these campaigns have even been nicknamed: the 'Bulldozer revolution' in Serbia in 2000, the 'Rose revolution' in Georgia in 2003, the 'Orange revolution' in Ukraine in 2004 and the 'Tulip revolution' in Kyrgyzstan in 2005. It should be noted, however, that similar campaigns were observed in Latin America as early as the late 1980s and early 1990s, and in the Middle East and Northern Africa as late as the mid 2000s. While the Latin American struggles have not been defined as electoral revolutions, the ones in the Middle East and Northern Africa were claimed as ones even by their participants (Bunce and Wolchik 2006a; Beissinger 2007).

6. This notion also resembles Vachudova's (2005) understanding of 'watershed elections'.

7. The first round of the presidential elections in Bulgaria was on 27 October 1996, the second on 3 November 1996; in Romania, the first round was on 3 November 1996 and the run-off on 17 November 1996.

8. Tactics borrowed from Serbia ranged from the theatrical – blowing a whistle at the police – to the strategic – lining up young women with flowers at the frontline to keep the protests peaceful.

9. Many of the 1996 protest tactics were used – from large street demonstrations that demonstrate prowess and create demonstration cascades to mocking the regime through small, well-planned performances highlighting its authoritarian character. However, many of the voter mobilisation tactics were borrowed from Slovakia, for example, encouraging the participation of young first-time voters through rock concerts and poster campaigns.

10. For instance, Slovak graduates began training the Belarusian opposition as early on as 1999 on an invitation by US donors. In the category of revolutions never attempted, the Soros Foundation brought Serbian youth movement leaders to Russia in 2002.

11. Here, the pro-Western orientation is in part meant to make the regime shift to democracy irreversible.

12. Such a claim also parallels to some extent Westphal, Gulati and Shortell's (1997) finding that early adopters customise innovative practices for efficiency gains, while later adopters gain legitimacy from adopting the normative form of these practices.

References

Beissinger, M. 2002. *Nationalist Mobilisation and the Collapse of the Soviet State.* Cambridge: Cambridge University Press.

———. 2007. 'Structure and Example in Modular Political Phenomena: The Diffusion of Bulldozer, Rose, Orange and Tulip Revolutions'. *Perspectives on Politics* 5(2): 259–276.

Bieber, F. 2003. 'The Serbian Transition and Civil Society: Roots of the Delayed Transition in Serbia'. *International Journal of Politics, Culture and Society* 17(1): 73–90.

Birch, S. 2002. 'The 2000 Elections in Yugoslavia: The "Bulldozer Revolution"'. *Electoral Studies* 21(3): 499–511.

Brady, H.E. and D. Collier, eds. 2004. *Rethinking Social Inquiry: Diverse Tools, Shared Standards.* Lanham: Rowman & Littlefield.

Bujosevic, D. and I. Radovanovic. 2003. *The Fall of Milosevic: The October 5th Revolution.* Houndmills: Palgrave Macmillan.

Bunce, V. and S.L. Wolchik. 2005. 'Bringing Down Dictators: American Democracy Promotion and Electoral Revolutions in Postcommunist Eurasia'. *Transnational Politics in Postcommunist Europe,* Syracuse, 30 September–1 October 2005.

———. 2006a. 'International Diffusion and Postcommunist Electoral Revolutions'. *Communist and Postcommunist Studies* 39(3): 283–304.

———. 2006b. 'Defining and Domesticating the Electoral Model: A Comparison of Slovakia and Serbia'. *Waves and Troughs of Post Communist Transitions: What Role for External vs. Domestic Variables?,* Stanford, 28–29 April 2006.

Carothers, T. 2002. 'The End of the Transition Paradigm'. *Journal of Democracy* 13(1): 5–21.

Chabot, S. and J.W. Duyvendak. 2002. 'Globalization and Transnational Diffusion between Social Movements: Reconceptualizing the Dissemination of the Gandhian Repertoire and the "Coming out" Routine'. *Theory and Society* 31(6): 697–740.

Dawisha, K. and B. Parrott, eds. 1997. *The Consolidation of Democracy in East-Central Europe.* Cambridge: Cambridge University Press.

Deheryan, S. 2005. 'Voice of Youth: Former Student Activist Enters National Assembly'. *ArmeniaNow,* 11 February.

Diamond, L. 2002. 'Thinking About Hybrid Regimes'. *Journal of Democracy* 13(2): 21–35.

Eckstein, H. 1975. 'Case Studies and Theory in Political Science'. In *Handbook of Political Science,* eds. F. Greenstein and N. Polsby. Vol 7: 94–137. Reading: Addison-Wesley.

Fairbanks, C.H. 2004. 'Georgia's Rose Revolution'. *Journal of Democracy* 15(2): 110–124.

Forbrig, J and P. Demes, eds. 2007. *Reclaiming Democracy. Civil Society and Electoral Change in Central and Eastern Europe.* Washington, DC: German Marshall Fund of the United States.

Gamson, W. 1992. *Talking Politics.* Cambridge: Cambridge University Press.

Gerring, J. 2007. *Case Study Research.* Cambridge: Cambridge University Press.

Herd, G. 2005. 'Colorful Revolutions and the CIS'. *Problems of Postcommunism* 52(2): 3–18.

Huntington, S. 1991. *The Third Wave: Democratisation in the Late Twentieth Century.* Norman: University of Oklahoma Press.

Jasper, J. 1997. *The Art of Moral Protest.* Chicago: Chicago University Press.

Kandelaki, G. 2005. 'Rose Revolution: A Participant's Story'. *United States Institute of Peace, Peaceworks* (November): 1–2.

Karatnycky, A. 2005. 'Ukraine's Orange Revolution'. *Foreign Affairs* 84 (2): 35–52.

Katz, M.N. 1997. *Revolutions and Revolutionary Waves.* New York: St. Martin's Press.

Karumidze, Z. and J.V. Wertsch, eds. 2005. *Enough! The Rose Revolution in the Republic of Georgia 2003.* New York: Nova Science Publishers.

Koopmans, R. 2005. 'Protest in Time and Space: Evolution of Waves of Contention'. In *The Blackwell Companion to Social Movements,* eds. D. Snow, S. Soule and H. Kriesi, 19–46. Oxford: Blackwell Publishing.

Kubicek, P. 2005. 'The European Union and Democratisation in Ukraine'. *Communist and Post-Communist Studies* 38: 269–292.

Kuzio, T. 2005. 'From Kuchma to Yushchenko: Orange Revolution in Ukraine'. *Problems of Postcommunism* 52 (2): 29–44.

MacWilliam, I. 2005. 'Kyrgyzstan's Friendly Revolution.' *BBC News,* 26 March.

Markoff, J. 1996. *Waves of Democracy: Social Movements and Political Change.* Thousand Oaks: Pine Forge Press.

McAdam, D. 1995. '"Initiator" and "Spinoff" Movements: Diffusion Processes in Protest Cycles'. In *Repertoires and Cycles of Collective Action,* ed. M. Traugott, 217–239. Durham: Duke University Press.

McAdam, D. and D. Rucht. 1993. 'The Cross National Diffusion of Movement Ideas'. *Annals of the American Academy of Political and Social Sciences* 528: 36–59.

McFaul, M. 2005. 'Transitions from Postcommunism'. *Journal of Democracy,* 16(3): 5–19.

Mendelson, S. and T. Gerber. 2005. 'Local Activist Culture and Transnational Diffusion: An Experiment in Social Marketing among Human Rights Groups in Russia'. *Post-Soviet Affairs* 23(1): 50–75.

Morris, A. and C. Mueller, eds. 1992. *Frontiers in Social Movement Theory.* New Haven: Yale University Press.

Mungiu-Pippidi, Alina. 2006. 'Europeanization without Decommunization: a Case of Elite Conversion.' *Waves and Troughs of Post Communist Transitions: What Role for External versus Domestic Variables?,* Stanford, 28–29 April 2006.

Myers, D. 2000. 'The Diffusion of Collective Violence: Infectiousness, Susceptibility, and Mass Media Networks'. *American Journal of Sociology* 106(1): 173–208.

Meyer, J.W. and D. Strang. 1993. 'Institutional Conditions for Diffusion'. *Theory and Society* 22(4): 487–511.

Offe, C. 1997. *Varieties of Transition: The East European and East German Experience.* Cambridge: MIT Press.

Petrova, T. 2010. 'A Postcommunist Transition in Two Acts: The 1996–7 Antigovernment Struggle in Bulgaria as a Bridge between the 1989–92 and 1996–2007 Democratization Waves in Eastern Europe'. In *Democracy and Authoritarianism in the Post-Communist World,* eds. V. Bunce, M. McFaul and K. Stoner-Weiss, 107–133. Cambridge: Cambridge University Press.

Silitsky, V. 2005. 'Is the Age of Post-Soviet Electoral Revolutions Over?' *Democracy at Large* 1(4): 8–10.

Snow, D. and R. Bedford. 1999. 'Alternative Types of Cross-National Diffusion in the Social Movement Arena'. In *Social Movements in a Globalizing World,* eds. D. della Porta, H. Kreisi and D. Rucht, 23–39. Houndmills: Palgrave Macmillan.

Soule, S. 2004. 'Diffusion Processes Within and Across Movements'. In *The Blackwell Companion to Social Movements,* eds. D. Snow, S. Soule and H. Kriesi, 294–310. Oxford: Blackwell.

———. 1999. 'The Diffusion of Unsuccessful Innovation'. *Annals of the American Academy of Political and Social Sciences* 566: 120–131.

Strang, D. 1990. 'From Dependency to Sovereignty: An Event History Analysis of Decolonization'. *American Sociological Review* 55: 846–860.

Strang, D. and J.W. Meyer. 1993. 'Institutional Conditions for Diffusion'. *Theory & Society* 22: 487–512.

Tarrow, S. 1989. *Democracy and Disorder: Protest and Politics in Italy, 1965–1975.* Oxford: Oxford University Press.

———. 1991. *Struggle, Politics, and Reform: Collective Action, Social Movements, and Cycles of Protest, Western Societies Program.* Occasional Paper No. 21, Center for International Studies, Cornell University, Ithaca.

———. 1994. *Power in Movement: Social Movements, Collective Action and Politics.* Cambridge: Cambridge University Press.

Tarrow, S. and S. Soule. 1991. 'Acting Collectively, 1847–1849: How Repertoires of Collective Action Changed and where it Happened'. *Annual Meeting of the Social Science History Associaiton,* New Orleans, 1–3 November 1991.

Thompson, M.R. and P. Kuntz. 2004. 'Stolen Elections: The Case of the Serbian October'. *Journal of Democracy* 15(4): 159–172.

Torbakov, I. 2005. 'Russia Hopes to Stem Revolutionary Tide in CIS by Strengthening Ties with Kazakhstan'. *EurasiaNet,* 23 February.

Tucker, J. 2007. 'Enough! Electoral Fraud, Collective Action Problems, and Post-Communist Colored Revolutions'. *Perspectives on Politics* 5: 535–551.

Vachudova, M. 2005. *Europe Undivided: Democracy, Leverage, and Integration after Communism.* Oxford: Oxford University Press.

Way, L. 2005. 'Ukraine's Orange Revolution: Kuchma's Failed Authoritarianism'. *Journal of Democracy* 16(2): 131–145.

Westphal, J.D., R. Gulati and S.M. Shortell. 1997. 'Customization or Conformity? An Institutional and Network Perspective on the Content and Consequences of TQM Adoption'. *Administrative Science Quarterly* 42(2): 366–394.

Wheatley, J. 2005. *Georgia from National Awakening to Rose Revolution: Delayed Transition in the Former Soviet Union.* Oxford: Oxford University Press.

Wilson, A. 2005. *Ukraine's Orange Revolution.* New Haven: Yale University Press.

Zald, M. 1996. 'Introduction'. In *Comparative Perspectives on Social Movements: Political Opportunities, Mobilising Structures, and Cultural Framings,* eds. D. McAdam, J. McCarthy and M. Zald. Cambridge: Cambridge University Press.

Methodology and Theory of Transnational Social Movement Research

Chapter Eight

National Constraints and Scale Shift in Current Transnational Activism

Marco Giugni, Marko Bandler and Nina Eggert

Introduction

Since Charles Tilly's path-breaking work on the emergence of the modern protest politics during the historical transformation from an old to a new repertoire of contention (Tilly 1984, 1986, 1995), social movements have been conceptualised as being inherently national or sub-national phenomena. Now, things seem to have changed. Over the past few years, transnational contention has increased considerably and a new collective actor has emerged. This new collective actor – which is defined variously as the no-global movement, anti-globalisation movement, alter-globalisation movement, global justice movement (GJM), movement for a globalisation from below, among other labels – includes a wide range of groups, mobilises various social networks and addresses many different, albeit interrelated issues relating to the struggle against neoliberalism (Sommier 2003). The most salient issues bear on social and economic injustice, North-South inequalities, international trade rules and barriers, fair trade, global environmental problems, sustainable development and so forth.[1] We use the label 'global justice movement' as we think that what unites the various organisations and groups mobilising on these issues is their willingness to bring about a new world order based on justice.

No matter how it is labelled, the growth of this kind of contention is undeniable and has been shown by a number of studies (e.g., Smith and Johnston 2002; Pianta 2004; della Porta et al. 2004; della Porta and Tarrow 2005; della Porta 2007). What is less clear, however, is the extent to which transnational contention is supplanting traditional patterns of claim-making and to which it oversteps the nation state. This chapter proposes to analyse the new form of contention represented by the GJM through the lenses of the classic social movement agenda for explaining contentious politics. This agenda represents the conceptual tools stemming from a synthesis of different approaches to the study of social movements. Each of the three core components of the classic agenda is adopted in order to ascertain their relevance for explaining transnational episodes of popular contention. To what extent are the emergence and development of this movement dependent on political opportunities that are created at a level located beyond the state, rather than being nationally bounded? To what extent does it rely on transnational organisations and networks, rather than national ones? To what extent does it convey broader collective action frames that allow for cross-national coalitions to be set up rather than country-specific frames? These are some of the questions whose answers require a systematic analysis of the conditions under which the mobilisation of the GJM takes place and of the mechanisms through which it occurs.

Underlying many analyses of the GJM and transnational contention is the idea of the emergence of a 'global civil society'. Thus, a certain number of scholars argue that the new (transnational) protest cycle attests to the emergence of a 'movement of movements' (Ceri 2002; Kaldor et al. 2003; Mertes 2004) and reflects a decline of the nationally based forms of contention. We are quite sceptical of this kind of argument. In our view, it overlooks the crucial impact of a number of domestic factors and overstates the idea of an emerging global civil society (Gobille 2005). In particular, every protest cycle rests on previous mobilising structures and episodes of contention (Agrikoliansky 2005). Nothing is reinvented from scratch. To a large extent, protest activities that occur at the transnational level, such as those carried by the GJM, rely on networks of actors that are embedded within national arenas of contention.

The Classic Social Movement Agenda

McAdam et al. (1996) identified an emerging consensus among students of social movements and revolutions toward three broad sets of explanatory factors: political opportunities, mobilising structures and framing processes.

Three of the most prominent scholars in the field – Doug McAdam, Sidney Tarrow and Charles Tilly (2001) – have added a fourth aspect, suggesting that much work since the 1960s and 1970s has focussed on four key concepts that form what they call the classic social movement agenda for explaining contentious politics: (1) political opportunities, (2) mobilising structures, (3) collective action frames, and (4) repertoires of contention. These four aspects are seen as mediating factors between social change (the ultimate origin of all contention) and contentious interaction (the outcome of such a change).

Although this synthesis has come under attack (Fillieule 1997; Mathieu 2002; Goodwin and Jasper 2004) and alternative explanatory factors have been proposed, most studies remain anchored to one or more of the three main aspects stressed by the classic agenda. Before they are applied to the analysis of the GJM, each of them will be introduced more precisely.[2]

Political opportunities can be defined broadly as 'consistent but not necessarily formal, permanent, or national signals to social or political actors which either encourage or discourage them to use their internal resources to form social movements' (Tarrow 1996: 54, emphasis removed). More specifically, they refer to all of those aspects of the political system that affect the possibilities that challenging groups have to mobilise effectively. As such, they have to be conceptually separated from the internal aspects of those groups that may also increase the likelihood of observing collective action. In this vein, Koopmans (2004: 65) has redefined opportunities as 'options for collective action, with chances and risks attached to them, which depend on factors outside the mobilising group'.

Although in the course of time, the concept of political opportunity structures has come to include an increasing number of different dimensions (Gamson and Meyer 1996) – indeed, nearly everything but the kitchen sink – the most influential works have focussed upon one or more of the four following aspects: (a) the relative openness or closure of the institutionalised political system; (b) the stability or instability of that broad set of elite alignments that typically undergird a polity; (c) the presence or absence of elite allies; and (d) the state's capacity and propensity for repression (McAdam 1996: 27). These are the dimensions of the political opportunity structures that, starting from the basic idea that 'political opportunity structures influence the choice of protest strategies and the impact of social movements on their environment' (Kitschelt 1986:58), have been used by various authors to explain the emergence of social movements, their development over time, their levels of mobilisation, and their forms of action or their outcomes.

While the emergence and mobilisation of movements depend on political opportunities, they do not emerge from scratch. Mobilising structures refer to 'those collective vehicles, informal as well as formal, through which people mobilise and engage in collective action' (McAdam et al. 1996: 3, emphasis removed). This aspect was initially introduced by resource mobilisation theory (see, for instance, Oberschall 1973; McCarthy and Zald 1977; Tilly 1978) as a criticism of the then dominant collective behaviour explanations that tended to see social movements as a (sometimes irrational) reaction to feelings of deprivation and grievances arising from social stress and change (see, for instance, Turner and Killian 1957; Kornhauser 1959; Smelser 1962; Gurr 1970). Against a view that saw collective action as a result of anomie and disorganisation, resource mobilisation theorists have stressed the role of organisation and the capacity of aggrieved groups to gather and mobilise various kinds of resources (for example, financial, human or symbolic).

Two basic types of mobilising structures can be distinguished: formal organisations – for example, the Association for the Taxation of Financial Transactions for the Aid of Citizens (Attac) and informal networks – that is, the web of interpersonal contacts and exchanges among movement activists and participants. Both represent crucial resources for any kind of collective action – whether contentious or not – that constitute the infrastructure of all social movements. Indeed, they are a component of the very nature of social movements, which can be defined as '(i) informal networks, based (ii) on shared beliefs and solidarity, which mobilise about (iii) conflictual issues, through (iv) the frequent use of various forms of protest' (della Porta and Diani 1999: 16). To what extent the GJM finds such resources at the transnational rather than at the national or local level is the empirical task considered below.

This definition introduces us to the third main component of the classic social movement agenda and that captures the cultural dimensions of social movements: framing processes. This is the most loosely defined among the three core concepts of the classic agenda for explaining contentious politics, as it has been used with such a varied array of meanings as to virtually become synonymous with culture. According to McAdam et al., in its original formulation, in the work of David Snow and his collaborators (see, for instance, Snow et al. 1986; see also Gamson et al. 1982; Gamson 1992 and 1995), it refers to 'conscious strategic efforts by groups of people to fashion shared understandings of the world and of themselves that legitimate and motivate collective action' (McAdam et al. 1996: 6, emphasis removed). However, since then, the framing perspective has evolved and today it 'focuses attention on the signifying work or meaning construction engaged in by social movement activists and participants and other parties (e.g. antagonists, elites, media, countermovements) relevant to the interests of social movements and the challenges they mount' (Snow 2004: 384).

Thus, framing processes refer to the signifying work by challenging groups whose resultant products are collective action frames. This may include activities aimed at motivating people for action (motivational frames) or designed for identifying causes (diagnostic frames) and consequences (prognostic frames) of a given problem, but also, more generally speaking, discursive practices relating to collective action itself and to its relation to societal issues.

One feature of the classic agenda for explaining contentious politics is crucial to our present purpose: it is firmly grounded in a nation-centred perspective. This, of course, is particularly true for political opportunities, which have been defined mostly as national opportunity structures, but it holds as well for mobilising structures and framing processes. As Smith has recently pointed out in her review of transnational processes and movements: '[m]ost social movement research takes for granted that the national state defines the relevant political space for political contenders. However, if globalisation is indeed amplifying the importance of remote decision-making arenas for local actors, then we must consider how global factors shape the political contests within states' (2004: 314). Later in her review, Smith puts forward an argument that underwrites our own view: '[i]n many ways, the movement forms and dynamics we see in the transnational arena resemble their national and local predecessors, even as they are adapted to fit a transnational political context' (2004: 320). In the remainder of the chapter, this argument is elaborated using the classic social movement agenda.

Political Opportunities

Perhaps the best way to inquire into the impact of political opportunities on the GJM is to examine the relationship between national and transnational opportunities. In this vein, looking in particular at the degree of openness or 'closedness' of institutions, Sikkink (2005: 156) has made a useful distinction between domestic and international opportunity structures, with the latter referring 'mainly to the degree of openness of international institutions to the participation of transnational NGOs, networks, and coalitions'. The attraction of this approach is that it looks at how the national and the international context open up new opportunities for the mobilisation of transnational actors, including the GJM, therefore acknowledging the fact that social movements, in the era of globalisation, often participate in what Sikkink (2005) calls a 'dynamic multilevel governance'. Therefore, the context of the GJM and other transnational movements can be characterised as a multi-level political opportunity structure (Tarrow and della Porta 2005). The question is, then, to what extent supra-national rather than national opportunity structures determine the mobilisation of the GJM and to what extent the latter remain relevant. This question can ultimately be answered only by looking at evidence coming from empirical research. In order to be assessed empirically, this broad question can be broken down into a number of more specific questions according to the various aspects of political opportunities available. Thus, referring to the four main aspects mentioned earlier, the task becomes one of determining to what extent supra-national political arenas are accessible to the GJM, to what extent the movement can take advantage of the instability in political alignments, to what extent it finds influential political allies at the international level and to what extent supra-national institutions have the capacity and propensity to exert repression on the movement. Our view is that the national context plays a crucial role even for an eminently transnational movement such as the GJM.

A first, although somewhat raw, indicator of the impact of national political opportunity structures on the mobilisation of the GJM is provided by the varying participation (intensity, type, etc.) and level of disruption of the movements' protest activities (often in the form of overt violence). These two aspects vary significantly according to the type of event. Here, the two main forms that mobilisations of the GJM take may be distinguished: mass demonstrations and protest activities addressed against governmental institutions or private organisations, on the one hand, and social forums, which are meetings and exchanges about different issues relating to globalisation, on the other (on counter summits see chapter 2, on social forums see the chapters 1, 3, 4, and 5 in this volume). Comparing the same type of events, substantial differences both across countries and within countries can be observed. For example, certain protests against international organisations, such as the one against the G8 Summit in Genoa in 2001, have been significantly more violent than others, and this is at least in part due to the different behaviours of the state and the police in particular vis-à-vis the protesters.[3] Similarly, certain events taking the form of social forums, such as the 2002 European Social Forum (ESF) in Florence, have mobilised a much higher number of participants than others. Furthermore, compared with the ESF that took place the following year in Paris, there are important differences in the type of actors mobilised (Agrikoliansky and Sommier 2005).

The impact of political opportunity structures on the mobilisation of the GJM can also be assessed indirectly at the individual level by looking at the participation within the movement. Indeed, the type of organisational participation of demonstrators reflects the protest traditions specific to each country, which depend in turn on the cleavage structures. Research undertaken by della Porta and collaborators on two GJM events that occurred in Italy relatively close in time to each other – the protest against the G8 Summit in Genoa in June 2001 and the ESF in Florence in November 2002 – provides evidence to understand cross-national variations in certain individual characteristics of participants in the GJM who are coming from different countries.[4] Their findings confirm the role of the political resources and opportunities peculiar to each country. Specifically, they stress the movement's greater appeal in countries characterised by closed political opportunity structures, especially in terms of the configuration of power, which seem to create a broad front for opposition (della Porta 2005a). For example, in Italy and Spain, the centre-right governments, by adopting neo-liberal positions, seem to favour broader coalitions within the movement as well as a stronger mobilisation than in Britain under a leftist government. The characteristics of the institutional Left also seem to have an impact on the mobilisation capacity of the movement. Indeed, where the Left is divided, such as in Italy, France and Spain, the movement is more present in the streets through mass demonstrations than in other countries, where it is much less visible (della Porta 2007).

Della Porta et al. also point to the traditions of the national social movement sectors in the countries from which the participants came. For example, new social movement (NSM) and environmental activists were much more present among British or German participants than among French ones. In contrast, French participants were characterised by a strong union component to a much greater extent than German or Spanish ones. Similarly, the identification with the GJM varied among participants in the same event. For example, the percentage of people strongly identifying with the movement was much higher among British participants than for other nationalities, whereas those not identifying or identifying only a little with the movement were more numerous among German and Italian participants (della Porta 2005a).

Findings stemming from another research (Fillieule et al. 2004),[5] conducted during the 2003 anti-G8 protest and reproduced in Table 8.1, show that during a transnational mobilisation taking place at the same time on both sides of the

Table 8.1. Organisational Networks of Participants in the Protest Against the G8 Meeting in Évian in 2003 (percentages)

	France	Switzerland	All nationalities
GJM organisations	34	25	31
Ecologists	19	30	25
Humanitarians	17	25	20
Political parties	19	16	20
Human rights	12	18	17
Against racism	14	14	16
Students	16	13	16
Unions	16	15	16
Pacifists	9	19	15
Youth organisations	11	17	14
Social help	12	15	14
Autonomous	6	11	9
Feminists	6	10	8
Religious movements	6	8	8
Neighborhood associations	8	8	8
Housing rights	5	8	7
Customers	4	7	5
Gays and lesbians	3	3	3
Unemployed	5	2	3
Farmers	2	2	2
Other networks	18	9	15
N	836	862	2280

Swiss-French border, opportunity structures play a critical role in the political composition of participants moved by the same issues. Thus, the setting-up of networks mobilised against the G8 summit reflects both the French and the Swiss political opportunity structures as already explored and pointed out by Kriesi et al. (1995). The Swiss mobilisation relies mostly on the NSM sector (ecologists, humanitarians, pacifists), while French activists stem mainly from the left wing political sector (unions, political parties).

Although systematic research on the impact of political opportunity structures on the mobilisation of the GJM remains to be done, these few examples suggest that the movement does not behave in the same way depending not only on the type of event staged, but also depending on the place in which it stages that event, be it a protest action or a social forum. National political opportunities may be responsible for a large part of such cross-national variations. A similar argument can be put forward with regard to the organisational networks, an issue that is addressed at more length in the next section.

Mobilising Structures

A growing number of international NGOs and social movement organisations (SMOs) have emerged in the past few years. For example, Johnson and McCarthy (2005) show that the density of national environmental SMOs has increased steadily between the mid 1960s and the early 1990s, but has since declined, whereas the density of international SMOs has continued to grow throughout the 1990s. This led them to conclude that 'expansion of the transnational environmental population comes later than growth in the population of national environmental SMOs' (Johnson and McCarthy 2005: 85). This trend, however, should not be overstated, as the number of national SMOs remains far higher than that of international ones, and the founding pace of the latter has also slowed down between 1995 and 2000.

A similar and perhaps even stronger trend can be observed for SMOs that are more directly addressing global justice issues. Indeed, since Seattle 1999 and the rising protest cycle against neoliberalism as well as for global justice and democracy, a dense network of organisations and groups has emerged, as attested by several emblematic SMOs. For example, Attac, created in France in 1998, is now present in more than 51 countries (George 2004). Similarly, less formalised groups such as Reclaim the Street, People's Global Action and Indymedia represent a large network of activists in many countries, and action campaigns such as Jubilee 2000[6] have mobilised strongly. At the same time, nationally specific networks such as SUD (Solidaires, Unitaires, Démocratiques) in France or the Lilliput Network in Italy have also emerged. These new kind of organisations and networks, which are very loosely structured, decentralised and horizontal (della Porta et al. 2006), cohabit with older ones within the GJM.

These examples convey the picture of a GJM formed by a network of organisations and groups that crosscuts national borders or at least that is part of a transnational cycle of contention in which actors from various parts of the world are involved. To be sure, there is a striking resemblance among the various protests arising across the globe and targeting supra-national organisations or intergovernmental summits. Such a resemblance can also be seen in the use of widely shared slogans such as 'Another World is Possible' (George 2004). However, it is at best too early to conclude that we are witnessing the emergence of a single world protest movement or the creation of a global civil society. In our view, these arguments overlook the crucial impact of a number of domestic factors on the GJM and the variation in the forms that this movement takes in different places. First of all, every protest cycle rests on previous mobilising structures and episodes of contention. To a large extent, therefore, transnational protest is carried by networks of actors that are embedded within national arenas of contention and whose strength varies from one country to another. Furthermore, transnational protest also depends on the work of core activists who have been engaged in previous movements and SMOs. For example, some have shown that, contrary to what one might think, the 'Battle of Seattle' did not gather a very heterogeneous and international network of actors, but rather was dominated by US activists (Levi and Murphy 2002). Similarly, others have shown that most of the activists in Seattle were Canadians or from the US and were mainly trade unionists (Lichbach and Almeida 2001). This shows that the supposedly global civil society mobilised in Seattle was in fact the result of a number of networks deeply rooted in the national or even local context in which the mobilisation took place.

Recent empirical research on participants in the GJM shows how its mobilisation relies on national structural and institutional factors. In particular, a look at certain characteristics of the networks involved in the mobilisation of the movement, shown in Table 8.2, allows us to show the importance of national traditions of contention on the multi-organisational field of the GJM. Specifically, a comparison of the organisational networks involved in the movements points to the impact of two factors on the mobilising structures of the GJM. First, the types of organisational networks that become involved in the movement depend very much on the pre-existing networks formed in other movements and during previous waves of contention (Passy and Bandler 2003), which in turn reflect the existing cleavage structure in a given country (Kriesi et al. 1995). Second, the movement's activities rest on different kinds of networks depending on the type of activity, that is, depending on whether it is a protest-oriented action (for example, a demonstration) or rather a more 'propositive' activity (for example, a social forum).

Table 8.2. Organisational Networks of Participants in Two GJM Events (percentages)

	Protest against the G8 summit in Genoa, June 2001	ESF in Florence, November 2002
NGOs	32.0	41.5
Unions	19.0	31.8
Political parties	32.2	34.6
Students organisations	52.0	57.5
Social centres	35.0	32.1
Religious movements	17.6	19.3
Ecological associations	24.2	43.1
Social volunteers associations	41.4	51.3
Sport or entertainment organisations	34.4	50.9
N	763	2384

The surveys, mentioned earlier, on the protest against the G8 Summit in Genoa in June 2001 and the ESF in Florence in November 2002 point to a similar direction (see Andretta et al. 2002; della Porta 2003a, 2003b and 2005a; della Porta and Mosca 2003). These surveys show a number of findings concerning the embeddedness in organisational networks of participants in these events that support our argument. Certain aspects are worth mentioning in this respect. First of all, it is obvious that the GJM mobilises a rather heterogeneous network of participants. Some networks are overrepresented in both contentious gatherings (for example, NGOs and voluntary associations), while others are much more weakly involved (for example, religious movements). Thus, certain types of networks seem to be prevailing, while others are more marginally involved. These findings also suggest that the mobilisation of the GJM depends on the national structure and implementation of existent social forces in the country. For example, political parties have traditionally patronised the social movement sector in Italy. Therefore, they represent an important part of the mobilising structures of the GJM in this country. Furthermore, student groups, which are overrepresented in the network structure of these two events, are also important in the Italian social movement sector, while they constitute a less developed organisational network in other countries, in particular in Switzerland. This suggests once more that national mobilising structures play an important role in the mobilisation of the actors that form the GJM.[7]

Thus, a movement may have a transnational or global nature, but the mobilising structures on which its mobilisation relies still vary according to the very place in which the protest occurs. Although it is clear that heterogeneity is one of the main characteristics of the GJM and, more generally, of the protest cycle around global issues, national structures and the particular history of the social movement sector in a given country have a prevailing impact on the organisational structure of transnational mobilisations. For example, although countries such as France and Italy have a long tradition of political mobilisation, they are characterised by a weak presence of the NSMs. Therefore, the national traditions of contention impinge not only on the type of organisations present at events occurring in a given country, but also express themselves in the organisational membership of activists coming from other countries, who tend to 'export' their own tradition of contention when they mobilise outside of their country. This influence on the organisational structure of the GJM also has implications for the collective action frames conveyed by it, as we try to show in the next section.

Framing Processes

In dealing with framing processes, we shift from the structural to the cultural aspects of contention. Building collective identities to be mobilised for contention is part of this process. Therefore, 'identity frames' are a particular and important kind of frame (Gamson 1995). Another kind is what may be called 'substantive frames', that is, frames bearing on more or less specific issues raised in political contention. The following discussion focuses upon these two types of collective action frames within the GJM.[8] In addition, it endorses the distinction between 'specific frames', which refer to particular issues and goals, and 'master frames', which are more general and encompassing (Snow and Benford 1992; Tarrow 1992).

As mentioned earlier, the struggle against neoliberalism is one of the central claims of the GJM. It can be considered what Snow and Benford (1992) call a 'master frame', that is, a symbolic construction of a public problem that allows many individuals, organisations and networks to get involved in a movement. The struggle against neoliberalism and the construction of this master frame began with the protest against the G7 Summit in London in 1984 (Massiah 2003). It has then continued since 1994 and the campaign against the Bretton Woods agreements (Fougier 2004). The Zapatistas have played an important role in this process, to the extent that they have constituted the first mass uprising against neoliberalism (Le Bot 2003). Since then, numerous issues have been added to the GJM, and country-specific matters have appeared. For example, mobilisation in Italy is very much focussed upon the promotion of 'democracy from below' (della Porta 2005b). Although the issue of democracy from below is addressed also on the local and transnational levels, it has a particularly important place in the claims and decisional processes within the movement in Italy. However, although it represents the common denominator of all of those involved in the GJM, not all organisations and groups consider the struggle against neoliberalism to be a sufficient motivation to mobilise. The heterogeneity of the GJM does not allow us to conclude that this common claim accounts for the presence of many different networks in the same movement or even in the same protest cycle. However, it would also be mistaken to consider that every network would join the protest based on a single issue. The gathering of such a variegated range of groups could hardly take place in the absence of shared beliefs about the 'world out there' and the creation of common meanings about the situation, which are brought about by the collective processes of interpretation, attribution and social construction stressed by framing theorists. We think that there are mid range or intermediate level frames that link the struggle against neoliberalism to more specific issues and claims and that allow for the mobilisation of different sectors. In other words, specific networks participate in a protest not simply because their own claims and the issues they raise resonate with the master frame of the GJM, but also because there are selective frames stemming from this master frame that mediate between the specific issues and the more general issues of the protest (Passy and Bandler 2003). For example, in Italy, Spain and France, the issue of global justice is linked to the struggle against neoliberalism on the national level, while in Germany and Switzerland the issue of global justice is mainly associated to North-South solidarity (della Porta 2007).

The framing perspective has taught us that a process of the construction of the 'problem' is necessary to activate the identities and motivations of actors to form social movements. However, this process is constrained and limited by previous mobilisations and ideas already expressed by previous social forces, most notably by previous social movements. In this view, the values and issues carried by the GJM do not differ fundamentally from those of the wave of contention that has preceded it. Indeed, although there are certainly several novelties, most issues already existed earlier. North-South solidarity, for example, is a typical NSM issue. Similarly, the struggle against economic liberalism is a long-standing claim of Marxist-oriented groups.

Thus, strands of the Old Left and the New Left – traditionally divided in their actions between a revolutionary and a reformist left – find a common ground within the GJM movement. We think that this common ground is found through the activation of 'selective frames' that are resonant with the master frame represented by the struggle against neoliberalism and that allow for the gathering of many different networks for a common cause (Passy and Bandler 2003).

To examine this argument, we can use a third dataset built in a fashion similar to the two mentioned earlier. The data come from research conducted during two protest events against the World Economic Forum (WEF) meeting in Davos, Switzerland, in January 2004.[9] They show the different values of activists according to the network to which they belong. As can be seen in Table 8.3, which shows the issues addressed by participants in these protest events by type of network, the two principal issues are core issues of the GJM: to establish democratic forms alternative to the state, and to abolish capitalism (with the last column taking into account all types of networks). Also belonging to these priorities of the GJM are the issues of strengthening international law and breaking radically with current models of economic development. Most of these issues were already addressed by the NSMs. Most importantly, when the distributions across types of networks are compared, we see that, whatever the type of network to which they belong, participants privilege certain issues rather than others. This means that these issues resonate with the master frame. In addition, the more the issues are vague and abstract, the more they meet the preference of participants.[10]

The fact that the ranking of issues is the same for every kind of network suggests that networks do not mobilise on specific frames, but on selective ones that are linked to the master frame. In other words, networks mobilise above all on thematically close issues or issues directly derived from the master frame.

This brief analysis of collective action frames in the GJM shows that, in spite of the national constraints and the traditions of contention, no matter where they come from, participants in this movement are able to put aside their specific identities in order to join the movement, displaying a similar priority order of issues on the level of the master frame. Indeed, in the specific case of the mobili-

Table 8.3. Issues Addressed by Participants in the Protests Against the WEF Meeting in Davos in 2004 by Type of Network (percentages)

	NSMs	Traditional organisations	Political parties	Unions and unemployed workers	No organizational affiliation	All networks
To strengthen international law	29	30	31	20	28	29
To reform financial and economic international institutions	20	18	14	22	21	20
To abolish financial and economic international institutions	20	19	20	17	18	20
To involve more the NGOs in international decisions	23	21	11	20	20	21
To reform capitalism	23	21	17	20	19	20
To abolish capitalism	39	35	46	41	31	38
To strengthen a larger state intervention in economic and social fields	20	18	14	20	15	18
To develop participative democracy	26	22	26	28	20	24
To establish a world parliament	20	17	11	13	13	17
To establish democratic forms alternative to the state	41	36	37	46	33	39
To break radically with current models of economic development	30	27	23	20	22	28
N	235	107	35	46	116	411

sation in Davos, sectoral issues such as homosexuals' rights, mine clearance and education were not considered as priorities because they were too specific. In contrast, general issues were much more emphasised in the mobilisation.

Conclusion

We have tried to apply to the analysis of the GJM the classic social movement agenda for explaining contentious politics. Thus, we examined the role of political opportunities, mobilising structures and framing processes for this movement in an attempt to show that the national context remains crucial even for transnational forms of contention, such as those staged by the GJM. In a nutshell, we have argued that the GJM acts within a multi-level political opportunity structure in which national contexts still impinge in important ways on its mobilisation. Country-specific contextual aspects, above all the cleavage structure, from which stem pre-existing social networks in which movement participants are embedded, allow us to explain why the characteristics of the mobilisation of the GJM vary from one country to another. At the same time, the creation of common ways of framing political, social and economic issues makes the gathering of a variety of different organisations, groups and networks possible.

In the light of our discussion, it thus looks like the scale shift of the GJM depends upon the angle from which one looks at it. Indeed, national political opportunity structures still play a relevant role in explaining the structure of the movement, and national mobilising structures are still relevant as well. The scale shift is to be found in the collective action frames elaborated by the GJM. However, the classic social movement agenda goes still quite far in explaining transnational contention. Of course, it must be adapted to some extent, for example, by taking into account supra-national political opportunities in addition to national ones. As of today, however, the imprint of the national context and characteristics seems so strong, after centuries of state formation, that even a genuinely transnational movement such as the GJM remains partly imprisoned in the cage built by the nation state.

Notes

This chapter is an adapted translation of an article previously published in French as M. Giugni, M. Bandler and N. Eggert, 'Contraintes nationales et changement d'échelle dans l'activisme transnational', *Lien Social et Politiques* 58 (2007): 41–57. It also draws from a paper previously published as M. Giugni, M. Bandler and N. Eggert, 'The Global Justice Movement: How Far Does the Classic Social Movement Agenda Go in Explaining Transnational Contention?', Programme Paper PP-CSSM-24 (2006), UNRISD, Geneva.

1. It should be noted that this actor is obviously not the only one to be engaged for another globalisation. NGOs are also part of the contention, but on a different ground, that of lobbying, which should not be confounded with mass protest (Siméant 2005).

2. Helpful reviews of these three aspects of the classic social movement agenda can be found in the *Blackwell Companion to Social Movements* (Snow et al. 2004). See, in particular, the chapters by Hanspeter Kriesi on political context and opportunities, the chapter by Bob Edwards and John McCarthy on resources and social movement mobilisation, the chapter by Mario Diani on networks and participation and the chapter by David Snow on framing processes, ideology and discursive fields. See also Benford and Snow (2000) on framing processes.

3. This is also the case for the demonstrations against the World Economic Forum (WEF), which are very conflictual and attract a number of particularly radical participants, precisely due to the risks involved and the transaction costs of participation.

4. The data were obtained by handing out individual questionnaires to participants in the two events. See Andretta et al. (2002), della Porta (2003a, 2003b and 2005a), and della Porta and Mosca (2003).

5. This survey, based on the same approach as the ones mentioned earlier, was conducted on both sides of the French-Swiss border near Geneva, where the protest events took place over approximately one week. This explains why the sample includes the same amount of French and Swiss participants (about 40 per cent each) and allows for a direct comparison of the two groups.

6. Jubilee 2000 was created for the G8 protest in Birmingham in 1998. Set up by Christian associations and various NGOs, the aim of this campaign was to put pressure on Northern countries to obtain the cancellation of the debt of Southern countries by the year 2000.

7. The study by Fillieule et al. (2004) shows that French and Swiss participants were embedded in different organisational networks. Specifically, GJM organisations were more present on the French side. This can be explained by the fact that France is one of the birthplaces of the GJM in Europe, as attested by the founding of the strong development of Attac there. No equivalent SMO exists in Switzerland in terms of size.

8. Identity and substantive frames are only two among a wider variety of collective action frames one can find in the literature. For example, Snow and Benford (1988) distinguish between diagnostic (problem identification and attribution of blame), prognostic (problem resolution) and motivational (recruitment and mobilisation) frames. In a similar fashion, della Porta (1999) distinguishes between four types of frames according to their function: a) protagonist field definition, b) antagonist field definition, c) diagnosis, and d) prognosis. Focussing more on what movement participants feel than on the strategic efforts by movement leaders aimed at consensus formation (Klandermans 1988), Gamson (1995) speaks of identity, injustice and agency frames. Finally, in a more dynamic and strategic perspective, Snow et al. (1986) identify four main 'frame alignment' processes, that is, four basic ways in which social movement activists and organisations present their messages congruent with prevailing views of certain social problems: a) bridging, b) amplification, c) extension, and d) transformation.

9. One of the two protest events took place in Zurich on 17 January and the other in Chur on 24 January 2004, for a total of 411 respondents.

10. The selective frames identified by Passy and Bandler (2003) in the protest against the G8 Summit in Évian were very similar to these ones.

References

Agrikoliansky, E. 2005. 'Du Tiers-Mondisme à l'altermondialisme: Genèse(s) d'une nouvelle cause'. In *L'Altermondialisme en France,* eds. É. Agrikoliansky, O. Fillieule and N. Mayer, 43–74. Paris: Flammarion.

Agrikoliansky, E. and I. Sommier, eds. 2005. *Radiographie du mouvement altermondialiste.* Paris: La Dispute.

Andretta, M., et al. 2002. *Global No Global New Global.* Rome: Laterza.

Ceri, P. 2002. *Movimenti Global: La Protesta nel XXI secolo.* Rome: Laterza

della Porta, D. 1999. 'Protest, Protesters, and Protest Policing: Public Discourses in Italy and Germany from the 1960s to the 1980s'. In *How Social Movements Matter,* eds. M. Giugni, D. McAdam and C. Tilly, 66–96. Minneapolis: University of Minnesota Press.

————. 2003a. *I New Global.* Bologna: Il Mulino.

————. 2003b. 'Politics, Anti-Politics, Other Politics : Conceptions of Democracy and the Movement for a Globalisation from below'. *ECPR General Conference,* Marburg, 18–21 September 2003.

————. 2005a. 'Multiple Belongings, Tolerant Identities and the Construction of "Another Politics": Between the European Social Forum and the Local Social Fora'. In *Transnational Protest and Global Activism,* eds. D. della Porta and S. Tarrow, 175–202. Lanham: Rowman and Littlefield.

————. 2005b. 'Making the Polis: Social Forums and Democracy in the Global Justice Movement'. *Mobilisation* 10(1): 73–94.

————. 2007. 'The Global Justice Movement in Context'. In *The Global Justice Movement. Cross-National and Transnational Perspectives,* ed. D. della Porta, 232–251. Boulder: Paradigm.

della Porta, D. and M. Diani. 1999. *Social Movements: An Introduction.* Oxford: Blackwell.

della Porta, D., et al. 2004. *Global Movements and Transnational Protest.* Minneapolis: University of Minnesota Press.

della Porta, D., H. Kriesi and D. Rucht, eds. 1999. *Social Movements in a Globalising World.* Houndmills: Macmillan Palgrave.

della Porta, D. and L. Mosca, eds. 2003. *Globalizzazione e movimenti sociali.* Rome: Manifestolibri.

della Porta, D. and S. Tarrow, eds. 2005. *Transnational Protest and Global Activism.* Lanham: Rowman and Littlefield.

Diani, M. 2004. 'Networks and Participation'. In *The Blackwell Companion to Social Movements,* eds. D.A. Snow, S. Soule and H. Kriesi, 339–359. Oxford: Blackwell.

Edwards, B. and J.D. McCarthy. 2004. 'Resources and Social Movement Mobilisation'. In *The Blackwell Companion to Social Movements,* eds. D.A. Snow, S. Soule and H. Kriesi, 116–154. Oxford: Blackwell.

Fillieule, O. 1997. *Stratégies de la rue: Les manifestations en France*. Paris: Presses de Science Po.

Fillieule, O., et al. 2004. 'L'altermondialisme en réseaux. Trajectoires militantes, multipositionnalité et formes de l'engagement: Les participants du contre-sommet du G8 d'Evian'. *Politix* 68:13–48.

Fougier, E., ed. 2004. *Le mouvement altermondialiste*. Paris: La Documentation Française.

Gamson, W.A. 1992. 'The Social Psychology of Collective Action'. In *Frontiers of Social Movement Theory*, eds. A.D. Morris and C. McClurg Mueller, 53–76. New Haven: Yale University Press.

———. 1995. 'Constructing Social Protest'. In *Social Movements and Culture*, eds. H. Johnston and B. Klandermans, 95–106. Minneapolis: University of Minnesota Press.

Gamson, W.A., B. Fireman and S. Rytina. 1982. *Encounters with Unjust Authority*. Homewood: Dorsey Press.

Gamson, W.A. and D.S. Meyer. 1996. 'Framing Political Opportunity'. In *Comparative Perspectives on Social Movements: Political Opportunities, Mobilising Structures and, Cultural Framings*, eds. D. McAdam, J.D. McCarthy and M.N. Zald, 275–290. Cambridge: Cambridge University Press.

George, S. 2004. *Un autre monde est possible si…*. Paris: Fayard.

Gobille, B. 2005. 'Les altermondialistes, des activistes transnationaux?' *Critique Internationale* 27: 131–145.

Goodwin, J. and J.M. Jasper. 2004. 'Caught in a Winding, Snarling Vine: The Structural Bias of Political Process Theory'. In *Rethinking Social Movements: Structure, Meaning and Emotion*, eds. J. Goodwin and J.M. Jasper, 3–30. Lanham: Rowman and Littlefield.

Gurr, T.R. 1970. *Why Men Rebel*. Princeton: Princeton University Press.

Johnson, E. and J.D. McCarthy. 2005. 'The Sequencing of Transnational and National Social Movement Mobilisation: The Organisational Mobilisation of the Global and U.S. Environmental Movements'. In *Transnational Protest and Global Activism*, eds. D. della Porta and S. Tarrow, 71–93. Lanham: Rowman and Littlefield.

Kaldor, M., H. Anheier and M. Glasius. 2003. *Global Civil Society*. Oxford: Oxford University Press.

Kitschelt, H. 1986. 'Political Opportunity Structures and Political Protest: Anti-Nuclear Movements in Four Democracies'. *British Journal of Political Science* 16: 57–85.

Klandermans, B. 1988. 'The Formation and Mobilisation of Consensus'. In *International Social Movement Research*, eds. B. Klandermans, H. Kriesi and S. Tarrow, Vol. 1: *From Structure to Action: Social Movement Participation across Cultures*, 173–197. Greenwich: JAI Press.

Koopmans, R. 2004. 'Political. Opportunity. Structure. Some Splitting to Balance the Lumping'. In *Rethinking Social Movements: Structure, Meaning and Emotion*, eds. J. Goodwin and J.M. Jasper, 61–73. Lanham: Rowman and Littlefield.

Kornhauser, W. 1959. *The Politics of Mass Society*. New York: Free Press.

Kriesi, H., et al. 1995. *New Social Movements in Western Europe*. Minneapolis: University of Minnesota Press.

Le Bot, Y. 2003. 'Le zapatisme, première insurrection contre la mondialisation néolibérale'. In *Un autre monde … Contestations, dérives et surprises dans l'antimondialisation*, ed. M. Wieviorka, 129–140. Paris: Balland.

Levi, M. and G. Murphy. 2002. 'Coalitions of Contention: The Case of the WTO Protests in Seattle'. *XV World Congress of the International Sociological Association,* Brisbane, 7–13 July 2002.

Lichbach, M. and P. Almeida. 2001. 'Global Order and Local Resistance: The Neoliberal Institutional Trilemma and the Battle of Seattle'. Working Paper. Riverside: University of California.

Massiah, G. 2003. 'Le G8, un club de riches très contesté'. *Manière de voir* 75: 22–25.

Mathieu, L. 2002. 'Rapport au politique, dimensions cognitives et perspectives pragmatiques dans l'analyse des mouvements sociaux'. *Revue Française de Science Politique* 52: 75–100.

McAdam, D. 1996. 'Conceptual Origins, Current Problems, Future Directions'. In *Comparative Perspectives on Social Movements: Political Opportunities, Mobilising Structures, and Cultural Framings,* eds. D. McAdam, J.D. McCarthy and M.N. Zald, 23–30. Cambridge: Cambridge University Press.

McAdam, D., J.D. McCarthy and M.N. Zald, eds. 1996. *Comparative Perspectives on Social Movements: Political Opportunities, Mobilising Structures, and Cultural Framings.* Cambridge: Cambridge University Press.

McAdam, D., S. Tarrow and C. Tilly. 2001. *Dynamics of Contention.* Cambridge: Cambridge University Press.

McCarthy, J.D. and M.N. Zald. 1977. 'Resource Mobilisation and Social Movements: A Partial Theory'. *American Journal of Sociology* 82: 1212–1241.

Mertes, T. 2004. *A Movement of Movements.* London: Verso.

Oberschall, A. 1973. *Social Conflict and Social Movements.* Englewood-Cliffs: Prentice-Hall.

Passy, F. and M. Bandler. 2003. 'Protestation altermondialiste: Une nouvelle vague de contestation? Une analyse des cadres narratifs et des réseaux d'action'. *Annual Congress of the Swiss, German and Austrian political science associations,* Bern, 14–15 November 2003.

Pianta, M. 2004. *UN World Summits and Civil Society: The State of the Art.* Programme on Civil Society and Social Movements, Paper number 18. Genève, UNRISD.

Sikkink, K. 2005. 'Patterns of Dynamic Multilevel Governance and the Insider-Outsider Coalition'. In *Transnational Protest and Global Activism,* eds. D. della Porta and S. Tarrow, 151–173. Lanham: Rowman and Littlefield.

Smelser, N.J. 1962. *Theory of Collective Behavior.* New York: Free Press.

Smith, J. 2004. 'Transnational Processes and Movements'. In *The Blackwell Companion to Social Movements,* eds. D.A. Snow, S. Soule and H. Kriesi, 311–335. Oxford: Blackwell.

Smith, J. and H. Johnston, eds. 2002. *Globalisation and Resistance: Transnational Dimensions of Social Movements.* Lanham: Rowman and Littlefield.

Snow, D.A. 2004. 'Framing Processes, Ideology, and Discursive Fields'. In *The Blackwell Companion to Social Movements,* eds. D.A. Snow, S. Soule and H. Kriesi, 382–412. Oxford: Blackwell.

Snow, D.A. and R.D. Benford. 1988. 'Ideology, Frame Resonance, and Participant Mobilisation'. *International Social Movement Research* 1: 197–217.

———. 1992. 'Master Frames and Cycles of Protest'. In *Frontiers of Social Movement Theory,* eds. A.D. Morris and C. McClurg Mueller, 135–155. New Haven: Yale University Press.

Snow, D.A., et al. 1986. 'Frame Alignment Processes, Micromobilisation, and Movement Participation'. *American Sociological Review* 51: 464–481.

Snow, D.A., S. Soule and H. Kriesi, eds. 2004. *The Blackwell Companion to Social Movements.* Oxford: Blackwell.

Sommier, I. 2003. *Le renouveau des mouvements contestataires à l'heure de la mondialisation.* Paris: Flammarion.

Tarrow, S. 1992. 'Mentalities, Political Cultures, and Collective Action Frames: Constructing Meanings through Action'. In *Frontiers of Social Movement Theory,* eds. A.D. Morris and C. McClurg Mueller, 174–202. New Haven: Yale University Press.

———. 1996. 'States and Opportunities: The Political Structuring of Social Movements'. In *Comparative Perspectives on Social Movements: Political Opportunities, Mobilising Structures and, Cultural Framings,* eds. D. McAdam, J.D. McCarthy, and M.N. Zald, 41–61. Cambridge: Cambridge University Press.

Tarrow, S. and D. della Porta. 2005. 'Conclusion: "Globalisation", Complex Internationalism, and Transnational Contention'. In *Transnational Protest and Global Activism,* eds. D. della Porta and S. Tarrow, 227–246. Lanham: Rowman and Littlefield.

Tilly, C. 1978. *From Mobilisation to Revolution.* Reading: Addison-Wesley.

———. 1984. 'Social Movements and National Politics'. In *Statemaking and Social Movements,* eds. C. Bright and S. Harding, 291–317. Ann Arbor: University of Michigan Press.

———. 1986. *The Contentious French.* Cambridge: Harvard University Press.

———. 1995. *Popular Contention in Great Britain, 1758–1834.* Cambridge: Harvard University Press.

Turner, R.H. and L.M. Killian. 1957. *Collective Behavior.* Englewood Cliffs: Prentice-Hall.

Chapter Nine

Individual Surveys in Rallies (INSURA)

A New Tool for Exploring Transnational Activism?

Olivier Fillieule and Philippe Blanchard

Introduction

Social movement understanding has been dominated for a long time by a legitimist bias that conceived of demonstrators and protest actions as the product of deprivation and abnormal conduct. With the emergence of resource mobilisation theory (RMT), these interpretations have been radically replaced by models that emphasise the costs and benefits of participation in collective action as well as the importance of social movement organisations (SMOs) in mobilising resources and distributing positive or negative incentives. RMT was further refined by the growing importance in explanatory models of the so-called 'political opportunity structure', which helped to stress contextual factors in collective action. To date, structural factors, political contexts, organisations and not the actors themselves, have been at the centre of social movement research for more than thirty years. That direction has been further reinforced by the quasi-exclusive recourse to methods such as organisational surveys or protest events analysis (PEA).

As a result, scholars have certainly gone too far in the rejection of the actors themselves, those who engage in collective action, their social and biological characteristics, their very motivations and their irreducible heterogeneity. Even the more recent developments of social movement theory, by taking into account the cultural turn and further hybridising between US and European research, has left unexplored the individual who actually participates in demonstrations, protest activities and, broadly speaking, social movements.

On the contrary, students of political participation, in addition to studying voting behaviour, have also investigated the so-called unconventional forms of social and political participation. Based on opinion polls conducted in many Western countries, researchers have tried to study political attitudes toward protest. The modes of actions investigated, ranging from signing petitions and lawful demonstrations to damaging property, have since become a permanent item in many national election studies almost everywhere in the United States and Europe, through World Values Surveys and European Social Surveys. The most significant findings of these cross-national opinion polls can be summed up by the so-called Socio-Economic Standard model (SES), which establishes that age, gender and level of education are the most important factors of protest behaviour (Fillieule and Tartakowsky 2008: ch. 2).

The advantage of population surveys is that they allow cross-national and historical comparisons. But, most of the time, they measure the willingness to protest rather than the actual participation in the protest. As a result, there are no figures on actual rates of mobilisation. Moreover, in these surveys, people are asked about their participation in general, which makes it difficult to distinguish between different protest issues. As Van Aelst and Walgrave (2001: 463) state, 'declared willingness to participate in a demonstration is a poor indicator of actual participation in collective action. "The action potential of individuals reflects not what they will do but what they think they ought to do" (Topf 1995: 59)'.[1] The difference between willingness to act and actual behaviour can be explained by a whole set of factors, among them the relational context, which seems to play a central role (Fillieule 1997; Favre, Fillieule and Mayer 1997). Finally, one should note that even in the most recent studies, which try to measure the actual past participation in protest actions, biases remain since one knows that there can be discrepancies between what people say about what they did in the past and what they actually did.

Coming back to social movement research, one knows that the development of the so-called political process approach has been backed by a parallel expansion of the PEA method, which has the advantage of focussing on protest actions themselves and, as a consequence, on actual participation to demonstrations. Yet, as we just said, PEA was never meant to answer any questions about the demonstrators, but was used more to determine, in a historical sociology and macro-comparison perspective inspired by the work of Charles Tilly, broad trends in protest activity. In any case, since newspaper cuttings have massively been chosen as source materials and, in some rarer cases, police archives, the material gathered is of little interest for those who would try to provide consistent information about the people involved in the protest actions.

To date, it seems that only by interviewing people during protest events can we gather substantial information about participants. However, as Favre, Fillieule and Mayer (1997: 11) stated, we are here confronted with 'a strange lacuna in the sociology of mobilisation'. Before the end of the 1990s, actually, very few students tried to collect individual data directly in the course of protest events.

The central reason for that situation is certainly to be found in epistemological considerations. Having recourse to an individual survey during protest events could at first sight seem paradoxical or contradictory, since the individual survey technique appears incompatible with the situation one wants to explore. As a matter of fact, individual surveys are by nature individualistic: the interviewee is isolated from its environment and is asked to express an opinion about questions he has not been forcibly informed about in advance. Moreover, answering the questions does not mean he is personally involved in the issue at stake. And finally, expressing an opinion will in no way have any personal consequence for the interviewee. In a demonstration, on the contrary, the interviewee is not isolated at all, since the march in itself is instituting a collective, and also because people usually demonstrate within small groups of friends, relatives, etc. (McPhail and Miller 1973; Fillieule 1997; Drury and Reicher 1999; Van Aelst and Walgrave 2001); also, the interviewee is already expressing an opinion by the very fact of demonstrating, he expresses that opinion in a visible manner, which means he is concerned by the issue at stake and ready to assume the possible risks and costs of his acts. From all of these differences, it follows that the recourse to an individual survey in the course of collective events collides with the economists' well known 'no bridge problem' between a micro- and a macro-level of analysis.

As a result, prior the middle of the 1990s, interviewing participants in protest events had only been used in a few studies.[2] Individual Surveys in Rallies (hereafter INSURA) did not enter the social researcher's usual toolkit until the following decade. It was at the beginning of 1994 that Favre and his colleagues conducted such a survey, with the primary ambition of building a solid methodological framework that could be subsequently applied by other researchers interested in gathering representative data on crowd participants (Favre, Fillieule and Mayer 1997).[3] Van Aelst first used their method in 1998 for research on the normalisation of protest in Belgium (Van Aelst and Walgrave 2001).

The new century marked a new era in the use of INSURA. More precisely, with the public emergence and tremendous development of alter-global protest events and forums, researchers began to have a recourse to that method that appeared particularly suited to that object of study. In effect, one knows the importance of events as epiphanic moments for the movement, the public debate that emerged around the qualification of participants as mere losers, terrorists or politically unaware people, the debate about the consistency of the ideology of the movement and its constituency (are these people 'rooted cosmopolitans' (Tarrow 2001) or 'modernisation losers'?), and finally, the question about how to measure and assess the heterogeneity of the 'movement of movements', in terms of organisations as well as constituencies. The INSURA technique seems appropriate to answer all of these questions.

To date, and apart from some data on demonstrators collected here and there (e.g., Lichbach and Almeida 2001; Levi and Murphy 2002), the *Gruppo di Ricerca sull'Azione Collettiva in Europa* (GRACE) was the first to launch an ambitious program to survey the so-called 'noglobal movement' in Italy at different settings (e.g., Andretta et al. 2002), followed by Bedoyan and Van Aelst (2003) on an alter-global demonstration that was held in Brussels on 14 December 2001; and our own surveys during the protest in Geneva and Lausanne against the Évian G8 summit and at the Saint-Denis European Social Forum (ESF) in France (Fillieule et al. 2004; Agrikoliansky and Sommier 2005; Fillieule and Blanchard 2005). More recently, the project 'Democracy in Europe and the Mobilisation of Society' (DEMOS) also included a workpackage dedicated to INSURA (della Porta 2009),[4] and finally, a group of researchers co-ordinated by Stefaan Walgrave has conducted the most ambitious INSURA ever at the global action day against an imminent war in Iraq on 15 February 2003 (see Walgrave and Rucht 2010). The survey was conducted at the same time in some cities of the US, Great-Britain, Spain, Italy, Germany, the Netherlands, Sweden and Belgium. More than 6,000 participants answered the questionnaires in eight countries and eleven cities.[5] Walgrave and Van Lear (chapter 1 in this volume) also realised a large-scale international questionnaire survey among participants of the ESF in 2006. Currently, they are engaged in a European project on the role of protest issues in determining who will participate in protest events, why they do so, and how they get to do so (Caught in the act of protest: Contextualizing contestation).

After some years of the intensive use of INSURA, one is entitled to wonder whether or not that technique has fulfilled the researchers' hopes. We learned from the past that, in social movement theory, due to an intensive and fertile competition that often drives us to quantity instead of quality, new methods of inquiry have been used at length without always ensuring a sufficient degree of epistemological vigilance and methodological scruple. It is certainly too early to decide whether INSURA will mark a real progress in social movement theory. Yet, some remarks can be made and some questions can be asked.

In this chapter, we use some results of a collective work on alter-global rallies in Évian and Saint-Denis[6] to first answer some basic methodological questions about how to collect data on crowds and then demonstrate the strengths and weaknesses of INSURA in exploring the transnational dimension of alter-global protests based on our work.

INSURA: Technical Problems and Sampling Strategies

Assessing the entire realm of methodological and epistemological questions raised by INSURA would largely exceed the framework of this chapter. We will only deal here with some questions centred on specific problems applied to alter-global events. Three main questions will be addressed: what are the specific constraints of interviewing people at the very moment they are 'expressing' a political opinion? What specific constraints result from the morphology of the covered events, that is to say, how to build a valid sampling frame? We then turn to a more general point about the questions that can or cannot be solved by using that technique.

People attending a protest event or a political rally are in an expressive situation. They actually express their feelings and their opinions, if only by being there, by chanting and shouting slogans, by raising their fists, by wearing masks or costumes, by holding banners or placards. This results in two consequences. One is that the peoples' willingness to participate in a survey is generally optimal, apart for those groups and individuals who reject poll techniques and sociological surveys altogether as part of the 'dominant order'.[7] The other is that in the case of face-to-face interviews, people will certainly pay little attention to the questions being asked since they are at the same time engaged in a collective action, surrounded by colleagues, friends, relatives and the whole crowd. The influence of fellow protesters will not be developed here. To allow for the turbulent situation, however, questionnaires must be short and too demanding questions, like multiple choice or open-ended questions, should be avoided. Participants might also be asked to fill in the questionnaire at home and to send it in by mail. That solution is very much in favour in contemporary INSURA practices and offers many advantages. However, one has to be aware that the answers will be of a different nature than those gathered in the course of the event, especially when the considered event has immediate consequences (e.g., clashes with the police). In these cases, media coverage of the event, organisers' press conferences and official declarations will certainly have an impact on attitudinal answers. The problem is all the more puzzling if the survey strategy is mixing face-to face interviews and a mail survey, at least when attitudinal data are not studied separately.

To date, INSURA has been used in four types of crowd gatherings. Outdoor static gatherings, indoor meetings (e.g., the ESF), protest camps or villages, and marches. In each case, constraints differ and adequate solutions must be found to conduct the survey. Most of the aforementioned events that were surveyed combined, more or less, the four morphological situations. It is not possible here to deal at length with technical solutions that have been used in each specific case. We will only deal here with surveys in demonstrations, since it is certainly the most complicated case.

To put it briefly, usual sampling strategies are useless in this context. In protest events, only some people are affiliated to organisations, and the number of organisations makes impossible any proximate to the research population. Since it is not possible to use a sampling strategy based on quotas, one has to use a probabilistic method, that is to say, to guarantee that all possible participants would have an equal opportunity of being interviewed. To achieve that, one must take into account the fact that participants' spatial and temporal distribution in a march is never aleatoric.

> For the most part of them, people do assemble at a meeting point, march under a banner, depending on multiple belongings, following a march order that is predetermined by organisers. Others are more erratic, travelling from one group to another, from the very heart of

the demonstration to its margins. These numerous spatial and temporal distributions have a clear consequence: one must use two different methods, depending on which stage of a demonstration is concerned, the assembling phase or the march itself. (Fillieule 1997, methodological appendix)

In the first phase, the best method is derived from Seidler, Meyer and MacGillivray (1976) and Favre, Fillieule and Mayer (1997). The gathering space (generally a square and its adjacent streets) is divided in advance into sectors clearly identified by some spatial distinguishing marks. One generally knows in advance where the different groups are due to their assembling under their banners, carts, etc. For big events, the press will even publish maps that indicate different meeting points. Sometimes, it is also possible to have an idea of the rough number of people per group or cluster of groups in advance. In each cell, interviewers (the number of which is defined depending on the expected density of demonstrators per cell) must randomly select interviewees. At that stage, a fixed number of interviewees per cell can be decided in advance or not, since the length of the assembling process is always difficult to evaluate.[8] As usually in probabilistic methods, the only criterion for the selection of the respondents is randomness. This can be achieved best by relying on a counting system, for example, approaching every Xth person in a group. Two persons who stand next to each other may not both be interviewed. In the case of a refusal, on the contrary, one should try to interview the nearest person in the group.

In the case of alter-global protest events, methodological rigor is all the more important as people usually attend different kinds of events. For some of them, certain activities are mutually exclusive. Villages, zaps and blockades, demonstrations, conferences and meetings can be held at the same time. That is why it is usually very fruitful to conduct interviews in the villages, as some of us did, since it is obvious that the kind of activity influences who participates. People who attend a meeting are not necessarily the same as the people who participate in the demonstration. Yet, both groups of people are and probably see themselves as participants in the same movement.

In the second phase of the survey, questionnaires must be distributed or interviews must be conducted during the protest march itself. Many solutions are available here and we have explored some of them (Favre, Fillieule and Mayer 1997). For technical reasons that will not be discussed here, the best solution is to divide the interviewers in two squads. One is placed at the front of the demonstration and the other at the end of it. The first group starts its interviews at the head of the march and gradually comes down to the end of the demonstration. The second group starts at the end and walks up to the head of the demonstration (Favre, Fillieule and Mayer 1997). Depending on the available resources, it is always possible to multiply the number of squads as long as they are intervening in a symmetrical way in the procession. Each squad of interviewers is supervised by two head persons, whose mission it is to offer spatial points of reference on each side of the demonstration and to decide who will be interviewed by whom and in what row (that rule could be of an utmost importance, especially if the interviewers are not professional staff or specifically trained personnel). Finally, experience proves that things never go exactly as previously planned. Crowd events are very awkward social phenomena and one must always be ready for alternative solutions.

One more problem to be solved in order to assure the reliability and validity of the data is connected to the response rate. Broad participation in the survey reduces the possibility that the group of respondents is systematically different from the population. Biases due to non-response are well identified in the survey literature. In INSURA, as said before, apart from those who are by definition hostile to any kind of sociological investigation, it seems that whenever activists are able to answer, people do accept the interview. However, one must take every possible step both to limit non-response bias (which means simple and short questionnaires) and, if possible, to understand its dimensions. That is why in face-to-face interviews, the interviewers must systematically register on a separate grid every person who refuses to cooperate or drops out after a while. Adding to that, interviewers should keep track of the spatial location of failed interviews (that will help, for example, in the assembling phase to identify the respective group). By doing that, the researcher can at a minimum determine whether the pool of respondents over-represents particular organisational affiliations, demographics, or any other pertinent categories. This knowledge can improve the validity of the conclusions from an imperfect sample by allowing a more accurate interpretation of survey results. For questionnaires sent in by mail, on the contrary, it is much more difficult to identify the non-response bias, apart from the total number of questionnaires returned out of the total number of questionnaires distributed. Technical solutions to secure that the interviewees' population does actually represent the people composing the crowd are certainly difficult to find, but still possible to attain.

Yet, one more central question remains. What does the crowd itself represent? Four statements could help to find the answer: first of all, INSURA consist of one-shot surveys with actual participants in a given event. A crowd can not be considered as equal to a social movement constituency. Its heterogeneity is far more important and different in nature. In SMOs, a number of empirical studies have called attention to the diversity of beliefs and motivations in the same social movement. In a crowd, heterogeneity does not only refer to that diversity of beliefs and motivations, but also primarily to the fact that only a limited part of the people, in a way or another, are part of the SMOs that organised the event. Moreover, participation in a protest event is generally not submitted to any condition. People do not need to be a member of an organisation, they usually do not have to register (apart from social forums where you have to pay fees), etc. That means that the reference population, the crowd itself, can be composed of core activists, sympathisers, bystanders, lost people, tourists, and sometimes even opponents of the demonstrators.

Secondly, and consequently, people attending a gathering may be participating for the first time in their life. Ladd and his colleagues (1983) were among the first to stress that point in their study of a national anti-nuclear rally in Washington, DC. They found that half of the sample were participating in their first anti-nuclear power activity (and we know from existing studies of alter-global events that this is usually the case in almost all of the events studied by INSURA). Still, the authors consider that the people interviewed are actually representing the anti-nuclear movement. In their opinion, 'by studying an actual movement demonstration, we are defining social movement membership in terms of participation in collective action' (Ladd, Hood and Van Liere 1983: 269). Yet, it makes no sense to assume that social movement participation can be epitomised in a one-shot participation, especially in the case of the alter-global movement, which is marked by a 'secular, inclusive and non-totalizing approach' and 'tolerant identities' (della Porta 2005), as opposed to the 'totalitarian', or at least organisational, identities of the past, which means that the 'entry costs' for such events or groups are particularly low.

Thirdly, INSURA, by definition, only captures the image of a crowd at one point in time and in one specific location. That very point has crucial consequences. To begin with, one can never assume that those who participate for the first time in a rally will stay involved in the movement, or even remain interested in the cause. Some certainly will, but one knows that all movements are marked by a high level of turnover. That means that newcomers cannot be considered as being part of the movement without further considerations. Only those who declare to have participated in previous alter-global activities (at least once) or to be a member of an alter-global organisation can be considered part of the movement. Furthermore, all INSURA dedicated to alter-globalisation events constantly stress the fact that about one-half of the interviewees are 'local people'.[9] Local people without organisational affiliation can certainly not be easily aggregated to other participants. For them, barriers to participation are significantly lower.

Finally and more broadly, movement participation and mobilisation are processes that evolve over time. Movements expand and contract in phases of mobilisation and de-mobilisation. Here again, it is all the more true in the case of alter-global events that gather people coming in from different countries. In each specific country, the position of the movement along the cycle can be different and submitted to very different contextual factors that affect the level of mobilisation. That very fact inhibits the ambitions to compare different national constituencies in one single event. We will come back to that point later.

If I Had a Hammer...

In INSURA, the unit of analysis is by definition the individual, not organisations. That means that INSURA are certainly not appropriate tools for addressing all research questions in social movements. As Klandermans and Smith (2002: 13) remind us:

> Research that takes the individual as its unit of analysis necessarily restricts itself to the explanation of individual opinions, attitudes and behaviour. It can help us to understand why individuals participate in social movements ... but it can tell us very little about the organisations and actors that stage movement events. ... The supply-side of protest is a different matter that cannot be assessed at the individual level with the individual as the unit of analysis.

In the remaining section, we show that INSURA is certainly well suited to explore the demographics of alter-global events, as well as relational networks of individuals and multiple belongings. We then argue that organisation networks and movement's boundaries are far more difficult to explore through INSURA, a fact that seriously limits cross-national comparisons of movements based on that tool.

Alter-global Demographics. Fighting Common Sense

The definition of the alter-global movement is without doubt ambiguous and is submitted to strategic consideration. Movement organisations, political elites, governments, journalists and social scientists, are all engaged in a symbolic fight for the right definition of what 'the movement' is, if one can talk about *a* movement (Sommier, Fillieule and Agrikoliansky 2008). At the very heart of that debate is the identity of those people composing the movement. At a very general level, can one speak of a 'transnational civil society', or an 'international working class' or 'modernisation losers'? At a more specific level, can one identify different kinds of groups involved, with different motivations and social characteristics? Globally speaking, the image of alter-global movements and constituencies is not that clear and is partially contradictory, depending on commentators' vested interests.

For sympathetic commentators, the alter-global movement is comprised of people with multiple geographic origins, being then truly internationalist. As a new social movement developing in the context of a crisis of representative democracy, it would be composed of new activists rejecting traditional affiliations to classical political parties, unions and voluntary groups. That 'political virginity' would be connected with a blurring of traditional class, gender and age cleavages usually structuring social conflicts and organisations. Hostile commentators, on the contrary, characterise alter-global activists as a bunch of heteroclite, naïve and unrealistic people rejecting modernisation processes because of their own dominated situation. They are perceived as being manipulated by small groups of political violent agitators, criminals and even terrorists. The development of INSURA, in that ideologically polarised context, has offered an opportunity to build objective descriptions of participants in alter global events.

Our own surveys show that respondents are more often men than women, especially at the No-G8. They are much younger than the average citizen: 40 to 60 per cent of them are less than 30 years old (two to four times more than the population of their respective country) and only 1 to 5 per cent is older than 64 (4 to 12 times less than the average). This goes along with the high proportion of students, especially at the No-G8, and few retired people. As universities and other higher education facilities are located in cities, anti-global activists do predominantly live in cities.

Although many of the activists are still studying, and therefore have not obtained their highest diploma yet, the average duration of studies is very high. Especially at the ESF, many participants have attended higher education and have or have had contacts with the sciences and other intellectual domains: they own a high cultural capital. At the same time, activists' religiosity is weak. Few of them believe in God or practice a religion, be it by praying alone, attending religious meetings or ceremonies, or engaging in religious groups. Activists who are not studying at the university level often work or they are unemployed. They are rarely stay-at-home moms or dads. The ones who work often have a favoured position: professionals, executives, managers and employees. These sociological properties can be summed up as pertaining to the 'middle class radicalism' described by Cotgrove and Duff (1980). Indeed, they place themselves clearly at the extreme left side of the left-right scale, while the distribution in the average population is rather symmetrical. Some of them also refuse the scale test. What usually appears as a lack of political competence proves to be another sign of a critical approach to classical politics in the alter-global movement, as the examination of the socio-ideological profile of 'no answers' to this question shows.

Individual Features of Cosmopolitanism… But Rooted Cosmopolitanism

Although more than four out of five respondents come from the countries where the two events took place, they show high levels of cosmopolitanism that is a propensity to keep up links with other countries. Table 9.1 shows that 75 per cent of the No-G8 protesters (respectively 77 per cent of the ESF participants) speak at least one foreign language and 50 per cent (respectively 45 per cent) speak at least two languages. The table also shows that 53 per cent (respectively 22 per cent of the ESF participants) have spent more than one year abroad and most of them keep up professional, friendship or family ties with people living

Table 9.1. Individual Evidences of Cosmopolitanism (percentages)

	ESF	No-G8
Foreign languages spoken		
0	23	25
1	32	23
2	30	32
3	12	14
>3	4	6
Spent time abroad		
No	59	22
Yes one year or less	19	25
Yes more than one year	22	54
Keeps up ties with people living abroad		
Professional ties		
Lots of ties	9	10
Some ties	28	29
No ties	63	62
Ties with friends		
Lots of ties	25	31
Some ties	51	51
No ties	24	17
Ties with family		
Lots of ties	17	22
Some ties	31	37
No ties	52	41
Travelled abroad for activist purpose		
Often	5	6
Sometimes	17	19
Seldom	19	20
Never	59	56

abroad; 50 per cent (respectively 41 per cent) have already been abroad for activist purposes. As a result, part of the people at the No-G8 and the ESF come from abroad. These activists already seem to belong to a social class that travels freely across borders and cultures.

Their ideological views seem to be in keeping with their social properties. In accordance with the alter-global label with which most of them agree, their ideological world is centred on worldly issues and their attacks target international institutions and phenomena. North-South inequalities and the fights against capitalism, multi-national firms and war are the first among the political issues that drove them to come to the events.

The organisational belongings they declare fit with these ideological stances. Some of them belong to international organisations. Several of the most important organisations they belong to aim at political transformations on the international level. Alter-global organisations in the strict sense logically come out first. This seems to confirm the existence of a specific alter-global activist field that would mainly exist at a transnational level. Then, the activists declare memberships to organisations that promote ecology, peace, human rights, in general, and migrants' rights, in particular.

At the same time, alter-globals declare several memberships to national organisations. There were 18 per cent of the No-G8 participants (22 per cent at the ESF) declaring membership to political parties, which seldom develop noteworthy links with foreign parties. Because of the intellectual and academic nature of the ESF, only three per cent of the activists are members of trade unions, compared to 17 per cent at the No-G8 protests. In both events, some people declare to be involved in other rather nationally rooted movements: movements advocating local issues, homeless and unemployed people, or farmers. Their political practice appears to be based on strong local belongings, from which they gain information, competence and access to social networks that are necessary to engage in global politics. As Tarrow (2001) put it, they are 'rooted cosmopolitans' (see also chapters 3 and 4 in this volume for members of the alter-global movement).

This is confirmed by the political integration of the ESF and No-G8 activists. They are much more involved in politics than the average citizen (Table 9.2). More often, they discuss politics or current affairs, which appears as evidence of political competence: they did not come to the events by accident; they know alter-global events are fully political events. Most of them declare that they take part in all ballots, which is noteworthy in countries such as France, where there are six levels of power, and above all in Switzerland, where the number of elections is outrun by the number of federal and local *votations*. Moreover, activists share high levels of conventional and non-conventional political participation. Not only do they take part in large protest events like in Paris and Évian, but they also participate in smaller demonstrations, they go on strikes or sign petitions. A significant share also take part in confrontational actions: resistance to police, occupation of buildings or holding up of traffic. The ESF and the No-G8 look like steps in the continuity of coherent activist biographies, more than exceptional participation in the course of quieter political lives. In this context, one hardly thinks of a new activism that expands to newly open transnational spaces, but rather of a mix of activist generations that are more and more devoted to international issues.

Table 9.2. Political Properties of Alter-global Activists
Compared to General Population from European Social Survey 2003 when Available. (percentage of all respondents)

	ESF	No-G8	ESS CH	ESS F
Talking about politics				
Never	0	1	4	13
Seldom	9	7	19	23
Sometimes	36	32	30	29
Often	53	55	46	35
na	2	5	1	0
Vote				
Always	76	57		
Often	11	18		
Sometimes	2	6		
Seldom	2	4		
Never	2	7		
Not the right	4	8		
na	3	1		

Means of political action already used	ESF	No-G8
Sign petition	92	95
Take part in demonstration	90	97
Take part in discussion groups	76	75
Boycott goods, shops, country	68	64
Deliver leaflets	66	66
Take part in a strike	63	56
Take part in symbolic actions	56	80
Block traffic (sit-in…)	40	53
Occupy building (factory, school…)	34	36
Resist armed forces	26	35
Engage in fasting or say prayers	10	11
Cause material damage	5	12
Take part in hunger strike	2	4
Put physical pressure on somebody	2	5

Is Comparison Reason?

As far as the consistency is concerned, INSURA results must be nuanced by some methodological considerations. At least two questions can be asked. Firstly, can INSURA results be interpreted identically year after year and in the different countries where meetings have taken place? Linguistic and ideological contexts should bias answers, all the more so because the proportion of activists from different countries and languages will vary. The cultural and linguistic biases come out again at the event level. Spanish and German demonstrators, for instance, might not understand questions the same. Thus, differences related to the degree of 'confidence in regional authorities', to the wish to 'increase the state's intervention' or to 'break off with present development models' might be over-, under- or misinterpreted. As a consequence, comparisons between results from the ESF and the No-G8 events have to be handled with care. An inquiry based on 83 per cent French respondents, like what occurred in Paris, must encompass severe cultural biases compared to an inquiry based on activists from more diverse origins, even mostly European ones. The education variable, for example, is biased by strongly differing education systems in France, Switzerland and Germany: apprenticeship is unevenly developed and rated by students and employers; higher education is unevenly developed and homogeneous; the researchers share differing representations of what each diploma sociologically means. Our coding scheme, as an illustration, did not match properly with the ESS surveys. This well-known problem of comparative studies proves even more complex for religion, left-right positioning, values or policy opinions.

Secondly, do our results represent the anti-global movement as a whole? Anti-global events are all the more ephemeral because people participating in them are mostly young. Therefore, many participants are newcomers to protest politics, as the age structure shows. Part of them might persist in protest politics and be back at the next alter-global event: they will keep most of their sociological properties and simply move from the newcomer category to a category of older and more experienced activists. But part of them will drop out. They might be replaced by clearly different profiles. The replacement of cohorts reduces the capacity of sporadic surveys to represent a mobilised population in general.

We still do not know much about activist biographies, which have been proven decisive in explaining their engagement (but see chapter 2 in this volume). Tracing the exact succession of employments, family changes, political engagements and associational memberships would require much more thorough questions than what can be done during a street demonstration or a public conference. Biographies are all the more crucial to explain current activism and its transnational aspects. Contrary to general population surveys, social reasons of engagement cannot be considered as mere consequences of objective and subjective class belonging, religious faith and practice, cultural and ideological cleavages and so on; all of these properties are also determined by years of activist practice – this is a pretty powerful process of secondary socialisation inside political organisations.

The ESF took place near the city of Paris, which concentrates several large universities. It was a rather intellectual mobilisation, made of numerous conferences and debates about globalisation and related topics, while the No-G8 in the Geneva region combined conferences with street demonstrations and other outside performances. Not only are the activists locally rooted, but the events themselves are as well. They also aimed at different audiences, which brings down the possibility of a generalisation of the results. Many respondents declared that they came to the event with an organisation. As collective trips reduce the material cost of participation, a marginal organisation may be overrepresented, while a larger organisation that did not plan any collective travel will be represented by only a few well-off and/or very motivated members. All of these aspects reduce the longitudinal ambitions of event-focussed questionnaire studies significantly: one given survey does not necessarily represent a moment of the history of alter-globals.

INSURA as a Tool to Measure Multi-organisational Fields

Since the beginning of the century, in the context of a dramatic development of network analysis (Diani and McAdam 2003), social researchers have more and more used individual data on multiple belongings to formulate hypotheses and draw conclusions about organisational networks. Two questions arise here. First, on what ground can we use a measure of multiple belongings to determine an organisational web? Second, can we define a social movement as a network of people and/or organisations, a network that would be turning transnational?

The measure of multiple memberships can be converted into a coincidence matrix, which allows formulating hypotheses about the extent to which organisations and organisational fields are linked by means of multiple memberships, participation or identification. Such reasoning is based on the concept of 'multi-organisational field' (Curtis and Zurcher 1973). Curtis and Zurcher (1973: 53) suggest that:

> Organisations in a community setting approximate an ordered, coordinated system. Inter-organisational processes within the field can be identified on two levels, which conceptually overlap: the organisational level, where networks are established by joint activities, staff, boards of directors, target clientele, resources, etc; the individual level, where networks are established by multiple affiliations of members.

With INSURA data, one cannot identify the web of existing relations among individuals since no variable compiles the relationship with other activists, such as, for example, in McAdam and Fernandez (1990). One has to rely on a description of declared proximities or belongings of individuals to given organisations or clusters of organisations (e.g., environmental or human rights movement).

Although our questionnaire design aimed at individual participants to the ESF and to the No-G8 protests, we are interested in understanding the social logics of engagement (Table 9.3). It appears that a majority of the alter-global activists are closely embedded in social and organisational structures. In both

Table 9.3. Social Embeddings of Participants (percentage)

	ESF	No-G8
Are your colleagues, family, friends active activists?		
Count of groups that are rather or very active activists		
None	18	17
One	36	33
Two	30	32
Three	12	12
Don't know	4	6
Who did you come to the event with? First answer given		
Alone	32	13
With close friends	23	57
With acquaintances, neighbours	2	5
With colleagues	6	3
With member(s) of your family	8	7
With your organisation, group	23	15
Who or what impelled you to take part in the event? Up to 3 (ESF) or 5 (No-G8) answers possible		
Close friends	25	38
Colleagues	9	4
Acquaintances, neighbours	6	7
Family	9	8
The organisation, group you belong to	52	28
Another organisation, group	12	9
Internet	13	13
The media	14	16
Posters, handbills	7	15
Your convictions, ideals (only ESF)	—	23
Other	19	21

events, less than 20 per cent of them declare that neither their colleagues, nor their family nor their friends are 'rather active activists'. Also, 34 per cent of them declare that two or three of these social circles are overlapping. This structural embedment translates into the concrete circumstances of participation. When asked 'what impelled you to come', 23 per cent mention their convictions (G8 only), but 38 per cent (25 at the ESF) mention their friends and 28 per cent (52) the organisation to which they belong. Although in the end 13 per cent (32) came alone, 57 per cent (23) came (mainly) with close friends and 15 per cent (23) came with their organisation. Social constraints matter much more than forecast by theories of disorganised individuals.

This encourages further investigation about organisational networks. We recorded numerous multiple memberships. In both events, each activist declares on average about 2.5 present memberships, be they active or passive. This result calls for a thorough study of combinations of individual affiliations in order to scheme indirectly the organisational structure of the antiglobal field. This way, we follow the theoretical approach suggested by Doug McAdam (1986) in his study of the Freedom Summer anti-segregation action.

As for the method, both M1 (2,000 individuals x 20 memberships)[10] matrices are converted into M2 (20 x 20 memberships) matrices that are processed by means of ascending hierarchical cluster analysis.[11] Figure 9.1 translates, in the case of the ESF, the main resulting classes into clusters and proximity in the classification tree into two-dimensional spatial proximity. The size of organisational labels is proportionated to the raw total of memberships and the thickness of

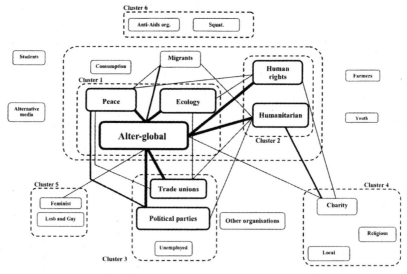

Figure 9.1. Network of Organisations Acccording to Their Constituencies Among 2003 ESF Activists

links between two organisations to the raw number of shared memberships. We obtain what can be labelled schemes of the network of organisations as represented in the events through their (declared and presumed) members.

While some organisations seldom combine with each other, some do frequently, gathering themselves into clusters that share distinct mean socio-ideological properties and distinct mean political attitudes.

The properties of clusters are extracted from their 'cores', namely, the 7 to 16 per cent of activists who represent each of them best.[12] As an example, the main cluster of the ESF organisational structure (Figure 9.1) gathers alter-globals in general, peace and ecology activists. Attac, one of the core organisations of the French alter-global field, logically provides a majority of these activists. They are younger than the mean, not very religious, with many full-time managers, who seldom vote, and, if so, they choose the Greens or the Ligue Communiste Révolutionnaire. They took part in former alter-global events and identify with this movement.

Table 9.4 compares six ESF organisational clusters according to their degree of cosmopolitanism, an index that synthesises the ability to speak foreign languages and the time spent abroad. This criterion proves clearly discriminating. The cluster most exclusively devoted to (conventional, traditional) politics (cluster 3) reaches a very low (and homogeneous) level of cosmopolitanism: these activists are most strongly rooted in national mobilisations and organisations. The feminist and gay and lesbian cluster (cluster 5) is composed of both very

Table 9.4. Mean Degree of Cosmopolitanism for Members of Clusters of Organisations Taking Part in the ESF

(Significant Positive Differences with all Respondents' Scores in Italics)

Clusters and the kinds of organisations they gather	Degree of cosmopolitanism					
	Null	**Low**	**Medium**	**High**	*Mean*	*s. d.*
Cluster 1: Anti-globalisation, ecology, peace	15	37	*41*	7	*2.8*	*2.2*
Cluster 2: Human rights and humanitarian	15	31	*44*	11	*3.3*	*2.4*
Cluster 3: Trade unions, political parties and unemployed	*37*	36	25	2	*1.7*	*2.0*
Cluster 4: Charity, religion and local	23	37	33	7	*2.5*	*2.3*
Cluster 5: Feminist and gay-lesbian	*30*	25	20	25	*3.0*	*3.0*
Cluster 6: Anti-AIDS and squatters	9	55	36	0	*2.4*	*1.7*
All respondents	**19**	**37**	**37**	**7**	*2.7*	*2.3*

strong and very little cosmopolitan activists, which does not contradict its marginal structural coherence. Human rights and humanitarian activists (cluster 2) as well as alter-globals, ecologists and pacifists (cluster 1) are very cosmopolitan, as if international causes would correspond to international activists.

Comparing the mainly French ESF graph with the French part of the No-G8 graph[13], one would overweigh local, temporal, contingent factors relatively to the system of organisations that irrigates each anti-global event. In both cases, alter-global organisations in the strict sense are heavy and central, which is no surprise. Moreover, ecology, humanitarian, trade unions and political parties are among the largest sub-fields. Unions and parties share a lot of members, as well as feminist and gay-lesbian organisations, or humanitarian and human rights. Comparing the No-G8 graphs according to the respondents' nationality, parties, unions and students compose one stable cluster, but differences are obvious, notably the centrality of French alter-global activists and the more federal looking Swiss graph. This tends to show that the existence of a transnational alter-global field, seen from the organisational point of view, is still a fiction.

Similarly, from the contrast between the two organisational webs (based on information given by French and Swiss activists), we dare not infer differences between national histories of social mobilisation. Several studies have established such differences. But above all, the analysis shows that organisations diversely tangle with the event, according to diverse political contexts. For example, taking part in the No-G8 events must have cost more to the French: the distance was bigger, many people were off during the long Pentecost weekend, and parallel protests concerned a large part of the potential participants.

Another crucial objection lies in the translation from individual multiple belongings to an organisational net. Organisational ties do consist in exchanges through individuals with multiple activities, these exchanges being linked with common ideological mottos, common conceptions of society, common generational roots and common conceptions of engagement. But they also encompass concrete political alliances, historical links, participation to common struggles, leaders working together and so on.

As a consequence, reducing the anti-global organisational field to our graphs would largely overinterpret its institutional value. The underlying assumption of such analyses is that activists' participation in multiple organisations helps foster participation between the organisations, and can serve as a fairly reliable predictor of actual inter-organisational linkages. As Diani (2005: 2–3) writes in a recent piece on the demonstrations on 15 February 2003: 'the web of the connections, produced by these involvements, constitutes the structural basis of the coalitions that promoted the demonstrations.... [It maps] the structure of the ties that linked the different types of organisational actors involved in the coalitions. This, regardless of whether they actually managed to establish publicly visible alliances on those specific occasions'. Such a conception is consistent with a number of recent studies tending to show that sustained communication and cooperation between people in a given milieu can foster a sense of solidarity and we-feeling, independently from organisational links (Bayat 1997; Bennani-Chraibi and Fillieule 2003). Diani is certainly right to stress 'the possibility that *recurrent patterns of interactions* generate the same type of solidarity and commitment that one experiences within associations. ... it is also likely that a distinct sense of commonality and specific bonds will arise linking people *repeatedly sharing the same experiences.* In this particular sense, it is not unreasonable to think of *sustained involvement in protest activities* as a particular type of group membership' (Diani 2005, emphasis added).

Ultimately, what is a social movement? Contemporary social movement theory lies upon a now challenged definition of the object. The political process perspective defines social movements as 'a sustained challenge to power holders in the name of a population living under the jurisdiction of those power holders by means of repeated public displays of that population's worthiness, unity, numbers, and commitment' (Tilly 1999: 257). For more than a decade, that definition, which finds its main operationalisation via protest event analysis, has been criticised for its exclusive focus on interactions between challengers and power holders, its objectivist and simplistic definition of the state (Fillieule 1997; Goodwin and Jasper 2003), its tendency to blend social movements and protest events, and its tendency to treat the former as aggregates of the latter (Armstrong 2002; Taylor and Van Dycke 2004; Fillieule 2006).

The definitional question is all the more puzzling in the case of the alter-global movement, which has large and fluid boundaries that are changing across time and national contexts. That is why the alternative definition of a social movement, offered by Diani (1992, 1995), who suggests that a movement is made up of a network of organisations and individuals with a collective identity that engages in collective action using semi- or non-institutional channels,[14] is widely used by researchers working on the 'movement of movements'.

In our opinion, Diani is absolutely right in stressing the fact that 'a movement is a form of collective organisation with no formal boundaries, which allows participants to feel part of broad collective efforts while retaining their distinctive identities as individuals and/or as specific organisations and at the same time, that collective identities are reproduced through actual or virtual interactions' (2001: 6). Yet, it remains that the belongings marked through INSURA do not measure the components of that definition. As we have shown before, most of the respondents are participating for the first time and because they live close to the location of the event. One cannot reasonably consider that the data gathered on multiple belongings accurately picture the web of organisations, except if one sets apart the first time and/or local people to concentrate only on people giving evidence that they form enduring links and commitments within protest activities.

Conclusion

Research about the transnationalisation of social movements might take two ways: either inquiries about structural efforts by organisations and individuals from different countries to collaborate across borders; or inquiries about particular moments when foreign organisations and individuals mix and combine their actions along common causes. INSURA conducted during international events, like the studies at the ESF and No-G8 presented here, supposedly belong to the second way, through a comparison between individual profiles from different countries, and from different national organisations and international organisations. Yet, this method can repeat, sometimes even increase, the problems met at the national level, that is, problems due to differential participation and relation to social science, differential contexts of mobilisation, differential behaviour during the event, and differential cultural background. Participation changes with distance from home and with the police opinion on their origin. Social science protocols might carry along differing opinions on questionnaire inquiries, varying reluctance to answer and varying liability to lie or distort answers. The ESF and the No-G8 do not have the same meaning and importance for activists from different origins; they do not insert the same way in national long-term mobilisation agendas and in national ideological backgrounds. Sampling obstacles come from different behaviours during the event, possibly tricking the sampling strategies of researchers. Linguistic, cultural and institutional aspects of distinct origins make it all the more difficult to come up with a wording that generates comparable answers for demographics, political attitudes or values; finding the right words comes even more knotty when thin biographical or ideological distinctions have to be made, requiring knowledge of multiple cultures. At the end, if one does not pay attention to all of these obstacles, one may produce 'Canada dry comparisons', that is, research that looks, smells and tastes comparative, but that is actually not.

Notes

1. See also Favre, Fillieule and Mayer (1997) for a systematic critique of the biases related to opinion polls about unconventional action.
2. See Fillieule and Tartakowsky (2008, ch. 4) for a review.
3. One should note that the design of the methodology as well as the administration of the questionnaires were realised in collaboration with Louis Harris France. All of the interviewers were paid staff and were trained long in advance. The research was financially supported by the CEVIPOF (Science-Po Paris) and by Louis Harris, who had a vested interest in developing a new technique.
4. See http://demos.iue.it, workpackage 5, on the ESF in Athens. One should also mention other specific INSURA that have been conducted, more or less in the framework of the DEMOS project, such as Giugni and Bandler's surveys in Zurich

on 17 January 2004 and for the Other Summit of Davos the same year; Rucht, Haug, Teune and Yang's research on the first national social forum in Germany (Erfurt) in 2005; and Saunders and Rootes on the Make Poverty History march in 2005.

5. If 15 February was not exactly an alter-globalisation event, it remains that 'it was coordinated and staged by an international network of movement organisations, most of which originated within the so-called global justice movement. It was on the European Social Forum meetings of the global justice movement that the protest was set up and organised' (Walgrave and Verhulst 2003).

6. The '*Groupe de recherches sur l'activisme altermondialiste*' (GRAAL, University of Paris – Sorbonne, France) and the '*Centre de Recherche sur l'Action Politique de l'Université de Lausanne*' (CRAPUL, Lausanne, Switzerland) have undertaken a series of studies about large alter-global protest events, where activists from all countries have recurrently been meeting since the beginning of the 1990s. This chapter deals with two events: the No-G8 protest in the French-Swiss region of Évian-Lausanne-Geneva in June 2003, and the second ESF in the Paris region, in November 2003. For both events, the same research design was applied: a four-language questionnaire (in French, English, German and Italian) distributed to activists who were to fill it in right on the protest place, except for a few of them who sent it back by mail. About 2,000 questionnaires where gathered in each event, without any strict statistical sampling. The research team only aimed at hitting the most diverse profiles in the different places where people met and discussed, demonstrated, lived: conference rooms, camping villages in Évian region, streets.

7. This means that in alter-globalisation events, a more or less reduced share of the participants will systematically refuse to be interviewed (activists in the black bloc and more generally anarchist activists).

8. For an alternative method also based on Seidler, see McPhail, Schweingruber and Ceobanu 2006.

9. That notion is not so evident to define. Nationality is certainly one, albeit insufficient, indicator. Depending on the location of the event, people living abroad can be closer to the event than national residents. For obvious reasons, that was the case for the INSURA in Lausanne and Geneva. Therefore, Bedoyan and Van Aelst's (2003) attempt to identify participation costs at demonstrations in Brussel by nationality is, among other reasons, pointless.

10. Respondents were asked about *active* or *passive* belongings. We assigned a double rating to the first in M1.

11. Our cluster analysis maximises the mean between-clusters distance, in order to discriminate clusters in the best possible manner. Distance between clusters i and j is the sum of squares of distances between the organisations they respectively include. Profiles of organisations in M2 are centred and reduced to control size effects. Other algorithms have been tested in order to check for stability: instabilities do exist but they reveal local structure, and do not alter the general structure.

12. For example, cluster 1 is made of 871 alter-globals, 393 ecologists and 376 pacifists, some of these cumulating in two or three of these belongings. The core of cluster 1 is composed of 270 activists who define it particularly well, that is, they belong to at least two of these three organisations, and they do not belong to too many organisations external to this cluster.

13. The graphs related to the No-G8 event are not published here because of a lack of space. The graph for all national origins can be found in Fillieule et al. (2004), or may be obtained upon request.
14. '[Social movements] are networks of interaction between different actors which may either include formal organisations or not, depending on shifting circumstances. As a consequence, a single organisation, whatever its dominant traits, is not a social movement. Of course, it may be part of one, but the two are not identical, as *they reflect different organisational principles*' (Diani 1992: 13).

References

Agrikoliansky, E. and I. Sommier, eds. 2005. *Radiographie du mouvement altermondialiste, le second Forum social européen.* Paris: La Dispute.
Andretta, M., et al. 2002. *Global, noglobal, new global. La protesta contro il G8 a Genova.* Rome: Laterza.
Armstrong, E. 2002. *Forging Gay Identities. Organising Sexuality in San Francisco, 1950–1974.* Chicago: University of Chicago Press.
Bayat, A. 1997. *Street Politics. Poor People Movements in Iran.* New York: Columbia University Press.
Bedoyan, I. and P. Van Aelst. 2003, 'Limitations and Possibilities of Transnational Mobilization. The Case of the EU Summit Protesters in Brussels, 2001'. *Les mobilisations altermondialistes,* Paris, 3–5 December 2003.
Bennani-Chraibi, M. and O. Fillieule, eds. 2003. *Résistances et protestations dans le monde musulman.* Paris: Presses de Sciences Po.
Cotgrove, S. and A. Duff. 1980. 'Environmentalism, Middle Class Radicalism and Politics'. *Sociological Review* 28(2): 333–349.
Curtis, R.L. and L.A. Zurcher. 1973. 'Stable Resources of Protest Movements: The Multi-Organisational Field'. *Social Forces* 52(1): 53–61.
della Porta, D. 2005. 'Multiple Belongings, Tolerant Identities, and the Construction of "Another Politics": Between the European Social Forum and the Local Social Fora'. In *Transnational Protest and Global Activism,* eds. D. della Porta and S. Tarrow, 175–202. Lanham: Rowman and Littlefield.
della Porta, D., ed. 2009. *Another Europe. Conceptions and Practices of Democracy in the European Social Forums.* London: Routledge.
Diani, M. 1992. 'The Concept of Social Movement'. *The Sociological Review* 40: 1–25.
———. 1995. *Green Networks. A Structural Analysis of the Italian Environmental Movement.* Edinburgh: Edinburgh University Press.
———. 2001. 'A Relational View of the Social Movement Organisation vs. Interest Group Distinction'. *ECPR General Conference,* Canterbury, 6–8 September 2001.
———. 2005. 'The Structural Bases of Movement Coalitions. Multiple Memberships and Networks in the February 15th 2003 Peace Demonstrations'. *American Sociological Association Centenary Meeting,* Philadelphia, 13–16 August 2005.
Diani, M. and D. McAdam, eds. 2003. *Social Movements and Networks. Relational Approaches to Collective Action.* Oxford: Oxford University Press.

Drury, J. and S. Reicher. 1999. 'The Intergroup Dynamics of Collective Empowerment: Substantiating the Social Identity Model of Crowd Behaviour'. *Group Processes and Intergroup Relations* 2(4): 381–402.

Favre, P., O. Fillieule and N. Mayer. 1997. 'La fin d'une étrange lacune de la sociologie des mobilisations: L'étude par sondage des manifestants: fondements théoriques et solutions techniques'. *Revue Française de Science Politique* 47: 3–28.

Fillieule, O. 1997. *Stratégies de la rue. Les manifestations en France.* Paris: Presses de Sciences Po.

———. 2006. 'Requiem pour un concept. Vie et mort de la notion de "structure des opportunités politiques"'. In *Les mouvements sociaux en Turquie*, ed. G. Dorronsoro, 201–218. Paris: Presses du CNRS.

Fillieule, O., et al. 2004. 'l'Altermondialisme en réseaux: Trajectoires militantes, multipositionnalité et formes de l'engagement: les participants du contre-sommet du g8 d'Evian (2003)'. *Politix* 17(68): 13–48.

Fillieule, O. and P. Blanchard. 2005, 'Le champ multiorganisationnel altermondialiste'. In *Radiographie du mouvement altermondialiste, le second Forum social européen*, eds. E. Agrikoliansky and I. Sommier, 157–183. Paris: La Dispute.

Fillieule, O. and D. Tartakowsky. 2008. *La manifestation.* Paris: Presses de Sciences Po.

Goodwin, J. and J.M. Jasper, eds. 2003. *Rethinking Social Movements: Structure, Meaning, and Emotion.* Lanham: Rowman & Littlefield.

Klandermans, B. and J. Smith. 2002. 'Survey Research: A Case for Comparative Designs'. In *Methods of Social Movement Research*, eds. B. Klandermans and S. Staggenborg, 3–31. Minneapolis: University of Minnesota Press.

Ladd, A., T. Hood and K.D. Van Liere. 1983. 'Ideological Themes in the Antinuclear Movement: Consensus and Diversity'. *Sociological Inquiry* 53(2–3): 252–272.

Levi, M. and G. Murphy. 2002. 'Coalitions of Contention: The Case of the WTO Protests in Seattle'. *International Sociological Association Meeting*, Brisbane, 8–13 July 2002.

Lichbach M. and P. Almeida. 2001. *Global Order and Local Resistance: The Neoliberal Institutional Trilemma and the Battle of Seattle.* Unpublished manuscript.

McAdam, D. 1986. 'Recruitment to High Risk Activism: The Case of Freedom Summer'. *American Journal of Sociology* 92(1): 64–90.

McAdam, D and R. Fernandez, 1990. 'Microstructural Bases of Recruitment to Social Movements'. in L. Kriesberg (ed.), *Research in Social Movements, Conflict and Change. Vol. 12*, ed. L. Kriesberg, 1–33. Greenwich: JAI Press.

McPhail, C. and D.L. Miller. 1973. 'The Assembling Process: A Theoretical and Empirical Examination'. *American Sociological Review* 38: 721–735.

McPhail, C., D.D. Schweingruber and A.M. Ceobanu. 2006. 'Bridging the Collective Behavior/ Social Movement Gap'. *American Sociological Association*, Montréal, 11–14 August 2006.

Seidler, J., K. Meyer and L. MacGillivray. 1976. 'Collecting Data on Crowds and Rallies: A New Method of Stationary Sampling', *Social Forces* 55(2): 507–518.

Sommier, I., O. Fillieule and E. Agrikoliansky, eds. 2008. *Généalogie des mouvements altermondialistes en Europe. Une perspective comparée.* Paris: Karthala.

Tarrow, S. 2001. 'Rooted Cosmopolitans: Transnational Activists in a World of States'. *Wisconsin University*, Madison, 2 November 2001.

Taylor, V. and N. Van Dyke. 2004. '"Get up, Stand up": Tactical Repertoires of Social Movements'. In *The Blackwell Companion to Social Movements*, eds. D.A. Snow, S.A. Soule and H. Kriesi, 262–293. Oxford: Blackwell.

Tilly, C. 1999. 'Conclusion. Why Worry about Citizenship?' In *Extending Citizenship. Reconfiguring States*, eds. M. Hanagan and C. Tilly, 247–260. Lanham: Rowman & Littlefield.

Topf, R. 1995. 'Beyond Electoral Participation'. In *Citizens and the State*, eds. D. Fuchs and H. Klingemann, 52–91. Oxford: Oxford University Press.

Van Aelst, P. and S. Walgrave. 2001. 'Who is that (Wo)Man in the Street? From the Normalization of Protest to the Normalization of the Protester'. *European Journal of Political Research* 39(4): 461–486.

Walgrave, S. and J. Verhulst. 2003. *Worldwide Anti-war-in-Iraq Protest: A Preliminary Test of the Transnational Movement Thesis*. Working Paper, Centre for Media, Movements, and Politics (M²P). University of Antwerp, Belgium.

Walgrave, S. and D. Rucht, eds. 2010. *The World Says No to War: Demonstrations against the War on Iraq*. Minneapolis: Minnesota University Press.

Chapter Ten

Prisoners of our Concepts
Liberating the Study of Social Movements

Jackie Smith and Rachel Kutz-Flamenbaum

> Oppression is a result of many conditions, not the least of which
> reside in consciousness.
> —Farmer 2004: 307

We, as social movement scholars, have become prisoners of our concepts and our professions. Conventions established within the academy to organise our professional lives and to discipline our thinking have prevented many social movement scholars from recognising important changes taking place in the world that we purport to be trying to understand. Privileging Western-dominated and bounded understandings of the state, organisations and social movements, we have overlooked, to a large extent, the important ways social movements are continuously transforming social and political relations. Although concepts such as social movements are defined in relational terms, they have remained fairly static in our minds. And whereas Charles Tilly (1984) argued that social movements evolved in tandem with national states, we have not fully accounted for questions of how they might continue to be transformed as national states and the inter-state system evolve.

For instance, most research focuses on movements within particular states, and frames conflicts largely within existing national (or diasporic) boundaries. The assumption that conflicts are bounded by national polities blinds the researcher to the ways these conflicts are shaped by a larger world system that affects, for instance, environmental or labour market pressures on national populations, the policy space available to targets (be they governments or corporations) and transnational flows of information and other resources to both challengers and targets.

Moreover, research focussing on individuals typically assumes national frames of reference that can obscure the ways transnational and global identities can and do affect social movement dynamics. For instance, most studies of the US civil rights or women's movements do not consider why the dominant actors in these movements have not attempted to mobilise around global human rights ideologies and institutional frameworks.[1] In both cases, some within the movement have attempted to use international human rights language to advance movement goals, but these efforts have been limited by both cultural and political constraints.[2] Just as states are embedded within a broader world system, so too are individuals and the identities they adopt. Thus, to fully understand social movements, our research must account for the potential system-level influences on the individual and collective actors involved (Kolb 2007). Applying conventional research methods typically forces the researcher to restrict his or her field of vision, precluding a more systemic perspective.

This chapter explores some of the ways research on transnational movements has been 'imprisoned' by disciplinary and conceptual frameworks and how this has limited our ability to fully appreciate the forces shaping these movements. We engage here in some broad generalisations that are meant to encourage a critical reflection on the ways the professional study of social movements may be limiting our understandings of contemporary struggles for social change. We recognise that our claims about the failures of social movement research are most relevant within the 'mainstream' of US and (to a lesser degree) European social movement research. Indeed, new social movements (NSM) scholars have long been exploring links between macro-level changes and shifts in culture, identities and political participation (see, for instance, Kriesi 1989; Melucci 1989; Offe 1999). The appeal of NSM approaches in the US has been limited, however, in part because NSM scholarship drew attention to identity and culture at a time when US research emphasised more structural and material approaches (Pichardo 1997; Goodwin and Jasper 1999; della Porta 2007b; Armstrong and Bernstein 2008). Sarah Waters (2008) links the relative neglect of NSM approaches to the static and reified treatments of social movements in much of the literature.

Disciplinary and Professional Prisons

> To the extent that we each analyze our social prisons, we liberate ourselves from their constraints to the extent that we can be liberated.
> —Wallerstein 2004: 22

As Immanuel Wallerstein and others have reminded us, the academy is an institution intimately linked to the emergence and spread of the modern world system. The segmentation of knowledge fields into disciplines aided the expansion of capitalism, and it led to a rationalised system of analysis and discourse and legitimated rule by experts (see also McMichael 2003). The separation of science and philosophy prevented social 'scientists' from asking questions about what is good, valued, or beautiful. It devalued disciplines focussing on such questions while privileging those employing scientific methods in the pursuit of some objective 'truth'. The notion that science can be value-neutral became normalised and prioritised.

Boaventura de Sousa Santos's (2007: 1) critique is more blunt: 'Modern Western thinking is an abyssal thinking'. Western academic institutions as we know them would not exist without the invisibility of non-Western realities that lie on 'the other side of the line':

> Whatever is produced as nonexistent is radically excluded because it lies beyond the realm of what the accepted conception of inclusion considers to be its other. What most fundamentally characterizes abyssal thinking is thus the impossibility of the co-presence of the two sides of the line. (ibid.)

Paul Farmer (2004: 308) notes that 'increasing specialization has often brought with it the erasure of history and political economy'. By forgetting history – especially the history that links Western societies' wealth and privilege to the continued exploitation of Southern peoples – scholars effectively 'de-socialise' the people who are the subjects of their research. They interpret Southern realities as somehow unrelated to their colonial legacies.

In reviewing sociological literature on globalisation, Raewyn Connell also speaks of an 'erasure' of the experiences of the global· South. She notes that: '"[e]rasure", to follow the early Derrida, does not mean obliteration; rather, it means an overwriting. The most important erasure in globalization theory concerns colonialism' (2007: 380). Erasure, according to Connell, can largely be attributed to the social structures within which analysts operate, which enables Western scholars to construct a 'performative unity of writer and reader' that excludes the voices and experiences of people and societies outside of the West.

Within the academy, feminists, cultural theorists and other scholars have critiqued dominant epistemologies and questioned the claims to objectivity in science. Disciplines such as peace studies, women's studies and critical global studies have emerged to actively challenge such claims. Despite these long and impassioned efforts, those of us in the academy still face strong pressures to downplay the values and political priorities that guide our research. Moreover, in many spaces of the academy, the market ideology has become normalised, and is even actively and uncritically promoted in business schools and economics departments. For instance, Dia Da Costa and Philip McMichael speak of a 'market epistemology' that 'infects' disciplines such as development studies and international relations (2007: 588). Such pressures have become even greater in the contemporary era of globalised capitalism, or advanced neoliberalism, as universities have been increasingly subjected to market discipline. This has meant the gradual corporatisation of the university whereby academic productivity is measured in terms of the numbers of high-prestige grants and academic articles, and where universities are governed more and more by professionals with training in management and marketing rather than by their faculties (Aronowitz 2000).

As Thomas Olesen observes in his contribution to this volume, social movement research is based in a 'tradition that rewards empirical analysis and theoretical and methodological rigor'. This has led, he argues, to a *professional parochialism* in our field, meaning that we provide detailed accounts and explanations of protest, but 'fail to relate this research to broader debates about the societies in which the protest occurs'. The emphasis on empirical analysis encouraged research designs that were shaped more by readily available concepts, measurement techniques and data sources than by the social phenomena that constituted the object of study (see, for instance, Crist and McCarthy 1996; Taylor 1998; della Porta 2007a). For example, research subjects tend to be individuals and organisations most readily contacted by telephone, email, or post. Individuals without access to computers or phones, and organisations without paid staff or offices, become invisible through such methodologies (e.g., Andrews and Edwards 2005). But many social movements operate in more informal, fluid and marginal contexts that are likely to escape the 'scientific' gaze of many Western social analysts (e.g. Oliver 1989). Without attention to these conceptual blinders, transnational research can exacerbate this problem by prioritising: a) organisations; b) that use English or some other dominant world language; c) that have access to technology that allows them to promote themselves in some way; d) that have resources that allows representatives to participate in transnational contexts; and e) that take some form that resembles researchers' conceptions of social movements.

In addition, how we theorise social relations and articulate our concepts can impact our ability to uncover important developments in the interactions between authorities and potential challengers. For instance, as Pamela Oliver (2008) observes, the efforts of US sociologists to distinguish dissent from crime led them to ignore how the US state has, since the riots of the 1960s, used crime control to repress dissent by the poor, and especially by African Americans. Also, the tendency in the US especially to distinguish social movement scholarship from that scholarship on labour organising contributed to a neglect of the ways formal labour laws have systematically disenfranchised the poorest – usually minority and immigrant – workers from the formal trade union movement itself (cf. Tait 2005).

As feminist and post-colonial theorists point out, positivism tends to privilege those with power and systematically marginalises the voices of the oppressed. Thus, while adoption of such methods by social movement scholars may have helped legitimate research on marginalised groups, it also turns our attention away from persistent and pervasive sources of inequality and oppression. In short, the conventions of Western social science have prevented us from appreciating the dynamic, interactive and multi-level nature of social movement analysis (more on these latter points below) and the relations of power and inequality implicated in them.

Acknowledging some of this conceptual messiness of social movements can make it harder to achieve professional legitimacy or to get one's work published in places that are valued by university authorities (Croteau, Hoynes and Ryan 2005). Thus, not only do we often fail to connect our research to broader societal debates, our research (and social science overall) tends to reinforce dominant modes of thought as well as professional hierarchies. This also serves to reinforce existing structures of inequality and domination. For instance, in his analysis of the genocide in Rwanda, Isaac Kamola accuses scholars of providing 'ideological cover' for neoliberal capital 'by depoliticizing interpretations of structural conflicts as "ethnic"' (2007: 588). Jackie Smith (2010) demonstrates how much of the literature on post-conflict peace-building similarly shifts attention away from the structural and economic forces that underlie most violent conflicts.

The organisation of our profession into distinct disciplines is one of the consequences of global capitalist dynamics, according to Wallerstein's logic. Certainly the study of social movements – particularly of the transnational sort – has been hindered by the separation of sociology from the field of international relations or international studies, which (in the US, at least) tends to be housed in political science departments. While some are hard at work attempting to chip away these disciplinary walls, they remain robust to the extent that many departments do not hire or even read much work by those from outside of their intellectual corrals. Professional associations that help credential scholars and provide networking opportunities reinforce disciplinary and sub-disciplinary boundaries. However, for the study of social movements this has meant, among other things, that questions about global institutions – such as the United Nations and the World Trade Organisation – and their role in shaping the contexts within which both national and transnational movements operate has been relatively under-studied.

While international relations scholars have explored the development of international institutions and regimes – many of which address the problems around which social movements organise – sociologists have investigated environmental, women's rights, or public health campaigns and organisations in isolation from their globalised contexts. These global contexts include major UN conferences on these issues and new trade regulations invalidating the state regulations that movements work so hard to win at local and national levels. In focussing on more immediate organisational, identity and (national) institutional structures, we have neglected how global capitalism and the world system have helped define the conflicts in which social movements engage. For instance, much scholarship defines movement boundaries along specific issues or policy arenas, thereby missing the ways movements might be defying existing institutional boundaries and developing new ways of organising in response to this global context.[3]

The pressures of academic life in many university settings dissuade researchers from devoting time and energy to thoughtful reflection on literatures and discussions outside of their main areas of research. Disciplinary structures thus confine our thinking and prevent the cross-fertilisation of ideas and the unfettered creativity necessary for the production and integration of knowledge in complex societies. Disciplinary sub-fields and their proliferation of specialty journals contain debates on particular subject matters, and networks of scholars typically cluster around defined and often limited realms, with few opportunities (or at least incentives) to interact with others outside of those boundaries. This has led, for instance, to the separation of social movement scholarship from political sociology and from the study of labour movements, for example, as well as created divisions from what may be called the 'mainstream' social movement literature and critical and interdisciplinary globalisation research, feminist, and post-colonial theories. More significant, however, are the national boundaries that remain important obstacles to the free flow of academic ideas. It is particularly ironic that scholars of globalisation celebrate and acknowledge the central importance of the flow of ideas and culture across boundaries and yet they (we) operate within academic networks that tend to be rigidly national – and Northern – in their orientation (Connell 2007).[4]

State Prisons

> Although the sovereign nation-state continues to be represented as the key to modernity, at this juncture, the nation-state, the nation-state system, and the United Nations may well have become key obstacles to the realisation of a more prosperous and more stable future for the majority of the inhabitants of the world.
> —Berger 2007: 1213

In his contribution to this volume, Marco Giugni and his collaborators echo a theme in much of the literature on globalisation and transnational social movements. They conclude that 'even a genuinely transnational movement such as the [global justice movement] remains partly imprisoned in the cage built by the national state'.

But the objective fact that every movement must be somewhere in the world and therefore must face a particular set of local or national institutions and systems of authority does not in and of itself mean that movements are prisoners of the state. Nor does it mean that the most important question for researchers is whether or not state influence declines as globalisation expands. As scholars of social movements have tended to reify the notion of states, activists themselves have transcended their confinement in a variety of ways. They have created transnational associations and networks, developed new forms of identity that privilege transnational over national allegiances and they have imagined and advocated for new institutional and normative arrangements designed to constrain state power (Finnemore 1996; Kriesberg 1997; Seidman 2000; Smith 2008; Khasnabish 2004). They do this, moreover, even as they continue to engage the national state and its institutions. The institutional and historical fact of the national state has not constrained social movement actors to the extent that our conceptual frameworks might suggest (Armstrong and Bernstein 2008).

Indeed, while social movements have been seeking to transform the nature of their 'cages', or the national state, capitalists have also been operating along a parallel track, with more obvious effects (Sklair 1997). William Robinson (2004: 77–79) refers to this as the 'revolution from above', whereby corporate elites and their allies have transformed national state structures in ways that further the aims of globalised capital. The resulting neoliberal state is 'lean and mean' (Evans 1997: 85–86), trimmed of its social welfare components, but with beefed-up military, policing and prison capacities (see also Harvey 2005). This revolution from above was even more brutal for people in the global South, where states were hollowed out (or rather, denied the ability to expand their capacities to provide for the welfare of their people), before they had developed effective systems of representation and distribution (Ferguson 2006, see also Tilly 1990, ch. 7). Advocates of globalised capitalism have shaped the global institutional order through their efforts both to counter the efforts of social movements and to advance institutional structures that support their aims (see, for instance, Bruno and Karliner 2002; Smith 2008, ch. 4). For instance, industry groups are largely responsible for blocking an effective international treaty on climate change, and for advancing international intellectual property rights and agricultural regimes (McMichael 2003; Sell 2003; Coleman and Wayland 2004).

The history of contemporary state-social movement interaction might be read in parallel with the story told by Tilly, whereby competition between authorities and challengers shaped the modern national state (Tilly 1984; see also Markoff 1996). Although Tilly's work contributed to contemporary, state-centric understandings of social movements, the underlying logic of conflict here suggests a multi-actor context that resembles the global system perspective we advocate for here. Today, and indeed throughout the history of the modern state, competitive dynamics between movements, states and other political actors are helping to define the global polity in important ways (Boli and Thomas 1999; Guidry, Kennedy and Zald 2000; Smith 2004). The perspective offered by this literature suggests that, while social movements are to a large degree defined and structured by the national state, the reverse is also true. The character and structure of states and international institutions are also an outcome of social movement actions.

Moreover, state-centric approaches ignore the fact that the national state can only exist within a larger system of states and institutions that recognise, legitimate and help to reinforce their authority and control over particular geographic regions. Dualistic frameworks suggesting that more globalisation equals less state power make little sense when one accounts for human history, or even existing theories of social movements and states. The reification of our concept of the state thus inhibits our understandings of social and political conflict (Armstrong and Bernstein 2008). Sidney Tarrow (2005) attempts to develop a more nuanced argument about the ways transnational activism is both shaped by and shaping the inter-state system, but our read of his argument is that it still suggests an autonomy and resilience of the state that downplays, if not overlooks, the ways states are constructed or constituted by transnational processes and through social movement challenges. Despite the fact that our theory tells us that states are particular, historically defined forms of social organisation (with a comparatively short history, we might add), we often treat them as if they are robust and enduring rather than dynamic, interactive and constantly undergoing transformation.

Some have offered critiques of this reification of the state, or the 'methodological nationalism' that characterises a considerable amount of the social science literature in political sociology and social movements. Methodological nationalism indicates a tendency of scholarship to remain within the statistical and conceptual confines (prisons?) of the modern national state (Beckfield 2003; Anheier and Katz 2005; Connell 2007). We might argue that, while many social movements have avoided incarceration by the state, many social movement scholars are wearing orange jumpsuits! We welcome emerging debates around this point, and see the 'multi-institutional politics approach' offered by Elizabeth Armstrong and Mary Bernstein (2008) as especially promising.

Feminist scholars in particular have reminded us of the importance of contextualising the actors we study. But as Connell observes, '[f]rom the 1940s to the 1970s, it was common to take the boundaries of a nation state as the boundaries of "society"' (2007: 369). We might question whether this tendency ended in the 1970s, since it seems prevalent in much academic discourse today. In any case, the idea that social organisation does not begin or end with the nation state is an important one that often gets lost in our analyses. And while we may know this in our roles as social actors, we are systematically forced to forget this in our academic practice. The debates in which we must participate to advance our scholarly careers and the concepts that we must use to guide our professional research serve as blinders that isolate particular variables. This can aid in our analysis of causal relations, but the process of putting the pieces back together – or contextualising our findings – is an essential step that is often left out. Professional norms and practices can help explain this, but real advances in our understandings will require some new approaches.

The point we make here is not trivial. By maintaining the 'ontological primacy' of the national state, and by defining relevant academic audiences in ways that exclude Southern voices, social science research helps normalise the Western state. As Connell reminds us: '[t]he shared experiences of metropolitan theorists and metropolitan readers do not include much of the sharp end of global social processes. The result is sociological texts that persistently underplay systemic violence' (2007: 378; see also Escobar 2004). Much social movement research, then, is guilty of what Peter Waterman calls 'westocentric universalism' (2001: 234–235).[5]

One could add, too, that it is guilty of 'capitalocentrism', in that it naturalises, or takes as unproblematic, the idea that world-historic social relations have always been and will continue to be based upon the capitalist mode of production (Gibson-Graham 2006). In other words, the methodological is political. As Heloise Weber observes:

> [A] critical re-evaluation of the formal [state-centric] comparative method is necessary not merely to rectify a methodological problem, but also to expose the politics of methodological choices. The formal comparative method is inextricably underpinned by temporal and spatial delineations that reproduce a particularly problematic framework with significant political implications, not least because it obscures the globally constituted social dimensions of struggles for recognition and redistribution. (2007: 559)

Feminist scholars are not alone in demanding attention to social context. For instance, Philip McMichael (1990) argues explicitly for a world-historical perspective in comparative methods, as have other scholars (e.g., Wolf 1982; Burawoy 1998; Farmer 2003; Korzeniewicz and Moran 2006). States must be seen as embedded within a broader system of relationships to globalised capitalism and resistance. They cannot be understood outside of this larger historical and relational context.

Breaking out of Prison

> For metropolitan [i.e., Western] sociology to become more inclusive in this sense is a major project. It requires breaking with professional customs such as the monocultural curriculum in graduate education. It requires an investment of time and resources, in which metropolitan institutions – controlling as they do most of the world's financial resources for social research – must give a lead. Among the tasks are to break the intellectual habits created by the deep eurocentrism of schools such as critical theory (Kozlarek 2001), a process involving risks for careers and reputations.

—Connell 2007

How can scholarship in transnational social movements overcome the limitations we have outlined in this essay? We might begin by observing that contemporary discussions within our professional disciplines are examining and debating the public roles of scholars. These debates are helping to bend the bars of our prisons (Bourdieu and Wacquant 1992; Bourdieu 1998; Santos 2003; Croteau, Hoynes and Ryan 2005; Blau and Iyall Smith 2006; Clawson et al. 2007; Kleidman 2008).[6] These discussions need to be broadened and extended to a wider audience outside of the academy. These efforts at social engagement must win greater legitimacy and acceptance within the professions themselves, in part to allow individual scholars (and their allies in social movements!) to devote adequate time to their pursuit. This will require considerable pressure from civil society itself to demand major transformations in educational policies and practices. In this sense, academics need public engagement in a struggle to democratise the academy and to restructure it in ways that will allow it to better support human needs.

Social science is a political activity. We must scrutinise our own choices of research topics and methods to assess the ways power and social inequality operate through them. We must be honest about the ways our own social position and perspective limit the conclusions we can make from our research, even as we strive to make some limited contribution to the wider search for knowledge and truth.[7] Just as some people speak of a need for 'social responsibility' by corporations, so, too, must social scientists consider more explicitly what it means to do their work in a socially responsible way. By this, we mean that they must do social analysis that contributes to the struggles against social structures that reproduce inequality and social exclusion. We must be sensitive to how our professions systematically 'erase' the histories and perspectives of non-Western people. And we must actively work to give voice to those made invisible by our dominant theories, conceptual frameworks and professional routines. Also, while the capitalist world-system promotes competition, hierarchy and exclusion, those of us committed to global justice must devote our energies to work that advances social solidarity and cooperation.

One way to start is for us to envision ourselves as people, citizens and workers first, and only then as social scientists. This goes against the dominant structures of the university, which fosters individualistic approaches to our work, and which encourages hierarchies within the faculty as well as between faculty and other university workers. Such divisions have enabled the corporatisation of the university and will continue to chip away what remains of value in these spaces. Equitable access to higher education, academic freedom and professional job security in the academy are all threatened by neoliberal globalisation. Only solidarity among workers on campuses and between academic workers and other elements of anti-systemic movements can effectively resist the subordination of universities to the logic of globalised capitalism. In other words, to defend academic principles of neutrality and objectivity, we must forge alliances with civil society groups to demand that our educational institutions operate independently of the global capitalist order. We must, in short, discard the notion that only the work that remains detached from social 'subjects' can be trusted as 'objective', 'neutral' and therefore 'valid'. Instead, we must see ourselves as essential players in the struggle 'to represent humanity's interest in containing the unbridled tyranny of market and state' (Burawoy 2004: 257). By failing to adopt a critical stance toward globalised capitalism, we not only abandon claims to neutrality, but we also help legitimate and sustain the dominant order.[8]

Once we accept our social responsibility and confront modernist notions of objectivity, part of what we need to do to break out of our various prisons is to radically transform our ways of thinking and acting (see, for instance, Stacey 2007). We are not suggesting that scholars should abandon all attempts at objectivity or that we must forego the practice of maintaining some distance between ourselves and the subjects of our research. Rather, with feminist scholars, we call for 'strong objectivity', which is an effort to situate ourselves, our subjects and our research claims or conclusions within the larger social context. This contextualisation, which is achieved by considering the perspectives of people from social positions other (less privileged) than those of the researcher, is sensitive to questions about how power and inequality shape institutions and ongoing social relations (Harding 1992). In other words, the ideal of objectivity remains, but it is strengthened by the recognition that knowledge and perspective are fundamentally political. Thus, it is only through recognition of our social location, acknowledgement of power relations and a thoughtful reflexivity (Bourdieu and Wacquant 1992) that we can fully attain the ideal of objectivity.[9]

Santos's call for greater attention to the 'sociology of absences' and the 'sociology of emergences' is instructive in this regard. We must use our sociological imaginations to examine how the various social structures in which we work have constrained our own thinking about our roles as scholars and about our approach to our subject matter. Those with more seniority and professional security can and should work to promote more cooperation across disciplines and to mentor younger scholars. More must clearly be done to facilitate cross-national exchanges among scholars, particularly between the global North and South. This requires attention to the ways professional practices and intellectual property rights restrict possibilities for Southern scholars to be full members of a global intellectual community. We need to break down the walls of the 'ivory tower' to engage in more egalitarian projects with activists, while attaching greater value to the mutual learning that occurs through these projects (Croteau, Hoynes and Ryan 2005). And finally, but importantly, we should teach in a way that reflects this perspective.

What is especially promising at this time in history, moreover, is that the social movements we have been studying have generated a process – the social forums – that can facilitate the kind of relationship building and identity transformation that is necessary. Santos (2006) speaks of the World Social Forum process as the 'epistemology of the South', recognising that the key ideas and models of organising have emerged from the 'periphery' of the world-system to influence the 'core' (cf. Markoff 2003). Further, reflecting the extent to which major social change initiatives depend upon resistance from those most marginalised by existing power relations, one finds strong links between the ideology of the forums and Third World feminism (see, for instance, Alvarez 2000, 2003). As a space and a model of organising, social forums at local, national, regional and global levels provide opportunities for scholars to both enact their identities as world-citizens and to contribute to the work of 'translation' that Santos sees as essential to the process. They can learn about others' struggles and experiences of economic globalisation, while also contributing to the collective work of developing alternatives.

We conclude by observing that the critique we offer here emerges from the work of countless social movement critics of capitalism, patriarchy and nationalism. While we claim 'authorship' for these ideas, they are more a reflection of the many conversations we have had with social movement activists, students and colleagues. They also parallel similar conversations between other critical scholars and practitioners. Indeed, the very practice of questioning basic modes of thought and the power relations implicit in these constitutes a form of struggle itself. It represents an attempt to critique and transform a culture that has been heretofore utilised in the service of global capitalism. To paraphrase organisers of the US Social Forum, if another world is possible, another sociology is necessary. If oppression resides primarily in our consciousness, then we must reflect critically upon how our own consciousness has been conditioned by relations of domination and oppression. Our research on social movements has taught us that the movements we study (and the people in them) may hold the key to our prisons.

Notes

We are grateful to Dawn Wiest and Simon Teune for comments on an earlier draft of this chapter.

1. Rachel Kutz-Flamenbaum, for example, found that the large and professional SMOs of the contemporary US women's movement have emphasised women's issues primarily in terms of the legal discourses and frameworks of the US system, rather than relating their struggles to global discourses and frames. The global women's movement, in contrast, stressed the problem of violence against women and broader reproductive rights, within the framework of the universality and non-divisibility of human rights (Keck and Sikkink 1998). Although these frames complemented the demands of the US women's movement, the institutional embeddedness of mainstream women's organisations in the US political system limited their attention to global contexts and opportunities.

2. Anderson (2003) and Kolb (2007) detail the challenges civil rights activists faced in linking their struggles to international human rights language. Early civil rights

efforts did use the Universal Declaration of Human Rights as part of their mobilising efforts. Contemporary organising by people of colour has sought to use international human rights language to advance demands for economic and racial justice (Cox and Thomas 2004; Smith 2008: ch. 8). On international feminist influences on US abortion discourse, see Ferree and Gamson (1999).

3. For instance, as noted earlier, there has been relatively little attention to the World Social Forums and even the US Social Forum among US sociologists.

4. Smith observed this in her work in Canada, where she found little dialogue between social movement scholars in the US and this proximate neighbour. Also, the American Sociological Association's attempt to integrate international scholars has consisted of an 'international scholars' reception' which drew participants who were from outside of the US, with little effort to draw in US members of the association (this is changing). And a 2007 meeting of the World Society Foundation, which focussed on globalisation and regionalism, involved just one (understandably frustrated) francophone African scholar, with the rest being based in the US or Europe (one or two were originally from the global South, but were trained in the West).

5. This bias in favour of Northern perspectives also tends to lead movement analysts to see social movements' relations with states as necessarily adversarial. In global contexts, it is Southern activists in particular who are calling for stronger and more capable states rather than seeking to push back state authority (e.g., Macdonald 1997; Guidry 2000; Seidman 2004).

6. European scholars, notably Bourdieu, have been highly influential in promoting an increased appreciation for the importance of the role of the public intellectual in civil society. We realise that the idea of 'public sociology' is less novel in other countries than the US.

7. This may require more adjustments to our epistemologies than our methodologies, although it is clear that innovative methodologies are also needed to remedy blind spots.

8. Indeed, it is the failure of academic workers to maintain a critical and objective perspective that allowed universities and other educational institutions to be subordinated to the logic of the marketplace and the demands of globalised capitalism.

9. This approach also encourages attention to right wing social movements that have been less attractive to social movement researchers. It is only by considering the larger context (and causes) of inequality and social exclusion that one can understand why some groups mobilise around racist and anti-social claims. Moreover, attention to the underlying structures that reproduce inequality and social division can help scholars and policy-makers to avoid framing resource-driven conflicts as more violence-prone identity conflicts, thereby reducing the likelihood that such conflicts will persist and/or escalate to violence.

References

Anderson, C. 2003. *Eyes off the Prize: African-Americans and the Struggle for Human Rights 1948–1954*. Cambridge: Cambridge University Press.

Andrews, K.T. and B. Edwards. 2005. 'The Organisational Structure of Local Environmentalism'. *Mobilization* 10(2): 213–234.

Anheier, H. and H. Katz. 2005. 'Network Approaches to Global Civil Society'. In *Global Civil Society 2004/5*, eds. H. Anheier, M. Glasius and M. Kaldor, 206–221. London: Sage.

Armstrong, E.A. and M. Bernstein. 2008. 'Culture, Power, and Institutions: A Multi-Institutional Politics Approach to Social Movements'. *Sociological Theory* 26(1): 74–99.

Aronowitz, S. 2000. *The Knowledge Factory: Dismantling the Corporate University and Creating True Higher Learning*. New York: Beacon Press.

Beckfield, J. 2003. 'Inequality in the World Polity: The Structure of International Organisation'. *American Sociological Review* 68 (3): 401–424.

Berger, M.T. 2007. 'States of Nature and the Nature of States'. *Third World Quarterly* 28(6): 1203–1214.

Blau, J. and K.E. Iyall Smith, eds. 2006. *Public Sociologies Reader*. Lanham: Rowman & Littlefield.

Boli, J. and G.M. Thomas, eds. 1999. *Constructing World Culture: International Nongovernmental Organisations since 1875*. Stanford: Stanford University Press.

Bourdieu, P. 1998. *Practical Reason: On the Theory of Action*. Stanford: Stanford University Press.

Bourdieu, P. and L. Wacquant. 1992. *An Invitation to Reflexive Sociology*. Chicago: Chicago University Press.

Bruno, K. and J. Karliner. 2002. *Earthsummit.biz: The Corporate Takeover of Sustainable Development*. Oakland: Food First Books.

Burawoy, M. 1998. 'The Extended Case Method'. *Sociological Theory* 16(1): 4–33.

———. 2004. 'The World Needs Public Sociology'. *Sosiologisk tidskrift* 12(3): 255–272.

Clawson, D., et al., eds. 2007. *Public Sociology*. Berkeley: University of California Press.

Coleman, W.D. and S. Wayland. 2004. 'Global Civil Society and Non-Territorial Governance Some Empirical Reflections'. *Global Governance* 12(3): 241–261.

Connell, R. 2007. 'The Northern Theory of Globalisation'. *Sociological Theory* 25(4): 368–385.

Cox, L. and D.Q. Thomas, eds. 2004. *Close to Home: Case Studies of Human Rights Work in the United States*. New York: Ford Foundation. Retrieved 30 August 2008 from http://www.fordfound.org/newsroom/humanrights/86.

Crist, J.T. and J.D. McCarthy. 1996. '"If I Had a Hammer": The Changing Methodological Repertoire of Collective Behavior and Social Movements Research'. *Mobilization* 1(1): 87–102.

Croteau, D., W. Hoynes and C. Ryan, eds. 2005. *Rhyming Hope and History: Activists, Academics, and Social Movement Scholarship*. Minneapolis: University of Minnesota Press.

Da Costa, D. and P. McMichael. 2007. 'The Poverty of the Global Order'. *Globalisations* 4(4): 588–602.

della Porta, Donatella. 2007a. 'The Global Justice Movement: An Introduction'. In *The Global Justice Movement: Cross-National and Transnational Perspectives*, ed. D. della Porta, 1–28. Boulder: Paradigm Publishers.

———. 2007b. 'The Global Justice Movement in Context'. In *The Global Justice Movement: Cross-National and Transnational Perspectives*, ed. D. della Porta, 232–251. Boulder: Paradigm Publishers.

Escobar, A. 2004. 'Development, Violence and the New Imperial Order'. *Development* 47(1): 15–21.

Evans, P.B. 1997. 'The Eclipse of the State? Reflections on Stateness in an Era of Globalisation'. *World Politics* 50(1): 62–87.

Farmer, P. 2003. *Pathologies of Power: Health, Human Rights, and the New War on the Poor*. Berkeley: University of California Press.

———. 2004. 'An Anthropology of Structural Violence'. *Current Anthropology* 45(3): 305–325.

Ferguson, J. 2006. *Global Shadows: Africa in the Neoliberal World Order*. Durham: Duke University Press.

Ferree, M.M. and W. Gamson. 1999. 'The Gendering of Abortion Discourse: Assessing Global Feminist Influence in the United States and Germany'. In *Social Movements in a Globalizing World*, eds. D. della Porta, H. Kriesi and D. Rucht, 40–56. New York: St. Martin's Press.

Finnemore, M. 1996. *National Interests in International Society*. Ithaca: Cornell University Press.

Gibson-Graham, J.K. 2006. *A Postcapitalist Politics*. Minneapolis: University of Minnesota Press.

Goodwin, J. and J. Jasper. 1999. 'Caught in a Winding, Snarling Vine: The Structural Bias of Political Process Theory'. *Sociological Forum* 14(1): 27–54.

Guidry, J.A. 2000. 'The Useful State? Social Movements and the Citizenship of Children in Brazil'. In *Globalizations and Social Movements: Culture, Power, and the Transnational Public Sphere*, eds. J.A. Guidry, M.D. Kennedy and M.N. Zald, 147–180. Ann Arbor: University of Michigan Press.

Guidry, J.A., M.D. Kennedy and M.N. Zald, eds. 2000. *Globalizations and Social Movements: Culture, Power, and the Transnational Public Sphere*. Ann Arbor: University of Michigan.

Harvey, D. 2005. *A Brief History of Neoliberalism*. Oxford: Oxford University Press.

Kamola, I.A. 2007. 'The Global Coffee Economy and the Production of Genocide in Rwanda'. *Third World Quarterly* 28(3): 571–592.

Keck, M. and K. Sikkink. 1998. *Activists beyond Borders*. Ithaca: Cornell University Press.

Khasnabish, A. 2004. *Globalizing Hope: The Resonance of Zapatismo and the Political Imagination(s) of Transnational Activism*. McMaster University Working Paper Series, Hamilton, Ontario. Retrieved 22 July 2008 from http://globalization.mcmaster.ca/wps/Khasnabish.pdf.

Kleidman, R. 2008. 'Engaged Social Movement Scholarship'. *Journal of Applied Sociology* 8(1) / *Sociological Practice* 23(1): 68–82.

Kolb, F. 2007. *Protest and Opportunities: A Theory of Social Movements and Political Change*. Frankfurt am Main: Campus.

Korzeniewicz, R.P. and T.P. Moran. 2006. 'World Inequality in the Twenty-First Century: Patterns and Tendencies'. In *The Blackwell Companion to Globalization*, ed. G. Ritzer, 565–592. Oxford: Blackwell.

Kriesberg, L. 1997. 'Social Movements and Global Transformation'. In *Transnational Social Movements and World Politics: Solidarity beyond the State*, eds. J. Smith, C. Chatfield and R. Pagnucco, 3–18. Syracuse: Syracuse University Press.

Kriesi, H. 1989. 'New Social Movements and the New Class in the Netherlands'. *American Journal of Sociology* 94(5): 1078–1116.

Macdonald, L. 1997. *Supporting Civil Society: The Political Role of Non-Governmental Organisations in Central America.* New York: St. Martin's Press.

Markoff, J. 1996. *Waves of Democracy: Social Movements and Political Change.* Thousand Oaks: Pine Forge Press.

———. 2003. 'Margins, Centers, and Democracy: The Paradigmatic History of Women's Suffrage'. *Signs: Journal of Women in Culture and Society* 29(1): 85–116.

McMichael, P. 1990. 'Incorporating Comparison within a World-Historical Perspective: An Alternative Comparative Method'. *American Sociological Review* 55 (3): 385–397.

———. 2003. *Development and Social Change: A Global Perspective.* 3rd ed. Thousand Oaks: Pine Forge.

Melucci, A. 1989. *Nomads of the Present.* Philadelphia: Temple University Press.

Offe, C. 1999. 'New Social Movements: Challenging the Boundaries of Institutional Politics'. In *Modernity: Critical Concepts,* ed. M. Waters, 336–372. London: Routledge.

Oliver, P. 1989. 'Bringing the Crowd Back in: The Nonorganisational Elements of Social Movements'. *Research in Social Movements, Conflict and Change* 5: 133–170.

———. 2008. 'Repression and Crime Control: Why Social Movement Scholars Should Pay Attention to Mass Incarceration as a Form of Repression'. *Mobilization* 13(1): 1–24.

Pichardo, N.A. 1997. 'New Social Movements: A Critical Review'. *Annual Review of Sociology* 23: 411–430.

Robinson, W. 2004. *A Theory of Global Capitalism.* Baltimore: Johns Hopkins University Press.

Santos, B. de Sousa. 2003. 'The Popular University of Social Movements to Educate Activists and Leaders of Social Movements, as well as Social Scientists, Scholars and Artists Concerned with Progressive Social Transformation'. Retrieved 24 June 2008 from http://www.ces.uc.pt/universidadepopular/Popular%20University%20of%20the%20Social%20Movements.pdf.

———. 2006. *The Rise of the Global Left: the World Social Forums and beyond.* London: Zed Books.

———. 2007, 'Beyond Abyssal Thinking: From Global Lines to Ecologies of Knowledges'. *Eurozine.* Retrieved 22 July 2008 from http://www.eurozine.com/articles/2007-06-29-santos-en.html.

Seidman, G.W. 2000. 'Adjusting the Lens: What do Globalisations, Transnationalism, and the Anti-apartheid Movement Mean for Social Movement Theory?' In *Globalisations and Social Movements: Culture, Power, and the Transnational Public Sphere,* eds. J.A. Guidry, M.D. Kennedy and M.N. Zald, 339–358. Ann Arbor: University of Michigan Press.

———. 2004. 'Deflated Citizenship: Labor Rights in a Global Era'. In *People Out of Place: Globalization, Human Rights, and the Citizenship Gap,* eds. A. Brysk and G. Shafir, 109–129. London: Routledge.

Sell, S.K. 2003. *Private Power, Public Law: The Globalisation of Intellectual Property Rights.* Cambridge: Cambridge University Press.

Sklair, L. 1997. 'Social Movements for Global Capitalism: The Transnational Capitalist Class in Action'. *Review of International Political Economy* 4(3): 514–538.

Smith, J. 2004. 'Transnational Processes and Movements'. In *The Blackwell Companion to Social Movements,* eds. D.A. Snow, S.A. Soule and H. Kriesi, 311–335. Oxford: Blackwell.

———. 2008. *Social Movements for Global Democracy.* Baltimore: Johns Hopkins University Press.

———. Forthcoming. 'Globalization and Strategic Peacebuilding'. In *Strategic Peacebuilding,* eds. D. Philpott and G. Powers.

Tait, V. 2005. *Poor Workers' Unions.* Cambridge: South End Press.

Tarrow, S. 2005. *The New Transnational Activism.* Cambridge: Cambridge University Press.

Taylor, V. 1998. 'Feminist Methodology in Social Movements Research'. *Qualitative Sociology* 21(4): 357–379.

Tilly, C. 1984. 'Social Movements and National Politics'. In *Statemaking and Social Movements: Essays in History and Theory,* eds. C. Bright and S. Harding, 297–317. Ann Arbor: University of Michigan Press.

———. 1990. *Coercion, Capital and European States AD 990–1990.* Oxford: Blackwell.

Wallerstein, I. 2004. *World-Systems Analysis: An Introduction.* Durham: Duke University Press.

Waters, S. 2008. 'Situating Movements Historically: May 1968, Alain Touraine, and New Social Movement Theory'. *Mobilization* 13(1): 63–82.

Waterman, P. 2001. *Globalisation, Social Movements and the New Internationalisms.* New York: Continuum.

Weber, H. 2007. 'A Political Analysis of the Formal Comparative Method: Historicizing the Globalisation and Development Debate'. *Globalisations* 4(4): 559–572.

Wolf, Eric. 1982. *Europe and the People without History.* Berkeley: University of California Press.

Contributors

Marko Bandler, Ph.D. student in political science at the University of Geneva, is currently head of the social action and solidarity department of the City of Vernier (Switzerland).

Philippe Blanchard is a post-doctoral student in the Department of Sociology of Pennsylvania State University, USA, and collaborates with the Institute of Political and International Studies of the University of Lausanne, Switzerland. His present research topics include the methods of social sciences, media and politics, party and protest activism, and parliamentary voting.

Donatella della Porta is professor of sociology in the Department of Political and Social Sciences at the European University Institute in Florence. Among her recent publications are: (ed.) *Democracy in Social Movements* (Palgrave, 2009); (with M. Caiani) *Social Movements and Europeanization* (Oxford University Press, 2009); (ed.) *Another Europe* (Routledge, 2009); (with Michael Keating) *Approaches and Methodologies in the Social Sciences* (Cambridge University Press, 2008); (with Gianni Piazza) *Voices of the Valley, Voices of the Straits* (Berghahn Books, 2008).

Nicole Doerr holds a Ph.D. from the European University Institute in Florence. Her research interests include democracy, language and communication in social movements and in transnational public spaces, feminist discourse theory, alternative media and the contentious visual and cultural politics of European integration. Her academic work has been published in journals such as *Mobilization, Social Movement Studies, Feminist Review* and *International Journal of Womens' Studies.*

Nina Eggert is a Ph.D. student at the University of Geneva (political science) and the University of Trento (sociology) and a research assistant at the Laboratoire de recherches sociales et politiques appliquées (resop). She is currently working on her dissertation on migrant's organisational networks and political integration. Her research interests include: social movements, immigration and integration and social network analysis.

Olivier Fillieule is a full-time professor in political sociology and head of the Political and International Studies Institute (IEPI) at the University of Lausanne. He is also Senior Researcher at CNRS Paris I Sorbonne. His work focuses on social movements and political activism, anti-HIV/AIDS and alterglobal movements. He has recently published (with Lilian Mathieu and Cécile Péchu) (eds.), *Dictionnaire des mouvements sociaux* (Presses de Sciences Po, 2009); (with P. Roux) *Le sexe du militantisme* (Presses de Sciences Po, 2009); (with D. Tartakowsky) *La manifestation de rue* (Presses de Sciences Po, 2008); (with I. Sommier and E. Agrikoliansky) *Généalogie du mouvement altermondialiste en Europe* (Karthala, 2008).

Marco Giugni is a researcher at the Laboratoire de recherches sociales et politiques appliquées (resop) and teaches at the Department of Political Science at the University of Geneva. He has authored or co-authored several books and articles on social movements and contentious politics. His research interests include social movements and collective action, immigration and ethnic relations, unemployment and social exclusion.

Christoph Haug is currently a post-doctoral researcher at the Gothenburg Centre of Globalization and Development (GCGD) at the University of Gothenburg, Sweden. At the Social Science Research Center in Berlin (WZB) he wrote his doctoral thesis about *Discursive Decision-making in Meetings of the Global Justice Movements*. He now works on poor people's movements and civil society organizations in South Africa. Haug's research interests include: the social forums, the role of meetings in organizing processes, theories of the public sphere, and the sociology of interaction. He is co-editor of *Kampf um Teilhabe* (VSA, 2008).

Ariane Jossin holds a Ph.D. in political science and is a post-doctoral fellow at the Marc Bloch Research Centre (Berlin). She is also affiliated to the Research Centre on Political Action in Europe (Centre de Recherches sur l'Action Politique en Europe/CRAPE, Rennes). Her research interests are the sociology of global justice and ecologist movements in France and Germany, and the sociology of migrants in both countries.

Rachel Kutz-Flamenbaum is an assistant professor in the Department of Sociology at the University of Pittsburgh. She recently completed her dissertation on the impact of the contemporary anti-war movement on the US women's movement. Her research focuses on intersections between movements, including the anti-war and global justice movements and women's peace movements. Kutz-Flamenbaum co-editor of *Strategy in Action* (University of Minnesota Press, 2010).

Thomas Olesen is associate professor, Ph.D., in the Department of Political Science, University of Aarhus, Denmark. His research interests are social movements, media, solidarity and globalisation. Recent publications include *Inter-*

national Zapatismo: The Construction of Solidarity in the Age of Globalization (London: Zed Books, 2005). He is currently working on two research projects: one on solidarity movements, distant issues and globalization in Denmark in the period from 1945 to 2008, and another on global activism and power.

Tsveta Petrova is a Ph.D. candidate at the Department of Government at Cornell University, USA. Her research interests include contentious politics and democratisation in EU member states. She is currently working on a doctoral dissertation studying the governmental and non-governmental efforts of the Eastern European members of the EU as democracy promoters at the national and the EU level.

Jackie Smith is associate professor of sociology and peace studies at the University of Notre Dame and a faculty affiliate of the Center for the Study of Social Movements and Social Change. She has recently published (with Dawn Wiest) *Social Movements in the World Political Economy* (Russell Sage Foundation, 2011); *Social Movements for Global Democracy* (Johns Hopkins University Press, 2008); (with several co-authors) *Global Democracy and the World Social Forums* (Paradigm Publishers, 2007). Smith teaches courses on globalisation, popular politics and the United Nations.

Simon Teune works at the Social Science Research Center, Berlin. His research interests are social movements, protest and culture. As a fellow of the Hans-Böckler-Stiftung he prepares a Ph.D. dissertation that deals with the communication strategies of global justice groups during the anti-G8 protests in Germany 2007. He is co-editor of *Nur Clowns und Chaoten?* (Campus, 2008), a book that unpacks the media event of the Heiligendamm protests.

Jeroen Van Laer is a research assistant at the University of Antwerp (Belgium) and a member of the Media, Movements and Politics (M²P) research group. He studied the impact of new communication technologies on transnational mobilisation and peace movement coalition formation. Since 2009, he has been preparing a Ph.D. thesis on mobilisation and frame alignment processes.

Stefaan Walgrave is professor of Political Science at the University of Antwerp (Belgium) and coordinator of the Media, Movements and Politics (M²P) research group. His research interests are social movements, political participation, political communication and elections. He is currently involved in several comparative projects on protest surveying, political representation and agenda setting.

Index